Industries and Global Competition

Changes in the dynamics of economic activities since the last decades of the 20th century have yielded major changes in the composition of industries and in the division of labor and production across different regions of the world. Despite these shifts in the global economy, some industries have remained competitive even without relocating their operations overseas.

Industries and Global Competition examines how and why the specificities of certain industries and firms determined their choice of location and competitiveness. This volume identifies the major drivers of this process and explains why some firms and industries moved to other parts of the world while others did not. Relocation was not the sole determinant of the success or failure of firms and industries. Indeed, some were able to reinvent themselves at their original location and build new competitive advantages. The path that each industry or firm took varied. This book argues that the specific characteristics of each industry defined the conditions of competitiveness and provides a wide range of cases as illustrations.

Aimed at scholars, researchers and academics in the fields of business history, international business and related disciplines, *Industries and Global Competition* examines the unique questions: How and why did the specificities of certain industries and firms determine their choice of location and competitiveness?

Bram Bouwens is an Assistant Professor at Utrecht University, Netherlands.

Pierre-Yves Donzé is a Professor at the Graduate School of Economics, Osaka University, Japan.

Takafumi Kurosawa is a Professor at the Graduate School of Economics, Kyoto University, Japan.

Routledge International Studies in Business History

Series editors: Jeffrey Fear and Christina Lubinski
For a full list of titles in this series, please visit www.routledge.com

Industries and Global Competition

A History of Business Beyond Borders

Edited by
Bram Bouwens, Pierre-Yves Donzé
and Takafumi Kurosawa

Routledge
Taylor & Francis Group
NEW YORK AND LONDON

First published 2018 by Routledge

2 Park Square, Milton Park, Abingdon, Oxfordshire OX14 4RN

52 Vanderbilt Avenue, New York, NY 10017

Routledge is an imprint of the Taylor & Francis Group, an informa business

First issued in paperback 2019

Routledge is an imprint of the Taylor & Francis Group, an informa business

Library of Congress Cataloging-in-Publication Data
Names: Bouwens, A. M. C. M., editor. | Donzâe, Pierre-Yves, editor. | Kurosawa, Takafumi, editor.
Title: Industries and global competition : a history of business beyond borders / edited by Bram Bouwens, Pierre-Yves Donzâe and Takafumi Kurosawa.
Description: New York : Routledge, 2017. | Includes index.
Identifiers: LCCN 2017020386 | ISBN 9781138680524 (hardback) | ISBN 9781315563909 (ebook)
Subjects: LCSH: Industries. | Competition, International. | International business enterprises. | International trade.
Classification: LCC HD2328 .I529 2017 | DDC 338.8/8—dc23
LC record available at https://lccn.loc.gov/2017020386

ISBN: 978-1-138-68052-4 (hbk)
ISBN: 978-0-367-87733-0 (pbk)

Typeset in Sabon
by Apex CoVantage, LLC

Contents

Figures

Tables

About the Contributors

Dimitry Anastakis is a professor of history at Trent University. His work addresses the intersection of the state, business and politics, particularly in the post-1945 period in Canada. He is the author and editor or co-editor of eight books and collections, including most recently *Death in the Peaceable Kingdom: Canadian History since Confederation through Murder, Execution, Assassination and Suicide* (2015), *Smart Globalization: The Canadian Business and Economic History Experience* (2014), *Autonomous State: The Struggle for a Canadian Car Industry* (2013). He also published in journals such as the *Business History Review*, *Canadian Historical Review* and *Michigan Historical Review*. He has also served as a co-editor of the *Canadian Historical Review*. His current project examines the 1970s-era Bricklin car company, and its broader meaning in North American society.

Bram Bouwens is a business historian at the Department of History and Art History of Utrecht University. He specializes in twentieth and twenty-first century business and has written studies on subjects including the Dutch paper and board industry, the alcohol industry and the dredging industry. In 2015 he published a corporate history of Heineken with Keetie Sluyterman. He published books on competition and concentration issues, ranging from business interest associations, cartels, and mergers and acquisitions. This research also appeared in international journals.

Pierre-Yves Donzé is a professor of business history at Osaka University, Japan, and a visiting professor at the University of Fribourg, Switzerland. His research interests focus on the history of medical business and the history of fashion and luxury industries, approached in a transnational and global perspective. His last books include *A Business History of the Swatch Group: The Rebirth of Swiss Watchmaking and the Globalization of the Luxury Industry* (Palgrave Macmillan, 2014), *Industrial Development, Technology Transfer, and Global Competition: A history of the Japanese watch industry since 1850* (Routledge, 2017) and *Making Medicine a Business: X-ray Technology and the Transformation of the Japanese Medical System (1895–1945)* (Palgrave Macmillan, forthcoming).

María Fernández-Moya is an assistant professor at Colegio Universitario de Estudios Financieros (CUNEF), where she teaches Economic History and Principles of Business Administration. Prior to joining CUNEF, María developed her research career at IESE Business School (Family Business Chair), and she has taught in the Department of Economic History at the University of Barcelona (Spain). Her research examines the analysis of business practices from a long-term perspective, with a focus on family-owned companies, internationalization of Spanish firms and the publishing sector. She is currently working on the evolution of the European and the US publishing industry in the twentieth century.

Rika Fujioka is professor of macro marketing at Kansai University, Japan. She is currently a visiting scholar at Erasmus University Rotterdam, Netherlands. She is a council member of both the Business History Society of Japan and Japan Society of Marketing and Distribution. While her academic base lies in marketing, Rika's research activities have extended into business history. Her publications include "European luxury big business and emerging Asian markets, 1960–2010," *Business History* (with Pierre-Yves Donzé), *The Development of Department Stores in Japan (in Japanese)*, Yuhikaku, and *Comparative Responses to Globalization: Experiences of British and Japanese Enterprises*, Palgrave Macmillan, (edited with Maki Umemura).

Tomoko Hashino is a professor of economic history at Kobe University. Her research interests are in the evolutionary process of the textile industry in Japan as well as the development history of weaving districts in modern Japan. Her recent articles have appeared in *the Economic History Review*, *Business History Review*, *Australian Economic History Review*, and *Journal of the Japanese and International Economies*. She received her PhD in economics from Hitotsubashi University in 2003. She has been a visiting fellow at the University of New South Wales, the London School of Economics and Political Science, George Washington University and Stanford University.

Takashi Hirao is a professor in the Faculty of Contemporary Business at Kyoto Tachibana University in Japan. He received his PhD in Commerce in 2003. His research interests are innovation management and human resource management from a historical perspective. He has written on research networks in semiconductor laser technology in the US and Japan, platform leadership of the Japanese mobile phone industry and British and Japanese labor management.

Takafumi Kurosawa is professor of economic policy at the Graduate School of Economics, Kyoto University, where he received his PhD in 2001. His dissertation analyzed the Swiss economy and the formation of the cross-border economic regions in the nineteenth century. His English publications deal with multinational enterprises and political risks, industrial clusters, the paper and pulp industry and industrial policy, examining European and Japanese cases. Since 2012, he has been managing a large-scale international project on the competitiveness of regions focused on industrial history, and organizing a series of conferences and publications on the issue of the political risks and organizational innovations of multinational enterprises, plus a comparative study on historiography of the business history.

Shigehiro Nishimura is the professor of business history at Kansai University, Osaka, Japan. He was the visiting fellow of the Business History Unit of the London School of Economics and Political Science from 2011 to 2012. He wrote his doctoral thesis on the international patent management of General Electric Company and received his PhD from Kyoto University. He is the co-editor of *Organizing Global Technology Flows: Institutions, Actors, and Processes* (Routledge, 2014), and the author of *International Patent Management in Japan: The Formation and Development of Local Patent Management via Cooperation between GE and Toshiba* (Yuhikaku Publishing, 2016).

Jari Ojala is professor of comparative business history and chair of the Department of History and Ethnology at the University of Jyväskylä in Finland. He specializes in economic, maritime and business history. Jari Ojala is currently Editor-in-Chief of the Scandinavian Economic History Review (2015–18) and previously served as Editor-in-Chief of the Scandinavian Journal of History (2004–2009). Among his recent publications are "Deskilling and decline in skill premium during the age of sail: Swedish and Finnish seamen, 1751–1913," in *Explorations in Economic History*, together with Jaakko Pehkonen and Jari Eloranta.

Nuria Puig is professor of economic history and institutions at the Universidad Complutense de Madrid, Spain, and visiting professor of History at The Ohio State University, United States. Her research focuses on the long term effects of foreign investment and the role of family firms and business groups in comparative perspective. She is the co-editor of two special issues: "Business Groups Around the World," *Business History* 57 (January 2016) and "Foreign Capital and The Development of Local Human Capital," *Business History* (forthcoming). Puig serves on the editorial board of *Business History Review* and *Revista de Historia Industrial. Economía y Empresa.*

Stig Tenold is professor of economic history at NHH—The Norwegian School of Economics in Bergen. His main research has been within contemporary maritime history, both from an economic history and from a business history angle. Stig Tenold's most recent book is *Geared for Growth: Kristian Gerhard Jebsen and His Shipping Companies*. At the moment, he is visiting The University of Washington, where he is writing a book with the provisional title *Twentieth century shipping: Norway's* *successful navigation of the world's most global industry*, scheduled for publication by Palgrave Macmillan.

Julia Yongue is a professor in the Faculty of Economics of Hosei University in Tokyo, Japan. Her research focuses on the development of the Japanese pharmaceutical industry and the policies and regulations that have shaped it from the Meiji period to the present. Her most recent work is a co-edited volume, *Encyclopedia of Pharmaceutical History*, published in Japanese in 2016. She currently serves as a trustee of the Japanese Society for History of Pharmacy and the Business History Society of Japan.

Acknowledgements

This volume is the result of seven years of work and discussions by dozens of scholars in many places around the world.

The most important foundation of this volume is a research project called 'CARIS': Competitive Advantage of Regions: Europe and East Asia in Comparative Studies on Industries, which was supported by the Grants-in-Aid for Scientific Research (KAKEN) (Project Code 23243055) by the Japan Society for the Promotion of Science (JSPS). The scope of research grew out of its name beyond Europe and East Asia, and it became truly global in the course of the project. Fourteen researchers from thirteen universities became the core members of the CARIS project and more than a dozen of scholars from all over the world joined as its affiliate members. It encompassed multiple subprojects, resulting in a collective book publication in Japanese (edited by Takeo Kikkawa, Takafumi Kurosawa and Shigehiro Nishimura), and many articles in different journals by its members. This volume in English highlights the main results of the whole project and includes a few additional contributions, with a different set of targeted industries. We would like to thank all the members of the CARIS project for their contributions not only to their own parts of the project, but also for their continued involvement with the project as a whole.

The CARIS project had a partner project in Europe, named "BEAT: Business in Europe and Asia during the Twentieth Century" with its official title: "Changing business systems and economic performance in Europe and Asia during the 20th century." The BEAT project was supported by the Netherlands Organization for Scientific Research. It organized various meetings in Glasgow, Utrecht, Frankfurt and other locations, in cooperation with the University of Glasgow and the Gesellschaft für Unternehmensgeschichte (GUG) in Germany. We would like to thank Andrea Schneider and Raymond G. Stokes, the organizers of those meetings, as well as all the contributors and participants.

The comments of multiple scholars at various workshops and conferences provided critical but supportive feedback to numerous papers. We particularly benefited from the discussion at EBHA in Athens (2011), Paris (2012, joint conference with BHSJ), Uppsala (2013), Utrecht (2014), Miami (2015, joint conference with BHC), BHSJ in Tokyo (2014), WEHC in Stellenbosh (2012) and in Kyoto (2015), BHC in Portland (2016), Takuetsu Workshop at Kyoto University (2013) and multiple workshops of CARIS in Osaka, Tokyo, Kyoto and Boston, which garnered valuable contributions and comments at various stages of the process. We are also thankful to Business History Society of Japan for the organizational support, including that for The International Conference on Business History (former "Fuji Conference") in 2013 in Kyoto.

Our special thanks go to Matthias Kipping for his support throughout the project. This volume would not have become a reality without his strong and thoughtful support both in academic and practical aspects.

Last but not least, we would like to thank all the authors who worked hard at shaping their contributions to fit into our design, Jeff Fear and Christina Lubinski, editors of *the Routledge International Studies of Business History*, the anonymous reviewers of the series, all the staff at Routledge and our partners and families for their support while we were preparing this volume.

Bram Bouwens, Pierre-Yves Donzé and Takafumi Kurosawa
Utrecht, Osaka and Kyoto
April 2017

Introduction
Industry History: Its Concepts and Methods

Takafumi Kurosawa

Introduction

The second decade of the 21st Century seems to be witnessing a turn away from globalization. A buzzword for the past several decades, it is now being supplanted with a dramatic surge in discussion of anti-globalism in world politics. This backing away from the global reveals how fundamentally people had been affected both by the reality and the notion of globalization. The global integration of the market delivered a remarkable expansion of the world economy and the improvement of life in many parts of the world. Although it seemed to offer a promising pathway to overcome nationalism, it has actually provoked a fundamental concern within nations for the future of their economic life and identity. The world-wide technology transfer and the diffusion of knowledge made possible the rapid catch-up by "the rest" (Amsden 2001), turning around the few centuries long trend of "Great Divergence" (Pomeranz 2000). While integration promoted development in some parts of the world, it also caused citizens in once dominant nations to fear they would face competition from lower cost labor and production from the less developed nations. Likewise, global integration of the capital market accompanied the increased inequality in many nations and left many people behind. The transformation of global value chains and the enhanced mobility of corporate activities triggered concerns about the de-coupling between the interest of globalized firms and the priority of local economies. Intensified mobility of a skilled workforce also triggered dread of competition with immigrants in rich countries and, at the same time, led poor economies to fear a brain drain of needed skilled workers.

We can gain a better understanding of these grave and complex issues by examining industrial competitiveness and dynamics of industries. Anxiety toward globalization was provoked especially by a dynamic change of the industrial landscape, where new winners and new losers emerged. These dynamics eventually impacted the employment opportunities and day to day life of people. Since this is a question of how the world was transformed, or not transformed, it should be addressed by historical analysis employing social scientific analytical concepts.

Industrial dynamics in global competition is a fascinating subject that raises a myriad of questions. Why do new entrants from emerging economies catch-up with first movers of rich countries in one industry, while mature economies and established firms remain competitive in others? Why do some industries witness a global scale of integration of markets and a high level of concentration, while others still maintain their national or regional characteristics? If a global value chain emerges and connects multiple locations in the world economy, who is competing with whom, and where and to whom does the competitiveness belongs? Focusing on a specific nation or industry may reduce the complexity to some extent, but may not provide a deep enough answer to these questions. A nation or region may improve its competitiveness in an industry while it loses it in another industry.

We adopt the **industry history** approach to address these questions. This approach uses industry, rather than firm or nation, as the starting point of analysis. This approach is especially useful when we focus on competition in the market because the industry is (a) an arena where the competition and cooperation among economic entities takes place, and (b) a sphere containing a unique set of economic resources and organizational capabilities. Studies focusing on competition among firms (or competition among relevant divisions of firms), or investigating competition among locations to become a home/host of corporate activities, or trying to capture the dynamic transformation of an economy need to take this "industry-centered" view. It pays attention to the specificity of individual industries. Since each industry may have its own unique dynamics, the industry-centered method can reveal industry-specific determinants of competitiveness. In this view, the basis of analysis is not a "one-size-fits-all" theory of competitiveness, but a diverse set of analytical concepts which are selected and customized to the industry specific conditions.

The search for a convincing interpretation of both the industrial and geographical dynamics must begin by asking the right questions. The above-mentioned questions on global competition can be summarized into two ways of asking questions. In the first, "industry-centered" way, we focus on a specific industry and ask, "what is the determinant of industrial competitiveness and locations, and how is it transformed over time?" In the second, "location-centered" way, we take one location (or any geographic unit such as nation or sub/supra-national regions) and ask, "what kind of competitive resource(s) does the location have, and in which industry is it exerted?" The combination of these two types of questions may lead us to our key research question: "how do specificities of a given industry and location-specific competitive resources interrelate, and how is the relationship transformed over time?" This book addresses this question from a historical perspective, taking a long-term horizon (from decades to centuries) and comparative and relational perspectives.

This is a daunting challenge, not only because of the complexity of issues and colossal scale of potential research targets, but also due to the lack of shared methods and the ambiguity in basic concepts and categories. Among many problems to overcome are: 1) concept of industry per se; 2) relationship among multiple approaches/viewpoints; and 3) spatial concepts and geographical framework. In the following three sections, I will discuss these issues to provide a better picture to explain the approaches and challenges of this book.

1 Industry as the Key Category

The primary problem of industry history is ambiguity of concept. Some studies that deal with a specific industry provide their own definition of the industry in question, and discuss general features of industries in some instances. However, surprisingly few works provide a conceptual or analytical framework to understand industry in general, and few scholars have elaborated the concept of industry per se. Unlike the concept of the firm, which has inspired many scholars to address theoretical questions and led to more than one "theory of the firm" (e.g. Penrose 1959), industry has not produced a "theory of industry." Although some pioneering works have addressed the concept of industry (Robinson 1958), and some recent works by historians demonstrated the advantageous position of historical research to reconsider the concept (Stokes and Banken 2015), the potential has yet to be tapped. This section takes up this challenge.

1.1 What Is Industry?

As briefly mentioned above, this book takes industry as the framework of analysis and positions it as the starting point of the study of competitiveness. However, this choice poses a problem. Unlike the firm, industry is merely a collective concept and it usually does not have a clear boundary. Interestingly, while a plethora of works have been published on diverse industries, and many studies on a specific industry define the targeted industry, almost none of these works have discussed "What is industry?" Accordingly, neither methods nor criteria to categorize an industry have been discussed. This section attempts to fill this gap by focusing on the greatest common factor of the concept.

First and foremost, industry is not a concept of actual entities, but an operational concept for cognition and understanding. It is defined and used according to the aim of the analysis. Unlike the term "enterprise" or "state," it does not have a real entity to embody it. Nevertheless, the industry concept is often treated as if it had a concrete reality. By using this concept, an economic entity (e.g. enterprise) understands its position in the economy, and it represents its interest in the society. Industry-wide organizations often transform this analytical concept into "visible" entities with their own will, interest and action. In addition, some legislations specify certain occupations or economic activities, and create an institutional foundation for the reality of the industry. However, industry is essentially not a subject of action, and it has neither its own will nor unambiguous boundary. Hence, taking this to an extreme, industry is a theoretical construct, if not a fiction.

Second, industry is a medium (meso-) level category, which is positioned somewhere between micro-level ones (individuals, enterprises and individual units of enterprises) and macro-level ones (regional, national or world economy). In the eyes of individuals and enterprises on the micro-level, it is a collective and relational concept to group multiple economic actors/ activities according to the homogeneity and/or relationship (competition and cooperation) among them. Conversely, from the view of the entire economy, it is essentially a concept for comprehending the social division of labor (i.e. occupational or organizational specialization). Once a type of specialized economic activity is established as an independent occupation or a specialized business in the market, it becomes possible to categorize it as an industry. This means that, while elements on the demand side also have to be considered, industry is basically a concept focusing on the supply side.

Third, from the perspective of micro-level economic entities, industry is a venue where competition and cooperation take places. A group of firms (or units of them), which are competing, cooperating and trading among themselves form this "arena," where those players get together and play the game. This arena usually does not have a single designer and it emerges evolutionally as an outcome of cumulative actions and reactions by the innovative firms/entrepreneurs, their followers and other related actors. The entry barrier to these activities forms the boundary of the industry. Both the shape of the boundary and its intensity (i.e. difficulty of new entry) constantly transform as a result of entrepreneurial activities in and out of the arena. Creative destruction (Schumpeter 1942) and disruptive innovation (Christensen 1997) make this transformation drastic and fundamental. On the other hand, for most firms and individuals in the industry, except for the very early phase of the industrial emergence or exceptional cases of monopolistic firms, the industry is a "given" condition that appears as the environment for the micro-level economic entities. Hence, the relationship between the industry and individual firms within it is mutual.

Fourth, similar to the firm, the industry can be regarded as a bundle of resources. As the "resource based view" in strategy studies argued, a firm can be deemed as bundle of resources, including capabilities to deploy them (Penrose 1959; Wernerfeld 1984). If so, an industry, a pool of individual firms, can also be positioned as a bundle of resources. If we introduce a longer time horizon, we may also argue that an industry is a bundle of resources guided by the evolutionary process of a specific system of knowledge. Furthermore, the industry is not merely a sum of individual firms. Firms' economic activities usually result in externalities. So an industry contains something additional to the activities of its firms. In fact, a large number of studies on industry and industrial competitiveness have been paying special attention to the inter-firm networks in a given industry, relationships of supporting and related industries, and regional clustering of firms (e.g. Porter 1990). While individual firms appear and disappear, their resources are usually released to the market when those firms exit and they often remain in the pool of the industry. In that sense, though it may sound paradoxical if we remember the previous assertion on the "constructed" nature of industry, it may have an even more tangible reality and substance than individual firms.

Fifth, the concept of industry has an inherently nested or multi-layered structure (hierarchy), as a logical consequence being a "meso" level category. Official standard industry classifications of major nations (e.g. SIC in the US, UKSIC in the UK, JSIC in Japan) and international organizations (ISIC by the UN) exemplify this structure with digital code systems. Typically, in the case of the Standard Industrial Classification (SIC) of the US, the hierarchy from the first to the fourth digit represents different categories, such as "economic division" (e.g. "Manufacturing"), "economic major group" (e.g. "Chemical and Allied Products"), "industry group" (e.g. "Drugs") and "industry" (e.g. "Pharmaceutical Preparations"). However, SIC is nothing more than one among a countless number of industrial taxonomies. Both differences among national SICs and constant revisions of each SIC suggest this fact. The criteria of hierarchy and grouping can be very diverse. In addition, multiple criteria are used in a single SIC code system: *products category* (e.g. "Food and Kindred Products" [SIC 20], "Beverages" [SIC208] and "Malt Beverages" [SIC2082]); *use, function and product* (e.g. "Transportation Equipment" [SIC37], "Motor Vehicles and Equipment" [SIC371] and "Motor Vehicle Parts and Accessories" [SIC3714]): *technological feature, processes and materials* (e.g. "Chemicals and Allied Products [28], "Plastic Material and Synthetic"[SIC282] and "Cellulosic Manmade Fibers" [SIC2823]); *scope of market* (e.g. "Health Services" [SIC80], "Hospitals" [SIC806] and "Psychiatric Hospitals" [SIC8063]); *social function* (e.g. "Engineering, Accounting, Research, Management and Related Services" [SIC87], "Management & Public Relations Services" [SIC874] and "Management Consulting Services" [SIC8742]).

Hence, the study of an industry needs to focus on the appropriate level of the multi-layered hierarchy, according to the aim of its analysis. It is also important to know what kind of factors (i.e. elements to form the boundary of industry) defines the layers of the hierarchy. Discussions on "product differentiation strategy" or "high-value-added product" are good examples. Such an analysis postulates a specific view of the boundary of the segment. One may conclude that the US machine tool industry lost its competitiveness since the introduction of NC-machines by its Japanese rivals during the 1970s, while others may argue that they are still highly competitive in the top niche segment for aerospace products.

In short, industry is an analytical concept to understand the inner structure and dynamics of economy and society. The concept reduces the complexity and groups wide-ranging actors and activities in the market into a large number of subsets with shared features. Hence, if it is defined in an adequate way, each industry though it may sound like a tautology—has its own specific features and dynamics ("specificity of industry").

1.2 Specificity of Industry and Its Elements

There is no "one-size-fits-all" criterion by which we can define all industries. As we saw above, the industry concept has an inherent ambiguity; the multiple functions of industry concepts mean that multiple types of elements are actually employed as criteria for the definition of diverse industries. Four elements can be listed: 1) products (goods and services); 2) technology and knowledge; 3) economic function or position in the value chain; and 4) market. These four often overlap, and they are not exclusive to one another. Many industries do not fall into just one, but several of these elements. More importantly, the specificity of each industry can be well described by a systematic study of the nature of these elements.

The primary category for the definition of industry is product (including services). The homogeneity among a group of products forms an arena for competition because the same types of products can usually be substituted for one another. It is also important to note that virtually no product stands alone. Almost all products become commercialized goods or services through multiple processes and inputs of a variety of intermediate goods and services. Therefore, it is meaningful to bundle multiple products and treat them as one group. The economic activities to supply this group of products (e.g. semi-finished products and parts) can be also categorized as an industry, as long as the individual items of the products do not have the versatility to be used for other sectors. Accordingly, not only the competition, but also supply-demand relationship and relatedness among different products are essential elements to form the boundary of industry.

Products have their specific features and these form an entry barrier. Accordingly, both the boundary of an industry and the major determinants of competitiveness are basically defined by the features of the product. Hence, the clarification of the basic features of the product at stake is the first step in the study of an industry and its competitive dynamics. Furthermore, each product category has its own historical context. Some products, especially basic commodities with a long and distinctive history, such as foodstuffs (e.g., salt, sugar, pepper, potato, oil, coffee, tea, etc.), minerals (e.g., oil, coal, iron, etc.), other materials (e.g., cotton, silk, etc.), basic industrial products (e.g., paper, etc.) have been popular targets for the intellectual tradition of commodity history. The systematic analysis of the specific features of the product is an essential part of the study of industries and competitiveness within it.

The secondary category for the formation of the boundary of an industry is technology, including knowledge. To some extent, this is a clumsy tautology, because any product requires a specific technology or knowledge for producing it. Let's take the examples of "chemical products," "plating products" and "insurance products." We may argue that even in these cases, the category of products defines industries (chemical industry, plating industry and insurance industry). However, in these cases, individual products may have diverse items, designs, shapes, uses and functions. In this case, it is more appropriate to say that "function based on chemical composition," "process of surface covering by thin metal coating" or "application of insurance principle" categorizes these products. Likewise, rather than a tangible or intangible product with specific design, a set of knowledge and/or technology can form the boundary of an industry. In addition, similar to the afore-mentioned "relatedness among products," the versatility of knowledge and technology applied to multiple products makes it possible and indispensable to categorize diverse products into one group. Technology and knowledge often play an important role in the classification of process industries, because a specific process (e.g., forging) is based on a specific technology. A process based on a specific technology or knowledge often becomes an independent sector and forms an industry.

The trajectories of technology/knowledge often differ from those of products. Electronic information and communication devices are a good example. While the mainstream products have been changing almost every decade (radio, TV, VTR, PC, flat TV and mobile phone), this industry has kept its identity over time. In this case, a systematic but sector-specific knowledge based on science, technological experience and related capabilities has served as the thread to connect multiple products over generations. The long-term shift in the actual products on one hand and the continuity of knowledge and capabilities on the other can also be observed in the chemical industry. The heterogeneity of products can be seen not only in the historical transformation, but also in a cross-sectoral application of versatile technology/knowledge into diverse products. Thus, together with the history of commodities, technology history can offer important insights into the history of industry (e.g. Hounshell 1984).

As the third category, the economic function and position in the value chain are used to define an industry. As discussed above, industry is a concept of social division of labor (or specialization). Thus, both specific economic function and the unit of occupational specialization, such as "retail," "finance," "telecommunication," "consulting" or "temporary staffing" form an important basis for a categorization into industries. Especially in service industries, the product is usually not defined by tangible products but by economic or social functions. In these industries, national or regional differences tend to be conspicuous, because the social structure and pattern of social division of labor often have a high degree of geographical diversity. The form of social division of labor is actually the social structure itself, and unlike tangible products or technological knowledge, it is hard to transplant into other societies. Accordingly, a significant part of such industries does not fit with the discussion of international competitiveness. Nonetheless, these sectors often have close relationships with other sectors with a high degree of global market integration.

The fourth element of the classification of industry is the market. If a market with a specific character creates a common base for diverse and heterogeneous products, technology and economic functions, it is meaningful to classify these economic activities into one group, and such a group is often called an industry. Both geographical scope and social needs are used to specify the market. The diverse business of a regionally specialized trading company is an example of the former. In this case, special know-how about the region (e.g. language skills, knowledge of local culture, the ability to mobilize region-specific economies of scope, etc.) creates an entry barrier. As examples of the latter, "hospitality industry," "beauty industry" and "luxury industry" can be listed. In these cases, specific needs on the demand side, rather than the elements on the supply side define the "industry." Here, the term industry is used in the broadest sense, drifting away from its original use as a concept on the supply side. However, this extended application of the concept of industry has its own merit; it is good at elucidating dynamics and structural changes in the economy.

1.3 Industry Specific Time and Space

Despite the lack of explicit discussion, there is a widely shared understanding of the specificity of industries. Both in economics and management studies, scholars usually postulate that economic and managerial conditions may differ from industry to industry. Studies often use dummy parameters to deals with possible qualitative differences among industries in their quantitative analysis, and some studies try to measure the impact of industrial differences (Rumelt 1991). In the field of business history for example, Alfred Chandler selected cases from different industries (Chandler 1962, 1977, 1990). It is a reflection of their understanding of the specificity of individual industries, though many of them also argued that there are cross-sectoral general patterns or phenomena. As soon as one starts to apply general analytical concepts, such as economies of scale, transaction costs, stickiness of knowledge transfer, types of architecture design to actual economic activity, it becomes obvious that there are none-negligible differences among industries. Furthermore, once observers carry out empirical studies, significant differences among industries often emerge based on many criteria, such as growth rate, profitability, degree of concentration, level of entrance barrier, intensity of international penetration, etc.

However, can we go beyond a mundane statement, "all industries are different in many aspects" and obtain a clearer way to comprehend more generally the individuality of each industry? Considering the aim of our research, namely the investigation of the dynamics of competition among diverse locations and their historical transformation, the specificity of industry can be paraphrased: *"each industry has its own time and space"* or "there is *industry specific time and space.*" In other words, economic entities that belong to the same industry live in the same temporality, and those that belong to a different industry live in a different temporality. In the same manner, economic entities of an industry are sharing the same type of spatial condition as other entities in the same industry, while such conditions are likely to differ in other industries. If the time horizon differs from industry to industry, the pattern of industrial maturity or catch-up may differ, accordingly. The difference in the constraints of distance may result in a different intensity of global competition.

This is a very simple argument. However, both social scientists and historians have been engaged in diverse types of temporality or concepts of time (Wadhwani and Jones 2014), and it is worth making at least a minimum inquest. For research on industry history, it is possible to list multiple categories, such as *absolute age* (time arrow), *stages, cycles, generations, life cycles, longevities, speeds*, etc. (e.g. Abernathy and Utterback 1978). For each of these, one may find industry-specific features (Kurosawa 2012).

In history, all events are unique and no event will be repeated in the same manner. Thus, historical study has to pay enough attention to the absolute age. Any industry is born at a specific point in the time arrow, and it is marked by its age. Thus, the pattern of industrial development of an industry born in the 19th century may differ from the one in the 20th century. Different industries experienced historically unique events, such as the World Wars, the Great Depression, urbanization, demographic transitions, and the emergence of mass production or IT technology at different stages of their development.

Likewise, in other types of temporality, such as *life cycle, speed* and *longevity*, significant differences among industries are likely to be observed. For example, the product life cycle theory (Vernon 1966) postulates a certain tempo and patterns for the development and maturity of products, and it is not applicable to industries with fundamentally different tempo and patterns. The silicon cycle of the semiconductor industry typically shows the industry-specific speed and cycle and exhibits a remarkable difference from other industries with a slower tempo and smaller fluctuations. Many elements constitute the industry-specific temporality: speed of innovation, usable life of production facilities, period of product development, life of product models, durability (turnover) of product items, speed and fluctuation of demand, etc. In most cases, all of these elements show considerable differences industry by industry.

We can make the same argument about the spatial dimension. Each industry has its own space, reflecting the feature of its products, technology, social function and markets. On the spatial dimension too, diverse elements produce industry-specific conditions: required space and locational condition for facilities, transportation cost, possibility of geographical separation of processes, required intensity of communication, etc.

2 Multiple Viewpoints and "Industry-Centered" Approach

The studies on industrial competitiveness and the history of industries are marked by a striking diversity of approaches. On the one hand, many studies limit their focus to a specific country/region and analyze industrial dynamics, including the competition among enterprises (Nelson 1993; Owen 1999; Whitley 1999; Fellman et al. 2008). On the other hand, for a countless number of studies, the unit of analysis is individual firms, rather than industry. These studies analyze how those firms interacted with other economic entities in- and outside the industry (Chandler 1962, 1977; Fear 2005; Owen 2010). Furthermore, a considerable number of studies start with industry, rather than individual firms or locations (e.g., Itami 1992; Mowery and Nelson 1999; Chandler 2001; Lamberg et al. 2012). Although all of these approaches are indispensable and are complementary to one another, it is essential to provide an easy-to-understand framework to position each approach within a larger picture.

2.1 Industry as Arena of Competition

In this book, we deem that competition and competitiveness are the most essential elements for understanding industrial dynamics. They play a pivotal role in the transformation of organizations and institutions. The competition among diverse economic entities and locations can be positioned as the most important driver of globalization.

If so, what kind of competition among what type of actors shall be analyzed? First of all, it is obvious that the actual players who compete in the market are enterprises, not industries. Thus we are supposed to focus on competition among firms, and firms shall be taken as a unit of analysis. By focusing on the perception, behavior and resources of firms, and on their strategy and organization including inter-firm networks, the entire picture of industry shall emerge. This is a standard method both in management studies and business history.

However, there is a perplexing issue, namely the diversification of firms. Diversified firms compete with a different set of competitors sector by sector. If a player participates in multiple events, how can one make a coherent analysis across different markets? This is not a marginal problem, because diversification is the central element for the modern corporation, as the classical studies by Alfred Chandler demonstrated. Even after the paradigm shift from integrated large firms to the networking among specialized firms, most multinationals and many internationally competitive medium-sized firms have multiple businesses in diverse sectors and segments. The diversification is even more prominent when we look at new challenges from the emerging markets. As a series of works in business history demonstrated, diversified business groups often have a dominant position both in mature and emerging economies (Colpan, Hikino and Lincoln 2010; Colpan and

Hikino 2017). Many of those studies discovered that resources and capabilities go beyond the boundary of single firms. Hence, even when we regard enterprise as the subject of competition, the setting of boundaries of actors and the unit of competitiveness are not easy issues.

One possible solution to this difficulty is a focus on earning power. By this view, an entire group is regarded as a unit to produce profit and it is treated as the unit of competitiveness, regardless of whether it is a diversified modern corporation or a family owned business group. As long as we position a company organization merely as a vehicle to produce profit, this approach has some validity.

Nevertheless, this approach is not the ultimate solution. Even in this case, one has to investigate competition in each individual sector to understand where the competitiveness resides, and from where the profit comes. Neither the competitiveness of diversified firms/business groups nor their earning power can be separated from the competitiveness of the firm (or a unit of it) in each sector (and their sum). Even if the economies of scope arise from the entire structure of the diversified businesses, the competitiveness of each section has to be investigated in each segment (Kurosawa and Nishimura 2016).

2.2 *Triangle of Viewpoints: Industry-Firm-Location*

The above-mentioned problem, namely the question of the unit of competition and the adequate framework of analysis, is a very basic issue. However, a clear and simple explanation is often missing and such omission makes debates in this field needlessly complicated. For this reason, I present a conceptual diagram to clarify the position of a variety of approaches (Fig. 0.1).

The diagram shows three viewpoints (enterprise, location [nation/region], industry) of studies on business and economies, together with multiple angles and related research questions. The levels of individual entrepreneurs, managers or workers are omitted for simplification. All of these angles can be applied both to static and dynamic analyses, or historical studies.

When one starts with an enterprise and asks where (i.e. location) it was founded and where it does its business, or how the enterprise connects multiple locations and markets, the viewpoints and angle of the question are shown by the arrow "1) Market/Location Strategy." The term "strategy" is used because enterprise is basically an actor with its own will and action. In addition, research on the geographical features of firms can be represented by the same arrow, even if it does not directly question the behavior of the company.

Conversely, when one focuses on a specific location (or any geographical unit of location such as nation or region), and asks what kind of enterprises (whether domestic or foreign) exist in the location, what type of business they do, or what features they have, the angle of the question is shown by the arrow "2) Enterprise Landscape." For example, here we can categorize

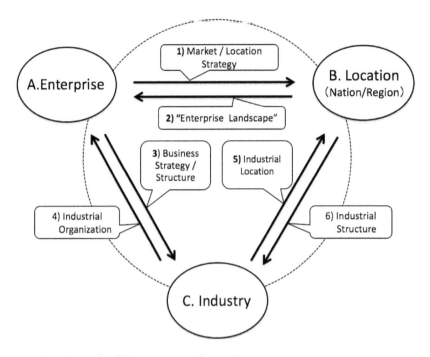

Figure 0.1 Triangle of Viewpoints: Industry-Firm-Location
Source: Designed by the author.

questions such as "Is German business characterized by small and medium-sized enterprises?"; "What was the function of the former bank-centered business groups in Japan?"; and "What are the advantages of start-ups in Silicon Valley?" Due to the lack of established terminology, we provisionally label it as "enterprise landscape."

Likewise, when one takes the viewpoint of enterprise and considers in which industry it does its business, or when one analyzes such a question as a third party observer, the angle can be classified as "3) Business Strategy/Structure." The afore-mentioned issue of corporate diversification belongs to this category. Both business strategy theory and business history have long traditions to address this type of questions.

The opposite direction, namely the arrow "4) Industrial Organization" is the viewpoint to take an industry as the starting point and observe the players in it. Industrial organization as a research field treats both industry and enterprises as abstract and quantitative entities. Even so, besides this established discipline, other types of studies, which pay more attention to the actual and individual feature of the industry and the enterprises, can be also classified into this section.

There are two directions of questions also between "B. Location (Nation/Region)" and "C. Industry." Once one specifies a certain industry, it is possible to ask the following questions: "Where are production and consumption located?" and "Which nation or region is competitive in production or the coordination of production?" We can also inquire as to what type of geographical structure the entire industry shows (e.g. is it a competition among nations or that among globally integrated networks? How are different locations connected to one another and who controls them? What kind of national or regional feature does the industry have?) We categorize this angle as "5) Industrial Location," although the term is usually used in a narrower sense and not sufficient to encompass all these issues.

Lastly, "6) Industry Structure" exhibits an approach by which one specifies a certain geographical category and analyzes the composition or characteristics of the industry inside the territorial boundary.

In this book, we analyze the global competition by positioning industry (C) in the center. Enterprise (A) and location (B) are channeled through industry (C). Thus a chain of "A-C-B" emerges as the main target of our analysis. The reason is simple; though actors in a competition are enterprises and the global reorganization of industries is an issue of location, the actual venue of competition is industry. The logic of the research and analytical steps are as follows; each chapter takes one industry and examines its geographical features and historical development by applying the viewpoints of "5) Industrial Location." Each chapter also analyzes the composition and characteristics of major players in the industry ("4) Industrial Organization"). By so doing, we reveal the firm-level actions that led to the outcomes (angles of "1) Market /Location Strategy" and "3) Business Strategy/Structure"); The remaining angles of "2) Enterprise Landscape" and "6) Industrial Structure" shall also be discussed, as long as it has a significant importance for understanding the central questions.

3 Industry and Geography: A Compact Birds-Eye-View

3.1 Spatial Categories

The spatial framework and geographical unit also contain both conceptual and technical challenges. The conceptual challenge is obvious: the international division of labor and global value chains of many industries have witnessed a fundamental change since the publication of Porter's influential work on the competitiveness of nations (Porter 1990). However, it is not clear to what extent the classical framework should be modified. Both the introduction of historical viewpoints and the conscious review of the unit of analysis may remind us of old but often marginalized questions: How have industries been geographically organized in the first place, and what kind of spatial/geographical categories were appropriate? If the national framework is not sufficient for the analyses, what type of geographical unit are we supposed to apply? The technical challenges in the geographical framework may seem less daunting, but they also require a series of systematic studies. Despite the massive amount of research on some industries, an overview of the global competitive landscape covering multiple industries is often missing.

For the first challenges, I make only a brief remark. Regarding the spatial unit of analysis, we are supposed to consider two types of special concepts. One is *territorial* categories, which have not only points and lines, but also spatial expansion. It has a boundary, though it can be unambiguous in some cases (e.g. the national economy), or blur more or less. Some territorial categories have the center-periphery structure, while others have only obscure ones. Many categories, such as small size industrial districts, sub-national regional clustering, national or supra-national economic areas can be classified into this. While the classical framework on the competitiveness of nations by Michel Porter was often mistakenly interpreted as the framework to emphasize only national units, his concept of cluster actually could be applied to the smaller or larger territorial unit. Hence, it is possible to discuss the industrial competitiveness of regional clusters, cross-border economic regions or supra-national regions, such as Europe or East Asia. Some chapters of this book will apply such an understanding to their analysis.

Another type of spatial category is *network*. It is constituted by specific locations/actors and relationships among them. In some cases, actors in such networks are only weakly bound to specific locations and thus have more mobility. However, even in such cases, economic activities tend to create some nodes in the network, which have more pivotal roles than others. If such nodes maintain their central role for a certain period, we can discuss the competitiveness of the location.

As for the second challenge, namely the task to provide an easy-to-comprehend overview of the global competitive landscape, the next section provides a tentative picture.

3.2 Geographic and Sectoral Distribution of the "Global 500"

Tables 0.1 and 0.2 show the geographical distribution of "Fortune 500" companies in each industry in 1990 and 2015. The regional classification is based on the headquarters of the companies.[1] These tables have serious constraints and they are subject to many biases. They show merely the position of large global firms and say little about the situation of entire industries. The inclusion into the "500" is based on revenues and it may have a large gap with market capitalization, profitability or competitiveness of those firms. Even diversified companies are classified into one industrial category and it may make any industry focused implication less reliable. The classification of firms and their revenues into each region/nation is merely based on the location of headquarters, thus neither the importance of each regional market nor FDI activities are reflected. From the perspective of our book, this table has a strong bias toward the "firm centered view," and it emphasizes too much the importance of headquarter locations.

For example, "Aerospace and Defense" in Table 0.2 (2015) shows 11 firms (5 from North America, 3 from Europe and 3 from China). Although Russia, Brazil and Canada have internationally active airplane makers, their numbers and revenues are not counted in the table, because they are out of the 500 ranking. In addition, while Boeing procures many components from their suppliers in Japan and other countries, and Airbus (EADS) manufactures also in China, all of their revenues are counted in the US and Europe (Netherlands) respectively.

Nonetheless, despite such biases and constraints, these tables are still useful to know "Which part of the world has large firms in each industry?" or "In which industry European, North American or East Asian firms have a larger presence?" These tables show a remarkable stability over a quarter century. The world's 500 largest firms have been concentrated in three regions, North America, Europe and East Asia (469 in 1990 and 464 in 2015). It is surprising that the position of "the rest" has not improved at all, even after a spectacular development of "emerging economies" since the early 21st century. The position of the three major regions witnessed some shifting though. In 1990, North America had the top position (181), followed by Europe (164) and East Asia (124). In 2015, the ranking reversed: East Asia (183), Europe (143) and North America (138). The most dramatic shift occurred inside East Asia. In 1990, "East Asia" was almost synonymous to Japan (111), and only Korea (11) had some position, while China had no company in the ranking. In 2015, however, China (98) had almost double the number of firms than Japan (54), and South Korea (17) and Taiwan (8) also improved their positions. It is true that the majority of those Chinese firms are state-owned enterprises and most of them are largely dependent on the domestic market. Their large presence does not necessarily mean international competitiveness of those companies. However, it shows a fundamental transformation in the region: from the dominance of Japan to a more balanced structure including China, Japan, South Korea and Taiwan. In contrast, the intra-regional composition changed little, both in the NAFTA countries and Europe. In 2015, only three firms are listed from Mexico, and none from Eastern Europe.

How is the situation of each industry? The regional distribution of competitive sectors is stable. North America and Europe have a strong presence in the sectors of energy, consumer goods/household goods, chemicals, pharmaceuticals and aerospace. East Asia has kept its strong position in metals and in electronics related industries. Europe and East Asia improved their positions in automobiles. In IT and electronic devices, Europe's position is constantly inferior to North America and East Asia. The table for 2015 shows a strong position of North American firms in retail, and a larger presence of East Asia in wholesales (e.g. trading company). In East Asia, except for China's presence in "Mining and Crude-Oil Production," where

Table 0.1 Geographical and Sectoral Distribution of the World's Top 500 Companies (Fortune Global 500) in 1990

Industries/Sectors	Revenue (Billion USD)	Number of firms ranked in	Regional Distribution of Headquarters of Fortune 500 Companies (Number of Companies)					Share of Revenue by the Regional Distribution of Headquarters (Share of each region by % and world as 100%)				
			North America	Europe	East Asia Sub-total	Japan	Others	North America	Europe	East Asia Sub-Total	Japan	Others
1 Mining, Crude Oil Production	74	12	1	5	0	0	6	5	65	0	0	30
2 Food	378	46	21	12	10	10	3	47	35	12	12	6
3 Beverages	91	17	5	8	3	2	1	46	36	12	9	6
4 Tobacco	44	5	2	2	1	1	0	23	59	18	18	0
5 Soaps, Cosmetics	52	9	4	3	2	2	0	64	21	15	15	0
6 Textiles	53	12	3	1	7	6	1	19	6	66	57	9
7 Forest Products	139	26	15	5	5	5	1	68	14	13	13	5
8 Petroleum Refining	759	52	16	14	12	7	10	45	34	12	8	9
9 Chemicals	381	50	17	23	9	9	1	31	55	13	13	1
10 Pharmaceuticals	94	17	10	5	2	2	0	62	28	9	9	0
11 Rubber and Plastics Products	53	8	2	3	3	3	0	26	39	35	35	0
12 Building Materials	81	16	3	8	3	3	2	13	67	13	13	7
13 Metals	307	38	10	18	7	6	3	16	57	21	19	6
14 Metal Products	84	18	3	8	7	7	0	19	35	47	47	0
15 Industrial and Farm Equipment	180	27	10	9	8	7	0	31	39	30	28	0

16	Scientific & Photographic Equip.	71	7	4	1	2	2	0	78	7	16	16	0
17	Electronics, Electrical Equipment	589	46	17	11	18	15	0	26	25	49	39	0
18	Computers	177	18	10	5	3	3	0	68	13	20	20	0
19	Motor Vehicles and Parts	745	42	7	14	19	18	2	38	31	30	30	1
20	Aerospace	157	17	11	6	0	0	0	77	23	0	0	0
21	Publishing, Printing	61	12	6	3	2	2	1	42	23	25	25	11
22	Others (Furniture, Apparel, Toys, Sporting Goods)	17	5	4	0	1	1	0	78	0	22	22	0
	Total	4,587	500	181	164	124	111	31					

Source: *Fortune Global 500*, in Fortune, July 1990. Compiled and classified by the author of the chapter.

Note 1) "North America" includes United States (168 companies) and Canada (13 firms). Europe includes United Kingdom (44), Germany (32), France (28), Sweden (15), Switzerland (10), Netherlands (8), Italy (8), Finland (7), Spain (5), Belgium (3), Norway (2) and Luxemburg (1). No firm from Russia is ranked in the list. Three firms from Turkey are classified in "others." East Asia includes Japan, China (including Hong Kong), South Korea, Taiwan, and South East Asian countries. However, in 1990, only Japan (111), South Korea (11), Taiwan (1), and Malaysia (1) had companies in the list and there were no Chinese firms. "Others" in 1990 include Australia (10), India (6), Brazil (3), Turkey (3), South Africa (2), Chile (1), Mexico (1), Venezuela (1), Kuwait (1), Saudi Arabia (1), New Zealand (1) and Zambia (1).

Note 1) "Industries/Sectors" are based on the original data of the "Fortune Global 500," except for "Others," in which three sectors are combined.

Table 0.2 Geographical and Sectoral Distribution of the World's Top 500 Companies (Fortune Global 500) in 2015

Sectors and Industries	Revenue Billion USD	Number of "500" Companies	Regional Distribution of Headquarters (Number of Companies)						Share of Revenue by the Regional Distribution of Headquarters (Share of each region by % and world as 100%)					
			North America	Europe	East Asia Sub-total	Japan	China	Other	North America	Europe	East Asia Sub-total	Japan	China	Others
1 Mining, Crude Oil Production	1,242	25	2	3	15	0	15	5	16	24	47	0	47	13
2 Petroleum Refining	4,738	38	7	8	14	4	2	9	22	29	33	4	20	16
3 Energy (others)	1,063	22	7	5	6	0	5	4	27	31	20	0	17	22
4 Utility	1,273	22	2	10	9	3	4	1	7	40	53	38	10	0
5 Engineering, Construction	759	13	0	3	10	1	9	0	0	19	81	3	77	0
6 Household Products	934	18	9	7	1	0	0	1	51	39	5	0	0	6
7 Apparel	116	3	1	1	1	0	1	0	24	36	40	0	40	0
8 Building Materials	121	3	1	1	1	0	1	0	22	45	34	0	34	0
9 Chemicals	420	8	2	3	2	1	1	1	22	48	18	8	10	12
10 Pharmaceuticals	455	10	4	5	1	0	1	0	42	49	9	0	9	0
11 Metals	716	17	1	3	13	2	10	0	3	22	74	12	54	0
12 Industrials	837	19	5	5	9	5	3	0	22	28	50	30	14	0
13 Technology	1,879	32	12	2	18	6	3	0	45	4	51	15	9	0
14 Motor Vehicles & Parts	2,700	34	4	11	18	9	6	1	14	38	46	26	14	1
15 Aerospace & Defense	541	11	5	3	3	0	3	0	48	24	29	0	29	0
16 Telecommunication	1,220	18	4	6	6	3	3	2	35	27	36	18	18	2
17 Media	138	4	2	2	0	0	0	0	58	42	0	0	0	0
18 Shipping, Railroad	216	6	1	3	2	1	1	0	11	65	24	12	13	0

19 Other Transportations	630	14	6	6	2	0	2	0	47	39	15	0	15	0
20 Wholesaler	1,014	19	5	2	12	5	6	0	19	16	65	27	35	0
21 Retailing	2,435	35	16	11	6	2	3	2	58	26	12	5	6	5
22 Finance	3,868	62	15	20	17	3	14	10	25	33	30	3	26	13
23 Insurance: Life	1,791	31	8	11	12	5	4	0	20	44	37	19	13	0
24 Insurance: Property	1,059	18	8	6	4	3	1	0	47	38	16	11	5	0
25 Services	132	5	1	4	0	0	0	0	79	21	0	0	0	0
26 Healthcare	965	13	10	2	1	1	0	0	91	6	3	3	0	0
Total	31,262	500	138	143	183	54	98	36						

Source: *Fortune Global 500*, http://fortune.com/global500/Compiled and classified by the author of the chapter.

Note 1) * "North America" includes United States (127 companies), Canada (11). "Europe" includes EU member countries, Switzerland and Norway, but does not include Turkey and Russia. "East Asia" includes China (98), Japan (54), South Korea (17), Taiwan (8) and South East Asian nations. Among South East Asian countries, Indonesia (2), Singapore (2), Thailand (1), Malaysia (1) have ranked companies. China includes Hong Kong. Among "others," Australia (8), Brazil (7), India (7), Russia (5), Mexico(3), Chile (1), Columbia (1), Saudi Arabia (1), Turkey (1), UAE (1) and Venezuela (1) have ranked companies.

Note 2) The original data of the *Fortune Global 500* has two levels of classification: "Sector" and "Industry." "Sector" includes one or multiple industries. In this table, both levels are used and some categories are merged, according to the aim of this book (see below for details).

Note 3) Details of classification adjustments; Categories from Nr. 1 to Nr. 4 correspond to the "energy" sector in the original dataset; "Energy (others)" in the table includes three industries in the original classification ("Energy," "Pipelines," and "Oil and Gas Equipment, Services"; "Household Products" (Nr. 6) includes the "Food, Beverage & Tobacco" sector and "Household Products" in the "Household and Personal Products" sector in the original dataset; "Industrials" (Nr.12) includes Industrial Machinery, Electronics, Electrical Equipment and Miscellaneous; "Technology" (Nr.13) includes the following industries: "Network and Other Communications Equipment," "Computers, Office Equipment," "Information Technology Services," "Computer Software," "Semiconductors and Other Electronic Components," "Electronics, Electrical Equipment," "Computer Peripherals" and "Internet Service and Retailing"; "Other transportations" (Nr. 19) includes "Airlines," "Mail, Package, and Freight Delivery"; "Retailing" (Nr.21) includes "Food and Drug Stores"; "Finance" (Nr. 22) includes "Banks," "Diversified Financials" and "Real Estate"; "Services" (Nr.25) is the sum of "Food Service," "Travel Services," and "Temporary Help" in the "Hotel, Restaurant and Leisure" sector. "Healthcare" (Nr. 26) includes "Health Care: Insurance and Managed Care," "Healthcare: Wholesalers," "Health Care: Medical Facilities" and "Health Care: Pharmacy and Other Services" in the "Healthcare" sector; however, it excludes "Pharmaceuticals" in the original category.

many Chinese coal producers are ranked, East Asian firms' strong presence is mostly limited to the industries in which Japan had a dominant position in 1990.

A comparison between the two tables reveals both dramatic changes and stability. A conspicuous difference is the range of industries in the two tables. The table for 1990 does not include firms in the sectors of utilities, telecommunications, airlines, railways and finance (banking and insurance and variety of services). This is partially due to the coverage of the original data, but it reflects more the outcome of privatization and the opening up of national markets. On the other hand, there is significant stability in regional advantages. Each region has a set of industries with stronger positions, and each has kept its positions for a quarter century. Similarly, though to a lesser extent, the position of each region in a given industry also shows some stability. Therefore, one may argue that we can discuss not only the competitiveness of individual nations, but also regions. Furthermore, this very tentative overview suggests the need for more historical and systematic studies with a longer term perspective. While the scope of this book is limited, quite a few chapters address this challenge.

4   Structure of the Book

This book is structured by industries, and each chapter analyzes a specific industry by reflecting the above-mentioned "industry-centered view." Some chapters observe the competitive landscape of the worldwide market (e.g. the chapter on watches and the chapter on the paper industry), while others focus on specific regions or nations, to exemplify the most essential phenomenon at stake in the industry. The analytical framework varies according to the nature of the industry. The scope of industry is also diverse and some chapters deal with a wide sector, while others analyze a small segment. The editors do not intend to compare this wide range of industries through a unified criterion. However, readers will discover both diversity and commonality among industries by reading through multiple chapters.

The book has three sections. The first section *"FDI and Global Competition"* focuses on multinational enterprises. The authors of this section concentrate more on the behavior of individual enterprises compared to authors in other sections. **Takashi Hirao** analyzes the "big three" firms of the global cigarette industry. The tobacco industry was mostly a business under monopolistic, state-control in many nations until the early 1980s. Since the 1980s, however, privatization, opening up of national markets, and waves of mergers and acquisitions redrew the competitive landscape. Hence, this is an industry to embody the globalization in the last three decades. **Dimitry Anastakis** sheds light on the Canadian automobile industry. Though often underappreciated, Canada's automobile sector was the world's fifth largest at the end of 20th century. With the absence of local car assemblers, the main driver for its development was the inward FDI by American firms, followed by Japanese multinationals. The Canadian case exemplifies the impact of national policy, the importance of the cross-border economic region and the emergence of the supra-national geographical unit as the spatial framework of competition. **Shigehiro Nishimura** studies turbine production for power plants, a section of the electric equipment industry. The competitive landscape of this industry is marked by a century-long stability, and old players from US, Europe and Japan still enjoy their dominant position in the global market. This chapter focuses on the strategy of Japanese firms, by examining the process of technology transfer and firms' FDI activities. **Julia Yongue** deals with a small but important sector in pharmaceuticals, namely vaccines. Vaccines are a special medicine with a public-goods like function, and French companies have kept their advantages in this market. This chapter analyzes not only the competitiveness of French multinationals, but also the features of competition in the Japanese market.

The second section, *"Localized Knowledge as a Lasting Competitive Advantage"* elucidates three cases in which a certain region or nation has held the dominant position in the world market for a very long period. Three relatively unknown industries, namely water construction, publishing and functional chemicals for electronics are examined. The geographic scope at stake varies: the clustering in a sub-national region (water construction), a nation (electro-chemical) and supra-national region (publishing) are considered as the geographic basis for competitiveness. **Bram Bouwens** analyzes water construction industry, a special segment in the construction business, where the technology of dredging, landfilling and maritime engineering forms the entry barrier. A small region in the Netherlands became a world-class leader in this sector and has maintained its dominant position over centuries. In this case, the transition from the classic sense of industrial district to an industrial cluster equipped with close ties with multinationals was observed. **Nuria Puig** and **María Fernández-Moya** examine the book industry, one of the most important segments of the publishing industry. Interestingly, rather than US firms from world's largest book publishing market, European firms from nationally or linguistically fragmented markets became the dominant global players. This chapter addresses this paradox by examining the role of historical and geographic conditions, together with entrepreneurship and innovations. **So Hirano** deals with specialty chemicals for electronic devices. They are not visible due to their nature as intermediate goods, but are universally used in many products including smartphones. In this market, Japanese medium-sized enterprises have had dominant positions for many decades. Such stability shows a sharp contrast with the situation of end-products, where the catch up by Korean, Taiwanese and Chinese firms entailed the industrial decline of Japanese firms. This chapter elucidates the reason for this contrast.

The third section, *"Shift in Global Value Chains"* investigates the most powerful driver of globalization in recent decades, namely the transformation of value chains. What kind of geographic unit should be adopted to comprehend the transformation of value chains and its impacts on competition? Did the unit of competition shift from the national economy to the transnational network? If a region keeps its dominant position even during such a transition, what was the mechanism that enabled the sustainable competitiveness? **Pierre-Yves Donzé** addresses these questions by focusing on the watch industry. In this case, the regional cluster in Switzerland maintained its dominant position for centuries, only with a short period of crisis, similar to cases analyzed in the second section. However, what is conspicuous in this case is the transformation of the character of the product (from precision instrument to fashion product) and the fundamental reorganization of the global production network. This chapter explains why Switzerland could maintain its advantage throughout the change. **Rika Fujioka** discusses a similar question by focusing on the retail industry dealing with apparel. Both department stores and fast fashion store chains are analyzed as actors in the competition, together with the role of apparel products suppliers in the emerging economies. A transformation of the value chain may have impacted not only the competition in the industry in question, but also in related industries, by reshaping the boundary of the industry. This chapter provides an eye-catching and insightful case for such a dramatic change. **Stig Tenold** and **Jari Ojala** elucidate how the European shipping industry surmounted challenges from new competitors by proactively reorganizing its value chain. Shipping is by definition a business to overcome distance, and it developed hand-in-hand with globalization. If a new form of global value chain contributes not only to the "latecomers" of the world economy, but also to the competitiveness of the old players, the mechanism in the background deserves special attention. **Takafumi Kurosawa** and **Tomoko Hashino** examine paper and pulp production, a typical "old" industry. While in this industry the national/supra-national markets still maintain a relatively high-level of self-sufficiency, an analysis focusing on global material flows can elucidate why some regions maintained their competitiveness and why others lost it. This chapter also demonstrates how customized analytical concepts can contribute to the explanation of the competitive landscape.

In the final section of the book, two co-editors, **Bram Bouwens** and **Pierre-Yves Donzé** provide conclusions by synthesizing the findings and implications of the analyses in the individual chapters.

Acknowledgment

I express my gratitude to Matthias Kipping and Kenneth Lipartito who offered me not only insightful feedback on my arguments, but also selfless practical support for the preparation of this section.

Note

1 By taking 500 firms in the "Fortune Global 500" as the total population, companies are classified into 22 (1990) and 26 (2015) industries and sectors. The third column "Revenue" shows the sum of revenues of the ranked in firms in

the industries. The fifth column "Regional Distribution of Headquarters" shows the number of firms in *Fortune Global 500* which has headquarters in each region and countries. The numbers for Japan (1990, 2015) and China (2015) are included number of "East Asia." The number of column "Share of Revenue by the Regional Distribution of Headquarters" does not show the share of regional revenue of the listed firms, but shows merely the percentage of aggregated sum of revenues of listed firms in each region to the one of total revenues of all listed firms in the 500 ranking.

References

Abernathy, W.J. and Utterback, J.M. 1978, 'Patterns of industrial innovation', *Technology Review*, vol. 80, no. 7, pp. 40–47.

Amsden, A. 2001, *The Rise of "The Rest": Challenges to the West From Late-Industrizalizing Economies*, Oxford University Press, Oxford.

Chandler, A. 1962, *Strategy and Structure: Chapters in the History of the Industrial Enterprise*, M.I.T. Press, Cambridge, MA.

Chandler, A. 1977, *The Visible Hand: The Managerial Revolution in American Business*, Belknap Press, Cambridge, MA.

Chandler, A. 1990, *Scale and Scope: The Dynamics of Industrial Capitalism*, Belknap Press of Harvard University Press, Cambridge, MA.

Chandler, A. 2001, *Inventing the Electronic Century: The Epic Story of the Consumer Electronics and Computer Industries*, Harvard University Press, Cambridge, MA and London.

Christensen, C. 1997, *The Innovator's Dilemma: When New Technologies Cause Great Firms to Fail*, Harvard Business School Press, Boston, MA.

Colpan, A., Hikino, T. and Lincoln, J. 2010, *Oxford Handbook of Business Groups*, Oxford University Press, Oxford.

Colpan, A.M. and Hikino, T. 2017, *Business Groups in the West: Origins, Evolution and Resilience*, Oxford University Press, Oxford.

Fear, J. 2005, *Organizing Control: August Thyssen and the Construction of German Corporate Management*, Harvard University Press, Cambridge, MA and London.

Fellman, S., Iversen, M., Sjörgen, H. and Thue, L. (eds.) 2008, *Creating Nordic Capitalism: The Business History of a Competitive Periphery*, Palgrave Macmillan, Basingstoke and New York.

Hounshell, D.A. 1984, *From the American System to Mass Production, 1800–1932: The Development of Manufacturing Technology in the United States*, Johns Hopkins University Press, Baltimore, MD.

Itami, H. 1992, *Nihon no Zosen Gyo: Sekai no Oza wo Itsumade Mamoreruka* (Shipbuilding Industry), NTT Press, Tokyo.

Kurosawa, T. 2012, 'Sangyo Koyu no Jikan to Kukan: Sangyo-shi no Houhou, Gainen, Kadai to Kokusai Hikaku Kenkyu no Kanousei' [Industry-specific time and space: Methodologies, concepts and challenges in industrial history and opportunities for international comparative studies], *Keizai- Ronso* [The Economic-Review], vol. 185, no. 3, pp. 1–20.

Kurosawa, T. and Nishimura, S. 2016, 'Gurobaru Keieishi towa Nanika [What is global business history?], in T. Kikkawa, T. Kurosawa and S. Nishimura (eds.), *Gurobaru Keieishi: Kokkyo wo Koeru Sangyo Dinamizumu* [Global Business History: Industrial Dynamism Beyond Borders], The University of Nagoya Press, Nagoya, pp. 1–30.

Lamberg, J.A., Ojala, J., Peltoniemi, M. and Sarkka, T. (eds.) 2012, *The Evolution of Global Paper Industry 1800–2050: A Comparative Analysis*, Springer, Dordrecht, Heidelberg, New York and London.

Mowery, D. and Nelson, R. 1999, *Sources of industrial Leadership: Studies of Seven Industries*, Cambridge University Press, Cambridge, New York, Melbourne and Madrid.

Nelson, R. 1993, *National Innovation Systems: A Comparative Analysis*, Oxford University Press, Oxford.

Owen, G. 1999, *From Empire to Europe: The Decline and Revival of British Industry Since the Second World War*, Harper Collins, London.

Owen, G. 2010, *The Rise and Fall of Great Companies: Courtaulds and the Reshaping of the Man-Made Fibres Industry*, Oxford University Press, Oxford.

Penrose, E. 1959, *The Theory of the Growth of the Firm*, Basil Blackwell, Oxford.

Pomeranz, K. 2000, *The Great Divergence: China, Europe, and the Making of the Modern World Economy*, Princeton University Press, Princeton, NJ.

Porter, M. 1990, *Competitive Advantage of Nations*, Free Press, New York.

Robinson, E.A.G. 1958, *The Structure of Competitive Industry* (rev. ed.) (first published 1931), Cambridge at the University Press, Cambridge and London.

Rumelt, R. 1991, 'How much does industry matter?', *Strategic Management Journal*, vol. 12, no. 3 (March), pp. 167–185.

Schumpeter, J.A. 1942, *Capitalism, Socialism, and Democracy*, Harper & Brothers, New York.

Stokes, R. and Banken, R. 2015, 'Constructing an "industry": The case of industrial gases, 1886–2006', *Business History*, vol. 57, no. 5, pp. 688–704.

Vernon, R. 1966, 'International investment and international trade in the product cycle', *Quarterly Journal of Economics*, vol. 80 (May), pp. 190–207.

Wadhwani, R.D. and Jones, G. 2014, 'Schumpeter's plea: Historical reasoning in entrepreneurship theory and research', in M. Bucheli and R.D. Wadhwani (eds.), *Organizations in Time: History, Theory, Methods*, Oxford University Press, Oxford, pp. 192–216.

Wernerfeld, B. 1984, 'A resource-based view of the firm', *Strategic Management Journal*, vol. 5, no. 2 (April–June), pp. 171–180.

Whitley, R. 1999, *Divergent Capitalisms: The Social Structuring and Change of Business Systems*, Oxford University Press, Oxford and New York.

Part I
FDI and Global Competition

1 Advantage of Being a Giant

The Global Cigarette Industry Since the 1980s

Takashi Hirao

Introduction

The tobacco industry is composed of many firms manufacturing a variety of tobacco products, such as cigars, pipe tobacco, chewing tobacco, snuff, and cigarettes. Among these, machine-made cigarettes are a special case of standardized products, and cigarette factories have become gigantic to gain economies of scale (Proctor 2012). After the emergence of machine-made cigarettes in the late 19th century, cigarette manufacturers succeeded in penetrating new markets and homogenizing their products through mass production and mass advertising around the world. As a result, cigarette consumption surpassed all other forms of tobacco consumption successively in the United Kingdom 1920, Japan 1923, Austria 1939, the United States 1941, and France 1943 (Goodman 1993; Japan Tobacco 1963). Today, about six trillion cigarettes are consumed worldwide, representing a 3% increase from the 2000s. China, the largest market, and the Eastern Mediterranean region are playing especially large roles in the growth of cigarette consumption despite reduction in smoking rates brought about by the passage of tobacco control laws that restrain the sale and advertising of tobacco and forbid smoking in public in other countries (The Tobacco Atlas n.d.).

Traditionally, the tobacco industry has developed either in the private sector or as a government monopoly. In the former case, since the late 19th century, mergers and acquisitions (M&As) were used as a major means to expand market share, particularly in the United States and the United Kingdom. In the United States, the American Tobacco Company (ATC) was established in 1890 by amalgamating five cigarette manufacturers. The ATC then entered Canadian, Australian, Japanese, and German markets through foreign direct investments (FDI) in the late 1890s (Cox 2000). In 1901, the ATC acquired the British company Ogden & Co. Ltd. and started conducting business in the United Kingdom. In reaction, the first mover in British tobacco industry, W.D. & H.O. Wills, merged 16 companies to form the Imperial Tobacco Co. (ITC) (Chandler 1990). Fierce competition between the ATC and the ITC led to an agreement between them and the creation of a new company in London in 1902 called the British American Tobacco

(BAT). ATC owned two-thirds of the capital of BAT, and ITC held one-third. The aim of BAT was to engage in the tobacco business in the world outside the United States and the United Kingdom. Therefore, BAT was born as a multinational enterprise (MNE) from the beginning (Alford 1973; Cox 2000). Yet, due to an antitrust case in the United States, the ATC was dissolved in 1911. Its shares in BAT were acquired by British investors, and it became 'the overseas arm of Imperial' (Chandler 1990, p. 247). In the United States, the ATC was broken up by the Federal Trade Commission into four companies (American Tobacco, R. J. Reynolds, Ligget & Myers, and Lorillard). Together with Philip Morris, a company founded in 1902, which succeeded in building a strong cigarette brand, Marlboro, these companies dominated the US market and became major players in the tobacco business throughout the world during the 20th century (Brandt 2007).

The next dramatic change in this industry occurred in the 1990s. The privatization of state-owned tobacco companies in many countries around the world provided the opportunity for a few MNEs, mostly American and British, to expand geographically in the context of an international cigarette market that had reached maturity. Gilmore, Fooks, and McKee (2011) stated that 30 countries privatized their tobacco business during the 1990s, followed by seven other countries in 2000–2008. Nearly all these former state-owned firms were acquired by the top four MNEs, namely Philip Morris International (PMI), British American Tobacco (BAT), and its associates, Japan Tobacco (JT) and Imperial Tobacco (IT). According to Physicians for a Smoke-Free Canada (2009), increased corporate concentration brought nearly 50% of the world's cigarette market under the control of these four MNEs (PMI, 16%; BAT, 16%; JT, 11%; and IT, 6%).[1] Thus, the global cigarette market is increasingly concentrated in the hands of a very few MNEs.

This chapter focuses on JT, drawing comparisons with two other giants, PMI and BAT. In contrast with these two Western MNEs, JT offers the rare case of a former state-owned enterprise that succeeded in transforming itself into an MNE after the privatization of 1985.[2] Consequently, this chapter intends to clarify how JT, whose overseas business had been the scanty export of its cigarettes to Southeast Asian countries until 1985, was able to become a top MNE in the cigarette industry. The main research question addressed in this study is as follows: How was JT able to build the necessary capabilities and adopt a proper global expansion strategy in a highly competitive market dominated by few British and American MNEs?

This chapter has two main purposes. One is to examine what competitive advantages JT has in the global cigarette market using a comparative analysis of the leading firms' three-pronged investments (production, distribution, and organizational capabilities) as defined by Chandler (1990). The other objective is to clarify how JT achieved its competitive advantages by exploring its history. Therefore, this chapter focuses on firm-level competitiveness in order to clarify how JT succeeded in expanding its business beyond Japan's borders to become one of the big three manufacturers despite its late entry into the global cigarette market.

The literature on international business and global management offers a broad range of theories and concepts that could be used to analyze JT's specific characteristics and sources of competitive advantage. This chapter builds in particular on the eclectic paradigm developed by Dunning (1979, 1995, 2000) to understand JT's ownership-specific and/or location-specific advantages that motivated its internationalization. According to Dunning, ownership-specific advantages of firms of one nationality over those of another include a benefit of some sort while operating and competing in unfamiliar foreign markets. For instance, intangible assets, access to the capacity of a parent company at favored prices, and economies of joint supply can be regarded as ownership-specific advantages over local rivals. However, FDI based on these advantages can be supplanted by export or licensing. Thus, firms that prefer FDI need location-specific advantages as well as ownership-specific advantages. Dunning argued that the former contains spatial distribution of inputs and markets, input prices, quality and productivity, transport and communications costs, government intervention, control on imports, and psychic distance. Namely, based on ownership-specific advantages, exploiting host-country-specific characteristics promotes FDI.

A second approach used in this chapter is the theory about global strategy developed by Porter (1986). Looking at the configuration of a firm's value chain, he identified two major types of organizations: multidomestic and global. A firm that employs a multidomestic strategy manages the entire value chain in each country, and thus each country's subsidiary has near or complete autonomy to tailor its activities to the country. In contrast, a firm that implements a global strategy selectively locates activities in different countries and coordinates among them to harness and extend the competitive advantage of the network. Thus, Porter pointed out the trade-off between global and multidomestic strategies: integration and uniformity vs. dispersion and fragmentation. There are many combinations of the strategies. Whether to concentrate or distribute individual activities, whether to configure them in any country or region, and how to coordinate them are all crucial decisions. Activities based on economies of scale or a continuity of activities such as a strong connection between research and development (R&D) and production can enhance the benefits resulting from integration rather than dispersion. On the other hand, as there are different needs in each country and the risk of the exchange rate and political instabilities exist, MNEs prefer dispersing over integrating their activities to respond to local needs and lower the risk.

This chapter consists of three main sections. Section 1 describes the historical development of JT, from state monopoly to MNE. Next, section 2 focuses on JT's competitive advantages today. Then, section 3 presents a comparative analysis of the three current giants, based on the works of Chandler (1990), Dunning (1979, 1995, 2000), and Porter (1986).

1 From State-Owned Company to MNE: Historical Development of Japan Tobacco

The competitive advantage of today's JT results from its unique development path in this industry. JT was the only former state-owned company to be able to internationalize and establish itself as a major player in the global market. This section explores the historical development of the firm and the challenge of privatization.

1.1 *JT in the Age of the State Monopoly*

JT's experience in the tobacco business dates back to March 1898, when the Japanese government established a monopoly bureau to exclusively sell domestic leaf tobacco. The government employed the bureau in order to prevent tax evasion through illegal cultivation and sales of leaf tobacco as well as to cover the expense of the Sino-Japanese War in 1894–1895. It extended this monopoly to include tobacco manufacturing in 1904, when the Russo-Japanese War broke out, and to the tobacco distribution business in 1931, due to financial difficulties from the Great Depression. As a result, the bureau operated all aspects of the tobacco business, from leaf tobacco cultivation to tobacco retail in the domestic market (Ueno 1998). In 1949, the monopoly bureau was incorporated as the Japan Tobacco and Salt Public Corporation (JTS) to support stable supplies and tax revenues for the government.

JTS actively facilitated the development of tobacco cultivation and production systems despite being a monopoly bureau. For example, the productivity of rolling and packaging cigarettes at JTS manufacturing factories was 28–40% of that of the foreign manufacturers before 1970. However, after 1970, JTS embarked on improving its productivity by restructuring its central research institute. In addition, agricultural experiment stations, as well as equipment such as drying facilities, nurseries for tobacco seedlings, and agricultural machinery, had been developed in order to improve agricultural productivity since 1970. JTS had been taking note that the European Economic Community (EEC), established in 1958, was trying to abolish tobacco government monopolies. Therefore, predicting that market-opening pressure would intensify, JTS created a long-term management plan titled 'Tobacco Business in the Future' [*Korekara no Tabako Jigyo*] in November 1968. This management plan not only included productivity improvement in its tobacco products but also aimed to expand JTS's tobacco business abroad and improve the quality of its tobacco products by introducing cross-licensing. As a result, JTS entered into cross-licensing agreements with PMI, Austria Tabakwerke AG, and Reemtsma Cigarettenfabriken GmbH in 1972 and with BAT in 1973 (Japan Tobacco 1990). Although cross-licensing was effective for overcoming tariff barriers, it did not lead to the development of the participants' overseas markets.

The Japanese cigarette market reached maturity in the mid-1970s as a result of decreasing population growth among the adult population and increasing concerns about health risks associated with smoking. While JTS sales went from 62.3 billion cigarettes in 1950 to 222.2 billion in 1970, it rose to only 303.9 billion in 1980 and peaked at 348.3 billion in 1996, before decreasing steadily until today (183.3 billion in 2015; Tobacco Institute of Japan n.d.). In addition to such structural changes in the domestic market, Japan's tobacco products were under pressure from market liberalization for foreign tobacco manufacturers who regarded the cross-licensing as a failure. Especially, the US government decided to appeal to the council overseeing the General Agreement on Tariffs and Trade in 1979 and put pressure on Japan to open its markets. As a result, the US and Japanese governments decided to reduce tobacco tariffs gradually. Thus, competition between domestic and foreign cigarettes in Japan's market could not be avoided (Japan Tobacco 1990; Miwa and Suzuki 2009).

1.2 Privatization in 1985

In March 1981, the first change to the monopoly tobacco system was proposed to the government. Namely, the government appointed a panel called *Rinji Gyosei Chosa Kai* (Provisional Commission for Administrative Reform) to deliberate on the public corporation system as well as financial reconstruction after the oil crisis. Its third report proposed abolishing the monopoly and public corporation systems in order to deal with the stagnation of domestic tobacco consumption and the demands for market liberalization (Japan Tobacco 1990; Miwa and Suzuki 2009). In response to this reform plan, the government drafted bills to establish a Tobacco Business Law (TB Law) and a Japan Tobacco Inc. Law (JT Law) to reorganize JTS as a joint stock company by abolishing the tobacco monopoly law and the earlier JTS law. These bills were passed in August 1984. As a result, in April 1985, JT was established and took over all the business operations and assets of JTS. At the same time, the Japanese tobacco market was opened to foreign tobacco manufacturers. Although the government monopoly was abolished, the government as the largest shareholder still influenced the corporate governance of JT. The following passage from the 2011 Annual Report illustrates this point:

> The JT Law provides that the Japanese government must continue to hold at least one-half of all of the shares that the government acquired by voluntary conveyance upon JT's establishment, as adjusted for any subsequent stock split or consolidation of shares, and that even if JT

issues new shares in the future, the government must continue to hold more than one-third of all of the issued shares.

(Japan Tobacco 2011, p. 50)[3]

The purpose of the TB Law enacted in 1984 was to achieve growth of the Japanese tobacco industry, stabilize government revenues, and contribute to the expansion of the Japanese economy. Moreover, the TB Law prescribed the cultivation and purchase of leaf tobacco as well as the manufacture and distribution of tobacco products because the biggest issue related to the opening of the domestic market was domestically produced leaf tobacco. Domestic leaf tobacco growers who feared competition from imported leaf tobacco strongly opposed privatization of the tobacco monopoly. As a result, with regard to leaf tobacco, JT was responsible for negotiating contracts with domestic leaf tobacco growers in order to determine the total area of tobacco cultivation and leaf tobacco prices. Furthermore, JT was required to purchase the entire usable domestic tobacco crop. In addition, the TB Law allowed JT to monopolize the production of tobacco in the Japanese market in order to make sure that the domestic tobacco crop was consumed. In making contracts with the producers, JT had to respect the opinion of the Leaf Tobacco Deliberative Council, which consisted of no more than 11 members appointed by JT from among representatives of domestic leaf tobacco growers and academic appointees with the approval of the Minister of Finance (Japan Tobacco 2011; Ueno 1998). The US government was dissatisfied with the continuation of such a manufacturing monopoly in Japan. In September 1985, it requested the abolition of either the regulations on foreign manufacturers' production in the Japanese market or tariffs on imported tobacco products. The Japanese government decided to totally abolish import duties on tobacco products starting in April 1987, because domestic leaf tobacco growers could not be protected unless JT maintained a tobacco manufacturing monopoly. Therefore, for its leaf tobacco procurement, JT relied on the domestic supply for about 60% of the tobacco, while certain types of tobacco that differed in aroma and flavor from domestic leaf were imported from various places such as the United States, Asia, Europe, and Africa. JT exported its tobacco products, mainly the highly popular brand 'Mild Seven' (renamed Mevius in 2013), to 30 countries through the Japan Tobacco International Corporation (JATICO), established in April 1984. Although tobacco exports totaled 1.5 billion cigarettes compared with 297 billion in domestic sales in 1987, JATICO sustained promotion of JT's products in overseas markets, with exports growing to 7.2 billion cigarettes in 1990. In addition, JT enlarged and enhanced the R&D functions of its laboratory by 1987. The major R&D areas were improvement of raw materials, research into the safety of tobacco-related materials and chemicals, development of new methods of cultivation to improve the productivity and quality of tobacco leaf, and refinement and testing of new tobacco manufacturing techniques and sophisticated control systems for highly automated plants (Japan Tobacco 1987). With respect to the relationship between JT and the Japanese government, JT had to obtain the approval of the Minister of Finance to set the maximum wholesale price of each class of tobacco released to the market. Tobacco product importers and wholesalers had to register with the Minister of Finance, and retailers of tobacco products were required to obtain approval from the Minister of Finance (Japan Tobacco 2011). Even after the privatization of 1985, government involvement in the Japanese tobacco industry was not necessarily over, because JT was also obliged to secure stable government revenues.

1.3 Diversification and Internationalization after 1985

In the 1970s, improving productivity was already a problem caused by pressure from the liberalization of domestic markets in the 1970s. After 1985, JT accelerated rationalization measures to enhance its cost-competitiveness and also pursued diversification led by its business development division, which was established to promote new areas of business such as pharmaceuticals and food. The business environment for JT changed drastically within two years after privatization. For example, The Plaza Accord in 1985 led to a very strong yen and weakened exports. Moreover, a tobacco tax hike in 1986 brought about a retail price increase for cigarettes. Finally, tariffs on imported cigarettes were totally abolished in April 1987. These changes led to a reduction in the price difference (previously ¥60–80 per pack) between domestic and foreign tobacco products in the Japanese market. As a result, JT's market share dropped from 97.6% in 1985 to 90.2% in 1987. In the 1990s, competition in the Japanese cigarette market intensified, after the liberalization of tobacco imports. In addition, the domestic cigarette demand peaked in the late 1990s due to a contraction of the adult population and growing concerns about health problems associated with smoking.

Since the domestic tobacco business's operating environment was becoming increasingly difficult, JT pushed forward with consolidation to achieve broad business diversification into the food and pharmaceutical businesses and a further expansion of its international tobacco business in order to maintain its current number of employees. In particular, as an international expansion strategy, JT took a positive attitude toward M&As in order to obtain access to local distribution channels and established cigarette brands around the world. For instance, in 1992, JT acquired Manchester Tobacco Company Ltd. to gain first-hand management experience and capabilities in its host country. JT acquired the non-US operations of R.J. Reynolds to establish Japan Tobacco International (JTI) as an overseas division of JT in 1999, and it also acquired Gallaher Plc in 2007. Moreover, JTI embarked on the integration of the tobacco leaf supply chain in 2009. Thus, JT obtained globally well-known cigarette brands through M&As and rapidly grew as one of the big three companies in the global cigarette market. JT's M&A

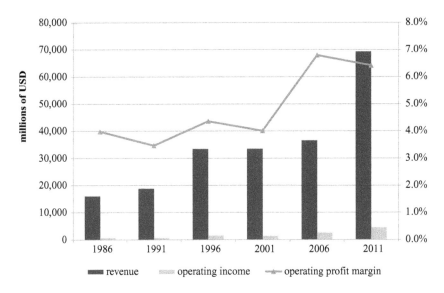

Figure 1.1   Japan Tobacco's Finances
Source: Japan Tobacco 1986, 1991, 1996, 2001, 2006, 2011.

activities—as it faced a shrinking domestic market—were intended as a means, in the short term, to become an international company under strict regulations on tobacco advertising in other developed countries (Shingai 2015).

As a result of its overseas expansion through active M&As, JT's international sales volume exceeded its domestic sales volume in 2006. Although such rapid growth in the global tobacco business brought about an increase in its total revenues, it did not contribute much to improving its profit margins (Figure 1.1). Even though, for example, the acquisition of the non-US tobacco business of RJR Nabisco in May 1999 and the purchase of Gallaher in April 2007 increased total revenues, the drastic increase in the operating profit margin in 2006 was brought about by domestic closedowns (decreasing from 25 factories to ten) in 2003, 2004, and 2005.

2 Japan Tobacco's Competitive Advantages

As the sole manufacturer of tobacco products in Japan, JT was devoted to boosting sales activities and developing new products in a domestic market that was facing both a stagnant demand and increasing competition from imported products. Especially, the strong yen after 1985 increased price differences between domestic and imported products. From the beginning of 1985, JT embarked on an effort to offset its production costs through efficient leaf tobacco procurement and effective operation of its 35 manufacturing factories located in Japan.[4] This section examines how JT promoted technical innovations and quality enhancement to turn the Japan factor into an advantage.

2.1 Home-Based Advantage

According to Dunning's eclectic paradigm, JT's history shows that ownership-specific advantages based on the home market allowed JT to increase its breadth in international tobacco markets. As a result, the integrated strategies and organizational structure of JT characterize it as an international company rather than a multinational or transnational company (Robinson 1984; Robinson, Dickson and Knutsen 1993). JT had some advantages over foreign rivals with respect to productivity because of its domestic industrial structure. However, JT also had some disadvantages related to its marketing and organizational structure. This raises the question of how JT actually acquired its competitive advantage.

JT had sold twice as many cigarettes outside Japan as within its home country since 2009, when Gallaher's tobacco business was merged into the company. The international tobacco business seems to have become the engine of JT's growth through its comprehensive brand portfolio. As shown in Figure 1.2, however, JT consistently earned profits from the sale of Japanese domestic cigarettes. This phenomenon arose from weak brands in the global tobacco market, JT's brands, and a distribution network inherited from the state monopoly age. Although a weak brand—called a 'discount brand'—will have low profitability, JT's monopolistic network in the domestic market allows such brands to contribute to its profitability.

2.2 Productivity in Domestic Cigarettes

In its tobacco manufacturing system, JT possesses domestic leaf processing factories as well as cigarette manufacturing factories. In particular, JT's relationship with its domestic tobacco growers is unique. According to the TB Law, JT is obliged to comply with the advice of the Leaf Tobacco Deliberative Council on the full purchase of the domestic tobacco crop and on tobacco leaf prices. Under increasing pressure to compete around the world and the necessity to reduce the negative impact of any increases in its purchase price, JT took a very positive attitude toward R&D investment, mechanization at factories, and even improvement of cultivation productivity.

In response to the difficult domestic operating environment, JT implemented rationalization measures to enhance its cost-competitiveness and pursued diversification. One of the rationalization measures was to eliminate excess production capacity. JT took over ten leaf processing factories and 35 cigarette manufacturing factories from JTS in 1985. These factories

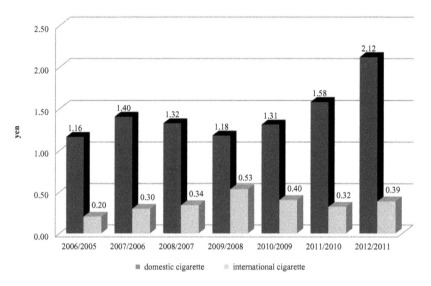

Figure 1.2 Profit per Cigarette

Source: Japan Tobacco 2012.

Notes: Values are averaged over each fiscal year ending March 31 (second year given) for Japanese domestic cigarettes and December 31 (first year given) for international cigarettes.

had excess capacities of about 50 billion and ten billion cigarettes, respectively. Therefore, JT closed or consolidated six leaf-processing factories and nine cigarette factories by 1993. In addition, JT developed high-performance rolling machines, such as the MMDP-8000 model, which had the world's best rolling capacity in 1988 (8,000 cigarettes per minute). Moreover, JT achieved a production cost reduction of about 40% through subsequent improvements to this machine (Miwa and Suzuki 2009; Proctor 2012).

JT's other main rationalization measure was to improve inventory management for leaf tobacco by optimizing its global supply chain. The government requested that JT used domestic leaf tobacco in principle. Leaf tobacco accounted for 60% of JT's raw material costs. Furthermore, as stated above, leaf tobacco prices were determined by the Leaf Tobacco Deliberative Council. Since JT was required to buy the entire domestic tobacco crop, these prices increased continually. JT had held a one-year stock of domestic leaf tobacco. One critical problem was how such over-stocking could be reduced. By introducing production adjustment incentives, JT promoted a policy of reducing the acreage under tobacco cultivation. However, this policy led to dissatisfaction among domestic leaf tobacco growers, and thus JT concluded a memorandum of understanding about leaf tobacco cultivation with the National Tobacco Cultivation Union in December 1989. As a result, JT declared that they would use the domestic crop as 50% of their total raw materials and would not reduce tobacco acreage further (Miwa and Suzuki

2009). Prices of domestic leaf tobacco were three times those of imported leaf tobacco. Therefore, enhanced productivity through realignment of the manufacturing process and the optimal level of inventory were inevitably necessary to ensure cost containment. To secure a stable and efficient supply of domestic leaf tobacco, JT embarked on the development of special purpose equipment, research on a new breed of leaf tobacco that required less labor, and the improvement of agricultural equipment while collaborating with domestic leaf tobacco growers. JT, which maintained domestic tobacco manufacturing as a priority, could also consume excess inventory by licensing the production of foreign cigarette brands such as Marlboro, which were very popular in the Japanese market. For example, JT had been granted exclusive licenses to produce and sell the following cigarettes in the domestic market: 'Old Splendor' from Austria Tabak in 1973–1983, 'Benson & Hedges' from BAT in 1974–1982, 'Milde Sorte' from Austria Tabak in 1983–1892, 'Gitanes' from SEITA (renamed Altadis after being acquired by Imperial Tobacco in 2008) in 1993–2003, and 'Marlboro' from Philip Morris in 1973–2005.

Thus, under contracts with domestic leaf growers to procure the entire domestic tobacco crop and fix its prices for the subsequent years, JT secured a supply of materials. It also reduced the negative impact of purchase price increases by implementing further integration in global leaf procurement and strengthened its relationships with suppliers. Moreover, it extended the use of common non-tobacco materials, increased its engagement with suppliers, and enacted flexible procurement to respond to attractive market prices. Finally, it improved its inventory management for both tobacco and non-tobacco materials. Thus, JT acquired its competitive advantages from a highly integrated manufacturing system under pressure to compete with foreign manufacturers in the domestic market.

2.3 Management of Business across Borders

JT's internationalization began in 1984, when JATICO was created to promote the export of its tobacco products under the demands of a more open domestic economy. Although the export of cigarettes, especially Mild Seven, increased mainly in Asia (Figure 1.3), increased cigarette exports could not balance the decrease in domestic cigarette sales.

Therefore, JT, which had faced the maturity of its domestic market since the 1970s, took a positive attitude toward M&As in order to obtain access to local distribution channels around the world. For example, in 1992, JT acquired Manchester Tobacco to manage its first experience and capabilities in a host country. JT acquired the non-US operations of R.J. Reynolds in 1999, when JTI was established as an overseas division of JT and was empowered to make decisions in international markets, except in Japan and China. In addition, JT acquired Gallaher in 2007. Thus, JT obtained

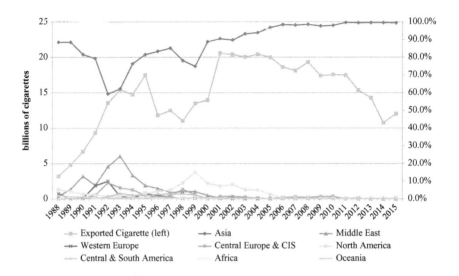

Figure 1.3 Japanese Cigarette Exports

Source: Ministry of Finance 2015, 'Trade Statistics of Japan'.

well-known global cigarette brands through M&As and rapidly grew as one of the big three in the global cigarette industry.

JT's headquarters in Tokyo has left overseas business management to JTI, whose headquarters are located in Geneva. Business plans are only discussed at biannual official meetings between the two headquarters. This suggests that JT, which has achieved rapid growth through M&As, faces a lack of human resources capable of making international business decisions. In other words, JT has not yet created an organization capable of managing its business in different, diverse countries.

3 Comparative Analysis of the Cigarette Giants

This section explores the competitive advantages of the big three in the global cigarette market by examining their annual reports with respect to manufacturing, marketing, and management in 2010 (Table 1.1). First, focusing on the differences in productivity among the giants, this section aims to see whether their production strategies depend on local responsiveness or global integration. Second, by comparing the number and share of their global brands, operating profit margins, and promotion activities among the giants, this section attempts to show how the giants have positioned themselves in the global cigarette market. Third, by investigating their organizational structure and the degree of diversity in the management of each firm, this section discusses the extent of their local responsiveness and global integration.

Table 1.1 Three-pronged Investments of the Big Three

Manufacturing

Company	Overseas sales volume (bn)	Domestic sales volume (bn)	Gross revenues (mn)	Earnings from overseas sales (mn)	Earnings from domestic sales (mn)	Factories	Average # of employees	Per-employee productivity	Labor equipment ratio	R&D intensity
PMI	899	–	67,713	11,200	–	56	77,800	11,566,272	82,834	0.6%
BAT	708	–	68,427	6,737	–	45	61,426	11,526,064	77,817	0.3%
JT	428	134	69,191	1,877	2,560	31	35,798	15,727,136	213,476	0.4%

Marketing

Company	# of the top 20 international brands	Sales share among the top 20 international brands	Sales share of GFBs* among all sales by company	Brands	Distribution (countries)	Operating profit margin (five-year average)	Earnings from domestic sales ($ per pack of cigarettes)	Earnings from overseas sales ($ per pack of cigarettes)	Promotion activities**
PMI	5	47.3%	58.9%	73	160	16.4%	–	0.25	0.6%
BAT	8	22.2%	50.6%	300+	180	10.4%	–	0.19	1.8%
JT	6	26.5%	44.4%	84	120+	6.4%	0.38	0.09	2.6%

Management

Company	Organizational structure	Directors	Nationalities represented among directors	Directors with external management experience	Executive officers	Nationalities represented among executive officers	Executive officers with external management experience	Regions in which company is engaged in business
PMI	M-form (region-based)	10	7	10	16	8	13	4
BAT	Holding company	13	8	10	10	6	5	4
JT	M-form (product-based)	8	1	1	21	1	0	1

Source: Philip Morris International 2010; British American Tobacco 2010; Japan Tobacco 2011.

Notes: All monetary values have been converted to US dollars for the fiscal year end. Units are billions (bn) of cigarettes and millions (mn) of US dollars. Earnings refer to operating income and operating profit. Gross revenues refer to tobacco sales including duty, excise, and other taxes. Per-employee productivity means the ratio of tobacco sales volume to average number of employees. Labor equipment ratio is the ratio of total assets to average number of employees. R&D intensity is the ratio of R&D expenditures to gross revenues. Factories include tobacco manufacturing and related factories. *GFBs means global flagship brands, which each firm tries to establish strong international brands through their brand portfolio.
**Promotion activities means the ratio of sales promotion and advertising costs to gross revenues.

3.1 Manufacturing

By focusing on the giants' geographical dispersion of manufacturing factories, productivity, and R&D intensity, this section will try to surmise their motivations to internationalize.

As shown in Table 1.1, PMI operated 56 factories around the world, sold 899 billion cigarettes in 160 countries, and had an average workforce of 77,800 employees. PMI reported revenues (including excise taxes on tobacco products) of over $67 billion and an operating income of nearly $11 billion. They posted an R&D intensity of 0.6%, the highest of the cigarette giants. BAT's total revenues (including excise taxes) were almost $68 billion, and about 10% of revenues became operating profit in 2010. BAT claimed to sell 708 billion cigarettes in 180 countries, have 45 factories around the world, and employ on average 61,426 workers in 2010. Their R&D intensity was 0.3%. JT increased its global market presence through M&As of other multinational tobacco companies such as the acquisitions of R.J. Reynolds' international tobacco business in 1999 and Gallaher in 2007. Consequently, in 2010, 76% of JT's tobacco sales were from international markets. JT reported revenues (including excise taxes) of over $69 billion and an operating income of about $4 billion. It operated 31 factories with an average of 35,798 workers in the period from April 2010 to March 2011. It had reduced the number of its domestic manufacturing factories from 35 to seven after privatization in 1985. Moreover, JT has gradually consolidated its international manufacturing factories after M&As. It posted an R&D intensity of 0.4%, concentrating its R&D activities on Japanese domestic tobacco; in 2011, its R&D intensity was 0.6% domestically but only 0.2% for international research.

PMI's factories were most widely dispersed throughout the world, while JT's were the most consolidated. In addition, JT's per-employee productivity and labor equipment ratio were the highest among the giants because JT did the most to rationalize and mechanize its manufacturing processes to enhance its cost-competitiveness. The per-employee productivity of BAT, which ranked lowest in terms of rationalization of its manufacturing, was the lowest among the giants, although BAT closed five of its manufacturing factories in 2010. As a result, both the per-employee productivity and labor equipment ratio of BAT were the lowest of the three, while JT's were highest because it implemented rationalization and mechanization measures to enhance its cost-competitiveness. BAT's performance was somewhere between that of PMI and JT.

3.2 Marketing

As Figure 1.4 shows, PMI manufactured five of the top 20 best-selling cigarette brands in the world in 2008, including Marlboro, L&M, Chesterfield,

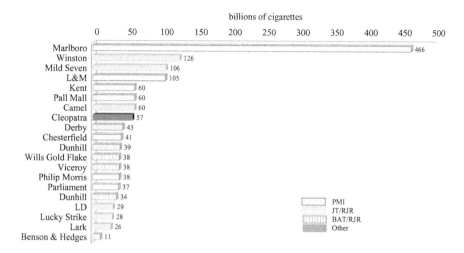

Figure 1.4 World's Top 20 Cigarette Brands (2008)

Source: Physicians for a Smoke-Free Canada 2009, *The global tobacco economy: a snapshot of the economies of multinational tobacco companies and of international tobacco control efforts in 2008*, Ottawa, pp. 4–6.

Philip Morris, and Parliament. Most importantly, PMI has an overwhelmingly strong brand, Marlboro. These top five PMI brands accounted for 47% of the total sales of the top 20 brands. In second place in total sales was JT, which held six of the top 20, including Winston, Mild Seven, Camel, LD, Lucky Strike, and Lark. These accounted for 27% of the total sales of the top 20. BAT produced seven of the top 20, namely Kent, Pall Mall, Derby, Dunhill, Wills Gold Flake, Viceroy, and Benson & Hedges, making up 22% of the total sales of the top 20.

In the cigarette industry, the prices of premium brands are 40% higher than those of discount brands, although they have approximately equal manufacturing costs (Moody's Japan 2011). According to Victor and Stewart (1991), discount cigarette brands require active advertising because profit from those brands is about one- to two-thirds that of ordinary cigarettes in the American market. As Table 1.1 shows, PMI sold 73 brands of cigarettes in 160 countries and obtained the highest operating profit margin among the big three. It earned $0.25 per pack of cigarettes from overseas sales. Furthermore, while the sales ratio of its global flagship brands (GFBs) to all brands was the highest among the giants, at 0.6%, its promotion activities were the lowest. This implies that PMI's earnings depended mainly on its strong premium brand, Marlboro. On the other hand, although JT was in second place in terms of market share of the top 20 cigarette brands, its operating profit margin was the lowest among the giants. Moreover, as its promotion activities were highest, JT needed a larger amount of money to promote its products than did other companies. This was because JT, which sold 84 cigarette brands in over 120 countries, retained many discount brands in its brand portfolio. However, it earned a great deal of profit from its domestic sales. JT has exercised self-restraint in advertising cigarettes in its domestic market since 1985, when the government announced guidelines for cigarette advertisements on television and magazines for women. However, Japan's regulations on tobacco advertising have been always too slow and too little compared with most other developed countries. In other words, such strong controls explain why JT took a positive attitude toward M&As, aiming to obtain existing brands to enter overseas markets. BAT, which sold more than 300 cigarette brands in 180 countries, managed a portfolio balanced between GFBs (50.6%) and many local brands.

Looking at the price premium of the big three firms' cigarette brands, PMI chose a global strategy to exploit the strong brand power of Marlboro. In contrast, BAT implemented a multidomestic strategy to efficiently manage their brand portfolio. PMI's premium brand—Marlboro—was strong in Europe and the Middle East. JT, which mainly possessed discount brands, was strong in the Commonwealth of Independent States (CIS) and Japan. PMI and JT concentrated their business on either high-income countries or low- and middle-income countries. In contrast, BAT, which obtained many local brands through M&A, dispersed its activities throughout the world.

3.3 Management

By investigating the organizational structure of the cigarette giants, the number of nationalities represented in their top management, and their external management experience, this section will describe the extent of their local responsiveness and global integration, that is, the diversity and uniformity of the organizations.

As Table 1.1 shows, PMI and JT employed a multidivisional structure, while BAT was a holding company. However, PMI's organization was region-based, while JT was product-based. PMI, which dispersed its factories the most among the giants, requires empowering the regional divisions to quickly and flexibly make decisions in order to keep up with the trend of each region under the control of headquarters. Although PMI's activities were restricted to within the tobacco industry, JT, which faced a mature domestic cigarette market, had carried out diversification by 1990. Therefore, JT developed the product-based M-form to efficiently respond to differences in the market and technology between their segments rather than respond to differences locally in foreign markets within the same segment. Actually, JT's international tobacco business has been organized into one of their tobacco divisions. According to MNE literature, this means a lack of organizational capabilities. In regard to management at the headquarters of MNEs, when managers who are responsible for multinational businesses lack international business experience and related expertise and when employees assigned to posts abroad are not familiar with local affairs, local people are employed and promoted to executive posts. However, accumulating knowledge of foreign markets at the headquarters accelerates the integration of decision making regarding companywide business strategies (Fayerweather 1969; Robinson 1984).

Table 1.1 indicates that PMI managers had the highest diversity of nationalities and the broadest management experience, while JT managers were most uniform in terms of nationality and had the narrowest management experience among the giants. In addition, the presidents of JT have always formerly been with the Japanese Ministry of Finance, which had authority to supervise its operations until 2000. Therefore, while the management characteristics of PMI and BAT were dispersive and professional, those of JT were uniform and amateurish in multinational business.

As Porter (1986) argued, these differences may indicate trade-off relationships between multidomestic and global strategies. In the multidomestic strategy, which locates production functions in different countries to respond to local tastes for cigarettes, economies of scale have less influence. Therefore, BAT's productivity was lowest among the big three in 2010, because BAT configured its factories in the various countries around the world to exploit host-country-specific characteristics by possessing over 300 brands. However, BAT has been able to coordinate these brands in its global network by using a holding company structure that provides higher empowerment than the M-form structure. In contrast, JT, which consolidated its manufacturing factories and rationalized the most, has been able to sell more cigarettes in overseas markets than in its domestic market. Despite this, JT gained more earnings from its domestic market than those overseas. JT employed a global strategy to highly integrate its activities uniformly under its headquarters, but it is rather amateurish in its multinational business. However, a global strategy that configures production functions to gain economies of scale in the global market weakens responsiveness to local tastes in cigarettes. As a result, JT's sales share (44.4%) of GFBs—positioned as strong international brands in its brand portfolio—was the lowest among the cigarette giants. PMI succeeded in coordinating its factories in the global network under its strongest brand, Marlboro. Although PMI's concentration of Marlboro in its brand portfolio was highest among the giants, it was flexibly managed by having factories that were most widely dispersed under headquarters that had high diversity and professional experience in multinational business.

Conclusion

The first purpose of this chapter was to clarify the competitive advantages of JT as compared to PMI and BAT. It showed that JT had positioned itself to require the most global integration, while BAT was under the strongest pressure to maintain local responsiveness and PMI put itself in a multifocal position.

PMI, which has an overwhelmingly strong brand, 'Marlboro,' operated 56 factories around the world under the control of a headquarters with the highest diversity of nationalities and most external management experience, and it thus earned the highest profit margin among the big three. JT, which has the most concentrated manufacturing system, obtained the highest productivity among the cigarette giants. However, JT's profit margin was the lowest due to the diffusion of its discount brands in the overseas markets. In contrast, BAT operated 45 factories throughout the world and sold over 300 brands across borders under the control of a holding company. Therefore, the advantages of JT in the global cigarette industry rely on high productivity under its integrated business system, which can produce high profitability from established brands in the domestic market, not from cigarette brands acquired in the overseas market.

The second purpose of this chapter was to examine how JT achieved its home-based advantages in internationalizing its tobacco business and to discuss the issue of privatization. The Japanese tobacco sales system formed after 1985 presented an entry barrier and provided government funds for FDI to JT. Such a system took over the role of the former state-owned tobacco company in the Japanese economy and politics. Actually, the JT Law required the Japanese government to continue to hold at least one-half of all the issued shares.[5] However, such home-based advantages provided JT with high profitability in its domestic business, which, in light of the difficulty in producing increased earnings from discount cigarettes in the overseas markets, were needed to meet its obligation to provide stable government revenues. In addition, JT's home-country characteristics contributed to improving its productivity. Under the leaf tobacco purchase system, which obliged JT to purchase all of the leaf tobacco produced domestically, JT faced competition with foreign rivals in the Japanese market after 1985. Therefore, JT needed to improve the productivity of agricultural work as well as its tobacco manufacturing factories and R&D activities under a highly integrated manufacturing system.

Notes

1 China has the largest production and consumption of tobacco products in the world. The China National Tobacco Company (CNTC), which held 39% of the global cigarette market in 2008, is vested by the State Tobacco Monopoly Administration, established in 1982, with rights to monopolize the domestic tobacco market, representing about a third of all smokers worldwide (Physicians for a Smoke-Free Canada 2009, p. 1; Zhang and Cai 2003, p. 17). However, this chapter excludes the CNTC because of its lack of FDI into business beyond China's borders.

2 In 1985, JT was established by the Japan Tobacco Inc. Law, under which JT is obliged to obtain approval from the Ministry of Finance for certain matters

regarding the issuance of new shares, appointment or dismissal of board members, distribution of surplus, M&A, and so on (Japan Tobacco 2015).
3 The shares of JT as a special joint-stock company were fully owned by the Japanese government for a short time after the privatization in April 1985.
4 JT consolidated its 35 domestic cigarette factories into seven through the rationalization of its business system in 2011.
5 This was changed to 33.35% of its shares in 2015 in order for the government to raise reconstruction funds in response to the Great East Japan Earthquake in 2011.

References

Alford, B.W.E. 1973, *W.D. & H.O. WILLS and the Development of the U.K. Tobacco Industry 1786–1965*, Methuen & Co LTD, London.

Brandt, A.M. 2007, *The Cigarette Century: The Rise, Fall, and Deadly Persistence of the Product that Defined America*, Basic Books, New York.

British American Tobacco 2010, *Annual Report*, British American Tobacco plc. Available from: <www.bat.com> [14 March 2013].

Chandler, Jr., A.D. 1990, *Scale and Scope: The Dynamics of Industrial Capitalism*, Harvard University Press, Boston, MA.

Cox, H. 2000, *The Global Cigarette: Origins and Evolution of British American Tobacco, 1880–1945*, Oxford University Press, Oxford.

Dunning, J.H. 1979, 'Explaining changing patterns of international production: In defense of the eclectic theory', *Oxford Bulletin of Economics & Statistics*, vol. 41, no. 4, pp. 269–295.

Dunning, J.H. 1995, 'Reappraising the eclectic paradigm in an age of alliance capitalism', *Journal of International Business Studies*, vol. 26, no. 3, pp. 461–491.

Dunning, J.H. 2000, 'The eclectic paradigm as an envelope for economic and business theories of MNE activity', *International Business Review*, vol. 9, pp. 163–190.

Fayerweather, J. 1969, *International Business Management: A Conceptual Framework*, McGraw-Hill, New York.

Gilmore, A., Fooks, G. and McKee, M. 2011, 'A review of the impacts of tobacco industry privatisation: Implications for policy', *Global Public Health*, vol. 6, no. 6, pp. 621–642.

Goodman, J. 1993, *Tobacco in History: The Cultures of Dependence*, Routledge, London and New York.

Japan Tobacco 1963, *History of Japan's Tobacco Monopoly Vol.4* [Tabako Senbaishi 4 kan (Shiryo-hen)], Japan Tobacco Inc., Tokyo.

Japan Tobacco 1986, 1987, 1991, 1996, 2001, 2006, 2011, 2012, 2015, *Annual Reports*, Japan Tobacco Inc., Tokyo.

Japan Tobacco 1990, *History of Japan's Tobacco Monopoly Vol. 6–1* [Tabako Senbaishi 6 kan (Jo-kan)], Japan Tobacco Inc., Tokyo.

Ministry of Finance 2015, *Trade Statistics of Japan*, Ministry of Finance, Tokyo.

Miwa, R. and Suzuki, T. 2009, *Japan Tobacco Industry* [Nihon tabako sangyo], Japan Tobacco, Tokyo.

Moody's Japan 2011, *Global Corporate Finance: Global Tobacco Rating Methodology*, Moody's Investors Service, Tokyo.

Philip Morris International 2010, *Annual Report*, Philip Morris International Inc., New York.

Physicians for a Smoke-Free Canada 2009, *The global tobacco economy: A snapshot of the economies of multinational tobacco companies and of international tobacco control efforts in 2008*. Available from: <www.smoke-free.ca> [27 February 2013].

Porter, M.E. 1986, *Competition in Global Industries*, Harvard Business School Press, Boston, MA.

Proctor, R.N. 2012, *Golden Holocaust: Origins of the Cigarette Catastrophe and the Case for Abolition*, University of California Press, Berkeley, Los Angeles, CA, and London.

Robinson, R.D. 1984, *Internationalization of Business: An Introduction*, The Dryden Press, Chicago.

Robinson, R.D., Dickson, J.P. and Knutsen, J.A. 1993, 'From multinational to transnational?', *The International Executive*, vol. 35, no. 6, pp. 477–496.

Shingai, Y. 2015, *M&A by JT: Textbook for Japanese Companies to Leap to International Companies* [JT no M&A: Nihon kigyo ga sekai kigyo ni hiyakusuru kyokasyo], Nikkei BP, Tokyo.

The Tobacco Atlas n.d., *Products: Cigarette consumption, industry: Tobacco companies* (4th ed.). Available from: <www.tobaccoatlas.org/> [13 August 2013].

Tobacco Institute of Japan n.d., *Data concerning tobacco*. Available from: <www.tioj.or.jp/> [8 August 2013].

Ueno, K. 1998, *A History of Tobacco* [Tabako no rekishi], Taishukan, Tokyo.

Victor, B. and Stewart, A. 1991, 'American cigarette industry: Its competitors and survey' [Amerika shigaretto sangyo: sono kyososya to tenbo], trans. K. Kawamura, *TASC*, no. 12, pp. 66–68

Zhang, H. and Cai, B. 2003, 'The impact of tobacco on lung health in China', *Respirology*, vol. 8, no. 1, pp. 17–21.

2 Access to Markets, Investment, Continentalization and Competitiveness

The Evolution of the Canadian Auto Sector

Dimitry Anastakis

Introduction

The purpose of this chapter is to utilize an example of the auto sector, more specifically the Canadian auto sector, to illustrate how and why certain industries determined their choice of location and their level of competitiveness. The overarching concept of this book perfectly epitomizes the dynamics of the Canadian industry, which was, from its start, profoundly "beyond borders," both in its creation and its development.

Why the Automobile Industry?

Globally, the auto sector remains a key foundational aspect of the world economy. A major component of advanced industrial capitalist economies, the auto sector historically has been the pinnacle of "industrial maturity," an aspirational goal sought by nations and regions since the beginning of the 20th century. As one of the major aspects of advanced manufacturing, investment, labour, supply chain, marketing and secondary industry, the auto sector is in many ways the progenitor and instigator of the modern global economy (Flink 1990).

In the 20th century, the auto sector was the leading industry in most advanced nations. In the post-Second World War period, in countries such as the United States, Germany and Japan, the auto sector has traditionally contributed the greatest single impact on gross domestic product, constituted the largest direct and indirect employment, and has often been the largest export sector. Politically, the auto industry remains at the centre of global economic considerations, and the role of automotive multinational enterprises (MNEs) are pivotal in a multitude of domestic and international aspects of political and economic development (Klier and Rubenstein 2008).

From a business history perspective, the auto sector was key to the development of Alfred Chandler's contributions on the managerial revolution (Chandler 1977) but also to understanding the development of modern corporate organization, finance and marketing (Clarke 2007), not to mention foreign direct investment and home-host relations of MNEs (Wilkins and Hill 1964). The auto sector has also featured prominently in a number of other business history literatures and paradigms, from Dunning's work on the location of MNEs to Porter's ground-breaking work on cluster theory (Porter 1990).

Why the Canadian Automotive Industry?

The first automotive MNEs were American firms that established operations in Canada at the dawn of the mass auto industry's emergence in the early 1900s. The Detroit-Windsor automotive corridor and the resulting emergence of an automotive cluster in Southern Ontario over the next thirty years were a direct consequence of the decisions of the United States automotive firms to enter into production in the Canadian market for a host of reasons. Though the Canadian industry emerged as a result of the foreign direct investment (FDI) decisions of US-based MNEs, the majority-US owned Canadian firms also embarked on their own FDI initiatives in an attempt to expand their own markets, such as Ford Canada's 1920s expansion into Australia, New Zealand and other British Commonwealth countries. This search for expanded markets was an important aspect of the Canadian industry, and, eventually, the continentalization of the industry allowing for direct access into the US market starting in 1965 meant significant growth and increased competitiveness for the Canadian industry, both in the assembly and parts manufacturing aspects of the sector.

As a result, for much of the 20th century, the Canadian auto sector was one of the largest global producers of automobiles, and in 1999 output reached a peak of over three million vehicles, ranking it fifth among auto manufacturers and ahead of traditional auto-making countries such as Italy

Table 2.1 Top 10 World Automotive Production in 1999 (Cars and Trucks)

		Population	Total production	Production per capita (vehicle per pop.)
1.	United States	276,218,000	13,024,010	.047
2.	Japan	126,505,000	9,904,298	.078
3.	Germany	82,178,000	4,994,723	.060
4.	France	58,886,000	3,190,227	.054
5.	Canada	30,857,000	3,048,693	.099
6.	Spain	39,634,000	2,772,416	.069
7.	South Korea	46,480,000	2,687,004	.057
8.	Great Britain	58,744,000	1,956,179	.033
9.	China	1,266,838,000	1,757,878	.001
10.	Italy	57,343,000	1,686,439	.029

Source: *Ward's Automotive Yearbook*, 2000

and Great Britain. Since the 1960s, the Canadian parts sector has grown dramatically, with major international firms such as Magna, Linamar and Wescast becoming significant players in the North American and global automotive supply chains. Automotive production has traditionally been the largest Canadian export and import category, employs the largest number of people and contributes significantly to Canada's GDP (Industry Canada).

Currently, in the Canadian auto sector cluster in southern Ontario, there are five manufacturers (GM, Ford, Chrysler, Toyota and Honda), and Ontario is the only subnational jurisdiction in the world with this many assembler MNEs. In total, these MNEs operate 11 assembly plants (three each for GM and Toyota, two each for Chrysler and Honda, and one for Ford). There are a number of global sole-source mandates of these plants, such as the Ford Flex (Oakville) and the Chrysler minivan (Windsor). The Toyota facility in Cambridge is also the only location outside of Japan that produces Lexus vehicles (RX 350, 450h). Total assembly employment in the early 2000s was approximately 30,000, including both union (Detroit Three) and non-union (Japanese). Significantly, all of these assemblers are foreign-owned. There are approximately 500 Canadian parts firms in this cluster, which range from small tool-and-die establishments to major near-assemblers, such as Magna. Total employment in the parts sector in the early 2000s was approximately 100,000 (largely non-unionized), and the sector contains both significant Canadian and foreign ownership.

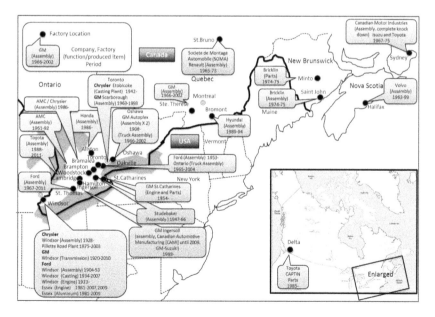

Figure 2.1 The Canadian Automotive Industry
Source: Drafted by the author.

From a global perspective, Canada's industry remains relatively under-studied. For example, a recent major volume on "Atlantic Automobilism" that examines the "emergence and persistence" of the car from 1895 to 1940 includes no mention of Canada, despite Canada's status as the second largest producer and consumer of automobiles by the 1920s (Mom 2015). Indeed, most surveys of the global auto sector have mostly examined the United States, Western Europe and Japan (Halberstam 1986). In part, this is because while Canada has been a G7 member since the 1970s, it is not traditionally considered a core economy, owing to its relative dependence upon the export of raw materials and the perceived underdevelopment of its manufacturing sector. Another key reason is that there are no Canadian-based assemblers. Further, industry output, particularly from the auto assemblers, is almost entirely focused on production for North American markets. Because of the almost complete continentalization of the sector, the Canadian assembly industry does not compete globally, in a traditional sense; the Canadian owned parts sector, however, does.

Two key determinants have shaped the Canadian industry. First is its proximity to the United States auto sector, both in terms of geography and ownership, which placed Canada in a position unique amongst auto industries in the world. Because of the overwhelming closeness and influence of the American sector, the Canadian industry provides an excellent example of early adaption, technology transfer, the importance of scale within an industry, the creation of an industrial cluster, and most significantly in the Canadian case, the shifting impact of FDI.

Second, public policy has had a significant role in addressing the problems and opportunities that emerged from the Canadian sector as a consequence of proximity to the United States. In this regard, tariff policy has played an important part in shaping unique corporate organizational arrangements in the industry, providing opportunities for access to markets, affecting productivity and competitiveness, and influencing the nature of FDI. Ultimately, the two most important factors in shaping the Canadian industry was access to markets and FDI. In terms of inward FDI, the chapter supports previous works that indicate an overall benefit of FDI in terms of productivity, knowledge transfer and competitiveness, particularly for developed economies (Caves 1974; Globerman 1979; Catherin 2000, Mordue 2007).

The chapter will illustrate these elements of the evolution of the Canadian industry through three parts. The first explains the emergence of the Canadian automotive cluster primarily as a consequence of industry factors, namely the proximity of the US sector resulting in the emergence of the Canadian sector in the shape that it eventually took. The second part of the chapter pauses to explain the emergence of formal continentalization of the industry after 1965. Part three addresses the impact that this continentalization had upon the sector's structure and competitiveness within North America. In doing so, this section also examines Magna International as a case study of the development of the Canadian parts sector, and ends with a look at how continentalization shaped inward FDI from Japan.

1 The Emergence of the Canadian Automotive Cluster

Why did US automotive MNEs come to Canada? There are a multitude of reasons: close proximity to Canada, the decisions of individual entrepreneurs to establish joint ventures and other cross-border corporate arrangements, desire to access Canadian and other British markets, and the failure of Canadian indigenous manufacturers to maintain a viable home industry.

1.1 The Problem of Scale: Proximity to the United States, Early Canadian Adoption and FDI

Unlike most traditional clusters, as established by Porter's "diamond" approach, the emergence of the Canadian automotive cluster at the end of the 19th and the beginning of the 20th centuries was a direct consequence of Canada's proximity to the United States, particularly the emergence of United States' own automotive large and growing industrial cluster in the Detroit area during this period (Anastakis 2004). The impact of US proximity was apparent in many economic sectors, not just automotive, and not solely manufacturing. Nonetheless, automotive was the most high-profile and visible Canadian sector that was dominated by the US industry.

Centered in Detroit and central Michigan, where the mid-western wagon industry had flourished, between 1890 and 1915 hundreds of American auto companies were founded. Across the Detroit River, a number of automotive ventures in Southern Ontario also emerged; the 1904–1933 period saw a host of car companies cluster in Windsor, as the town quickly became a magnet for automakers, both Canadian and American. Firms such as The Canadian Commercial Motor Car Company (1911–33), Dominion Motors (1910–15), Dodge Brothers (1920–24) and Maxwell-Chalmers (1904–25) all converged on the border town. By the First World War, Windsor had become Canada's undisputed "Motoropolis" (Roberts 2006). However, the emerging Canadian cluster was a fraction of the size of its US counterpart. Moreover, Canadian firms often lacked technological capabilities, were short on capital, or were simply unable to sell enough of their product in such a geographically large but poorly linked and sparsely populated national market (Traves 1987; Davis 1990; McDiarmid 1940).

As a consequence, by the 1910s, many Canadian firms were taking advantage of their proximity to the sizeable Detroit cluster by adopting US technology, developing joint ventures, and agreeing to corporate partnerships that resulted in US automotive branch firms and plants being established in Canada. The latter measure was, in part, to avoid the 35% tariff on completed automobiles imposed by Canada; even with the high protection of 35%, Canadian companies were hard-pressed to remain solvent. A few

Table 2.2 Some Early Producers in Canada

Firm	Location	Dates of Existence
McLaughlin Motor Car Company	Oshawa, ON	1908–22 (under McLaughlin brand, after 1918 GM)
REO Motors	St. Catharines, ON	1904–14 US firm in Canada
McKay	Kentville, Nova Scotia	1910–13 Imported US motors
Russell Motor Car Company	Toronto, ON	1904–16 After 1910, US engines imported
Brockville "30" and Brockville-Atlas	Brockville, ON	1911–15 Imported US parts
Chalmers Motor Car	Windsor, ON	1916–24 US firm
Canadian Motors Limited	Toronto, ON	1911–14
Tudhope Motor Cars	Orilla, ON	1909–14 Imported US parts
Willys-Overland	Toronto, ON	1915–33 US firm
Gray-Dort Motors Limited	Chatham, ON	1915–25 Imported US parts

Source: Hugh Dumford and Glen Baechler, *Cars of Canada.*

Canadian firms attempted to survive by importing cheaper American parts (the 30% duty was less than that for completed autos), but by 1925 the last of these, Gray-Dort, was out of business after its American parts-maker had closed its doors. By the late 1920s, there were no strictly Canadian-owned concerns left in the industry. While the tariff was not solely responsible for the end of the Canadian car manufacturer, it certainly hastened the demise of an indigenous industry and by the 1920s, the Canadian auto industry was clearly dependent on the American (Ankli and Frederiksen 1981).

Meanwhile, by the 1920s, American auto companies in Canada were flourishing, a consequence of economies of scale, capital needs and geographic location. The scale requirements and intense capital needs of mass auto manufacturing that hastened the end of indigenous Canadian production was also present in the American industry. By 1925, virtually all American auto manufacturers had failed or had been acquired by other companies, leaving the industry with only a handful of successful firms, especially the Big Three of GM, Ford and Chrysler (Hyde 1996). These firms dominated American auto production for the next five decades, and did so in Canada as well; by the time of the Great Depression, the sector was dominated by the Canadian subsidiaries of the US Big Three.

Three examples that illustrate the impact of US FDI in this period will suffice. First, there is the creation of the Ford Motor Company of Canada.

Gordon McGregor, an enterprising Canadian, visited Detroit and struck a deal with Henry Ford in 1904. In return for granting the use of Ford patents and drawings, and the right to sell Fords to other British nations (save for the UK), the stockholders of the Ford Motor Company received 51% of Ford-Canada. With the success of the Model-T, also built in Canada, by the 1920s Ford of Canada was the largest industrial enterprise in the British Empire (Anastakis 2004; Wilkins and Hill 1964).

General Motors of Canada, on the other hand, started as the largest indigenous Canadian car manufacturer, Oshawa's McLaughlin Motor Works. In 1908 Sam McLaughlin arranged with William C. Durant, the financial wizard who formed General Motors, for a contract to use David Buick's engines. Later, Durant offered McLaughlin the Canadian rights to the Chevrolet "Classic Six," a car designed by Louis Chevrolet, which became a sales success in Canada. But McLaughlin soon realized that maintaining Canadian independence was too costly and technologically demanding. In 1918, following Sam McLaughlin's decision to sell to Durant's company, McLaughlin became GM Canada, a wholly-owned subsidiary of GM (Robertson 1995).

Chrysler took the most traditional FDI route to Canada, directly buying its plant in Windsor and establishing Canadian operations as a wholly-owned subsidiary in 1925 (Moritz and Seaman 1981). Due to these branch plant operations, Canada was the second-largest motor vehicle producer in the world between 1918 and 1923. By 1926 Canadians were building over 200,000 vehicles a year, and the industry employed 12,000 people. While all of the assemblers were American, there were a few small Canadian parts makers that survived largely through tariff protection (Bladen 1961, p. 101).

Thus, the Canadian auto industry was, practically from its birth, both national and regional, a product of unique circumstances that saw the massive American auto industry located on an international border. Indeed, US automotive firms first became "multinational" because of their entry into the Canadian market during the industry's early period. By the interwar period, over ninety percent of the Canadian auto industry was American-owned. The pervasive American influence, however, was not entirely negative. Some scholars have argued that Canada's proximity to the US and the American presence in the Canadian industry actually helped to "democratize" the auto and helped to spread the motorization of Canada at a much faster and easier pace than Canadians could have done themselves (Davis 1990).

1.2 The Benefits of Branch Plants: Technology Transfer and Access to Markets—British Commonwealth

Beyond "democratizing" motor vehicle use for Canadians, the Americanization of the auto industry had other key benefits. First, there was the benefit of technology transfer, which allowed the Canadian subsidiaries to utilize the latest developments of the US firms in their own production for the Canadian market. For example, Ford Canada generally followed the schematics and production guidelines sent from across the river, and gained the benefits of production and technology advances that were being achieved in Dearborn. Sometimes, Ford-Canada's output varied form Detroit's: Windsor did not produce a two-door Model T in some years, while the Canadian company produced four-door Model T's before they were built in the US. Other unique Canadian-made additions, such as stronger headlights or heavy upholstery, emerged as a response to more difficult driving conditions and colder winters, and in the 1920s and 1930s the Canadian firm continued to offer vehicles which departed from US-produced models (Anastakis 2004).

Similar practices occurred at GM Canada and Chrysler Canada, which benefitted immensely from their parent firms production practices and technological innovations. The Canadian Big Three firms acted as "miniature replicas" of their American parents, utilizing many imported manufacturing techniques and building smaller batches of many of the same cars that were built on the US side of the border. Without this American technological and production transfer, no Canadian industry would have existed (Holmes 1983).

A second key benefit that resulted from Americanization—and benefitted the US owners of the Canadian branches—was the ability of the Canadian firms to sell their products to other British nations. The impact here was twofold: on the one hand, it allowed the Canadian producers to secure bigger markets, thus increasing their production and economies of scale; it also allowed these US MNEs to more easily establish themselves in markets that were otherwise protected by British Empire/Commonwealth tariffs. Thus, while much of the Canadian production was intended to supply the Canadian market, the industry also exported a significant amount of its output overseas to other parts of the British Commonwealth. As part of the imperial preferential system, the Canadian government maintained a lower tariff rate of 22.5% for its fellow dominions. This system encouraged American companies to assemble and export their wares from Canada to gain the benefit of the lower duties.

Ford of Canada, for instance, held exclusive rights under its 1904 agreement with the Detroit firm to market Fords in Australia, New Zealand, South Africa, India and other imperial destinations, and the Canadians quickly took advantage of the overseas arrangement (Anastakis 2004). In August, 1906, just two years after the company's founding, the first Canadian-built Fords (Model K's), were shipped to Australia. Of the 101 vehicles built in 1906, 25 were exported (James Mays 2004, 13) Ford Canada was soon exporting a significant portion of Fords built in Windsor overseas, regularly as much as a third of production before 1920. These exports provided Ford-Canada with greater economies of scale than would have been possible producing solely for its domestic market, and helps to explain the company's fantastic growth before 1930.

Table 2.3 Canada Auto Exports and Imports, 1904–1940

Year	Motor Vehicles: Units				Parts: Dollar Value	
	Passenger Cars		Motor Trucks			
	Exports	Imports	Exports	Imports	Exports	Imports
1904–1910	804	4,175	–	–	–	–
1911–1915	17,828	29,651	–	–	–	8,310,453
1916–1920	74,803	49,898	–	6,520	11,255,470	42,768,134
1921–1925	204,068	49,321	45,342	5,275	17,949,433	73,049,733
1926–1930	242,937	158,526	114,426	22,013	15,009,920	176,288,551
1931–1935	113,776	14,866	40,672	4,153	9,354,062	80,859,949
1936–1940	183,321	70,736	138,669	10,581	21,780,469	154,401,961

Source: *Statistics Canada (Cat. No. 65–004 and 65–007)*

In response to demands by colonial governments for local production, Ford-Canada shifted from exports to setting up assembly operations in these imperial destinations, and by the mid-1920s boasted wholly-owned subsidiaries in Australia, India, Malaya (Malaysia) and South Africa. The Canadian subsidiaries in these locales were established and managed almost exclusively by Canadians, and operated utterly free from Detroit influence. These imperial subsidiaries proved immensely lucrative, as dividends and production of Ford vehicles in these far-flung offspring were funneled back to the Canadian firm, which in turn were used for further expansion and were shared by Ford-Canada stockholders (Anastakis 2004).

By the mid-1920s, Canadian auto exports to British Commonwealth countries were significant, valued at over $33 million in 1924, while in 1925 nearly *half* of all passenger cars built in Canada were exported (Bladen 1961, p. 101). American-owned companies (usually wholly-owned subsidiaries as opposed to join ventures or having a Canadian ownership element) made hefty profits building cars in Canada and selling them to Canadians and overseas. Canadians reaped the benefits of this economic boom in the form of employment and production. The American firms that owned these Canadian subsidiaries also benefitted in ensuring their own market dominance in these far-flung locales.

2 The Role of Public Policy: The Shift from Tariff Protection to Regional Trade Agreements

After 1945, the need of the Canadian industry for access to greater markets resulted in an industry supported continentalization of the sector into that of the US. This continentalization meant the development of new corporate structures, increased productivity and investment, and a wholly new competitive environment, particularly for Canadian parts makers, who now could embrace economics of scale to build for the entire North American market.

2.1 Access to Markets II: Continentalization of the Industry after 1965

In the period after the Second World War, the Canadian industry experienced a boom, as it benefitted from the postwar prosperity that fueled domestic consumption and a renewed overseas market for cars. But by the early 1960s, the industry faced difficulties. A large auto trade deficit with the United States threatened Canada's balance of payments as US-owned Canadian Big Three branch operations imported from the United States an increasing number of cars and parts that were not made in Canada. Moreover, given the proliferation of styles and models, Canada's plants could simply not keep up with the demand of Canadian consumers for the latest models; they also could not keep up with the latest technological developments, such as the increasing popularity of automatic transmissions. A decline in the 1950s export market meant that Canadian manufacturers needed to gain access to larger markets, most notably the US market (Anastakis 2005).

As a result, in the early 1960s, the federal government in Ottawa embarked on a number of initiatives to boost exports from Canada to the United States, and also to prompt the US car companies—and the American government—to rethink the automotive trade and production relationship between the two countries. After a series of incidents, including a confrontation over imported parts and a tense round of negotiations, what emerged was the 1965 Canada-US Automotive Products Trade Agreement, or auto pact.

The shape of the agreement reflected the constraints faced by the industry and by each government on both sides of the border. Although the US administration was keen to enact a free trade agreement that created one continental market for autos, the Canadian government was far less sanguine about such a notion. The Canadian negotiators understood that unrestricted free trade could wipe out Canadian production in an industry already over 90% owned by American interests. For their part, the auto companies were interested in seeing an agreement that allowed them to rationalize their production and take advantage of North American economies of scale. Most importantly, they did not want to see Canada follow the onerous local content and ownership demands being put in place in countries such as Mexico, Brazil or Australia in the 1950s and 1960s (Keeley 1983).

Instead, the two governments and the industry came to a compromise: the Canadians succeeded in having local content, investment and output targets built into the agreement that guaranteed certain levels of Canadian production in the North American market. While they knew that the agreement marked the end of any notion of a "national" auto industry for Canada, they also understood that the new regime provided jobs, investment and, ultimately, survival for a threatened industry. The US government acceded to these as the price of solving a difficult problem with their closest economic partner which they hoped would eventually lead to unrestricted free

Table 2.4 Evolution of the Canadian Automotive Industry

	Institutional Element	Trade Policy	Owner of Canadian industry	Major markets	Production organization/Mode
19c–1930s	• Protectionism	• Import Custom • British preference	• Canadian Assemblers to 1918 (McLaughlin) • US Assemblers (GM 1918–, Ford 1904–, Chrysler 1921–) • US parts makers • Small Canadian Parts Makers	• Canada (60–90%) • British Empire, including Australia, New Zealand, Malaysia	• Small scale, local markets, limited efficiency • High cost
WWII	• Wartime production	• Export of wartime production	• US Assemblers	• none	• Wartime production; no commercial production
1945–1985	• Exchange rate fluctuation • Support for public/social programs: electricity costs, infrastructure, health care; • Trade Policy. • Cross-border union, the United Auto Workers.	• Canada-US Auto Pact (1965), managed trade	• US Assemblers + (Studebaker, 1948–66) • Sweden/US (Volvo, 1964–98) • Japanese (Isuzu, Toyota) • Canada (less than 30% of parts sector)	• Canada (70–90%) • British Commonwealth	• To 1965: local production, small scale, limited efficiency, lack of production or technology innovation; some export • 1965–89: Canada-US Tariff free, large scale production, increased productivity and efficiency; Canadian content requirements
1985–2001	• Investment Incentives/Subsidies • Labour nationalism, Canadian Auto Workers Union.	• Canada-US FTA (1989–) • NAFTA (1993–)	• Assembly: US, Japan • Parts: US, Japan, Canada • Japanese (Honda, Toyota, Suzuki, 1985–) • Korean (Hyundai, 1989–93)	• United States (80%)	• North American content requirement; large scale production • Emergence of major Canadian parts makers
2001–	• Partial nationalization (GM, Chrysler), 2008–2015	• NAFTA, WTO • Mexico major player	• US+ Japanese Assembly • Decline in US Big Three operations	• United States (80%)	• Decrease in US assembly; Canadian parts makers internationalize

trade in the auto sector—a significant step forward in the US policy of creat-ing a North American trade zone. For the industry itself, the new agreement avoided the far more punishing requirements being foisted upon them in other countries, and held out the possibility of integrating their operations on a continental scale (Beigie 1970).

Ultimately, industry support for the agreement, helped to smooth its pas-sage. The new arrangement allowed companies based in Canada or the US (essentially the Big Three and their Canadian subsidiaries) to import parts and autos duty free as long as they maintained a minimum 50% North American content for parts and autos imported into the US, or in Can-ada achieved minimum production targets and continued to build as many cars and trucks in Canada as they had before 1965. With the agreement, Canadian producers were no longer restricted to build only for the Cana-dian market, and could reorganize their production along continental, as opposed to national lines. Canadian firms—both the subsidiaries of the Big Three and the Canadian parts producers—now had access to the whole of North America for production (Thomas 1996).

2.2 Corporate (Re)Structures: From Branch
Plants to Complete Integration

With the continentalization of the industry through the auto pact, the Big Three moved to rationalize their operations. Administratively, the compa-nies reorganized their subsidiaries so that the Canadian entities were now completely integrated into their North American operations. All of the Big Three shifted decision-making for their Canadian facilities to their corpo-rate headquarters in Michigan. Chrysler reorganized its operations so that Canada, once a separate entity under its own administrative hierarchy, was now included under "US and Canadian Operations." In a special letter to shareholders in 1967, GM explained that due to the agreement, the com-pany had realigned production facilities between the US and Canada result-ing in increased expansion and some dislocation (Chrysler 1967; General Motors 1967).

With the creation of the auto agreement, the parent company moved to absorb Ford-Canada into a new North American organization. Ford-Canada was integrated into the North American Automotive Operations section under an executive vice-president responsible for continental opera-tions. The president of Ford-Canada, though he retained this largely sym-bolic title, now reported to the head of the sales group for North American operations, while the Group Director of the Canadian Overseas Group was now responsible to the parent company's Executive VP in charge of overseas operations. Ford of Canada's purchasing, research and development and personnel operations now became closely tied to the parent company's, and Dearborn had the final say on every major decision. While Ford Canada remained a separate profit centre within North America (it was still traded on the Toronto Stock Exchange), all production decisions were organized on a continental basis, and the Canadian company drew heavily on Ford US expertise to meet performance targets. By the end of 1967, Ford-Canada had become a mere division within Ford's North American operations (Wilkins and Hill 1964; Ford 1965–67).

As a result, a new form of subsidiary emerged within MNEs that was unique to the Canada-US continentalized relationship. The host country entity that was once a distinct subsidiary was now completely subsumed and integrated into the home country. With the consolidation of home/host entities, Canada's auto assembly industry became entirely North American in its ownership, organization and operations (Holmes 1983).

3 Competitive Impact of Continentalization

The competitive impact of continentalization on the Canadian industry could be seen in the increased productivity and competitiveness of the Canadian assembly sector, but particularly so for the Canadian parts industry. There, access to markets, corporate consolidation and innovation resulted in industry leaders such as Magna International. Continentalization also resulted in a new wave of FDI from Japanese MNEs, further benefitting the Canadian sector.

3.1 Productivity and Competitiveness of the Canadian Sector after 1965

In response to the auto pact, after 1965 the Big Three shifted a greater percentage of their North American assembly operations to Canada, and to take advantage of lower costs (a product of a lower-valued Canadian dollar and government-administered universal healthcare) and good productivity and quality results at its Canadian facilities. In 1965, Canadian production was 7% of the continental marketplace, yet by the 1990s, Canadian production was consistently over 15% of North America (Holmes 1996; Molot 1993; Perry 1982).

For example, at Ford, this meant that by the 1980s and 1990s its Canadian plants were the sole North American production source for its Windstar/Freestar minivan, and its important Crown Victoria/Grand-Marquis mid-sized cars, which made up a significant element of fleet sales in North America as police vehicles and taxicabs. Ford-Canada's Essex engine plant also became Ford's most important engine production centre, and since 1981 produced over 8 million engines for use in a wide range of its products. 85% of Ford-Canada's production was exported to the US in the 1990s. This was similar to GM's and Chrysler's Canadian operations, which also sole-sourced vehicles for all of North America.

Canadian productivity and competitiveness within the integrated sector correspondingly increased. In the 1970s auto sector employment was 30%

higher than in the rest of the economy, and that the parts industry had come within 10% of the productivity level of its US counterpart (far in excess of the rest of the Canadian manufacturing sector), while Canadian assembly operations actually exceeded those in the US by approximately 20%. Canadian Big Three production mostly grew, specialized and became far more productive (Roberts 2002).

The parts sector also flourished and saw the emergence of significant Canadian-owned firms. Able to take advantage of the "Canadian content" requirements of the auto pact and the ability to sell directly to Detroit (or to sell to the Canadian Big Three assemblers who were now building or all of North America) hundreds of Canadian companies increased their production and exports dramatically in the fifteen years after the auto pact's implementation. Parts exports from Canada to the US increased from 13% of total production of $690 million (about $90 million) in 1964 to 69% of total production of $4.4 billion in 1977—an astounding $3 billion (Reisman 1978, p. 79). Much of these exports were intra-company sales within the Big Three between their Canadian captive parts firms and their US operations. Another large percentage was constituted by sales of American parts makers with Canadian subsidiaries selling into the US (Reisman, p. 86). But Canadian-owned parts makers also experienced growth in this period.

The growth in the sector was also borne out by an increase in the number of firms and in the growth in employment. Before the auto pact, the Canadian parts industry consisted of less than 150 firms. In 1975, the number of establishments was 231, and in 1980 it was 342. By the mid-1980s, there were nearly 500 parts companies operating in Canada (statistics Canada, various years). Correspondingly, the number of workers in the parts sector nearly doubled in the fifteen years between 1964 and 1978, and in the mid-1970s surpassed the number of workers at assembly plants in the country.

Notwithstanding the initial and ongoing challenges faced by the industry, there was no doubt that Canadian parts makers were reaping the benefits of the integrated sector by the end of the 1970s. In 1978, Canadian parts industry topped $2 billion in sales for the first time. Three-quarters of this production were shipped to the US. By 1986, analysts estimated that the Canadian-owned segment of the industry was selling $2.5 billion in parts, nearly one-fifth of the total Canadian sector (*Report on Business Magazine* 1986, p. 104).

3.2 Supply Chain Development: The Case of Magna International and the Parts Industry

Magna International is the best example of the increased competitiveness of the postwar Canadian auto parts sector. Founder Frank Stronach emigrated from Austria in 1954, opening a tool-and-die shop in Toronto in 1957. Obsessively focused on quality machining, Stronach's first contract with GM Canada, to make a metal bracket for a sun visor, was worth $30,000.

From that point forward, Stronach slowly started to build an auto parts company. When the auto pact began in 1965, Stronach was well-placed to take advantage of the new competitive environment created by continental integration. The auto pact, "changed Frank Stronach's life . . . the Pact made it possible for him to build a profitable small business into an empire" (Lilley 2008; Gibb-Clark 1986).

Much of Magna's initial success was in consolidating a diverse and broad range of Canadian parts makers under its corporate umbrella. In 1968 Magna took control of Multimatic Investments Ltd., which at the time had five subsidiaries making parts. In the decade after 1968, Magna consolidated a number of firms in the parts sector, expanding its product lines and capacity. For instance, in 1969 the company bought an Orillia tool-and-die maker and a small stamping outfit, then a steel fabricator in 1970. In 1972 it bought a muffler maker, and the next year the company became Magna International.

In the 1970s, as continentalization continued to provide opportunities to Canadian parts firms, business boomed for Magna. When Magna landed a contract for a Canadian Big Three manufacturer (and the company maintained relationships with all of the Big Three), the scale of its sales far outstripped what Magna had been doing in the pre-auto pact period. Just as important was Magna's management approach: Magna's plants were organized in a uniquely decentralized structure which gave each individual plant significant autonomy, kept plant sizes small, and kept unions out. Instead, workers were part of a profit-sharing plan, one which included lump sum payments out of annual profits and shares in the company. Magna also maintained recreational and day-care facilities for its workers (Anderson and Holmes 1995; Lewchuk and Wells 2006).

The company also devoted a significant amount of funds to research and development, always seeking to achieve high technology value-added capabilities. This focus led to Magna's ability to build significant components and modules of vehicles when the Big Three began to outsource major parts development. By 1977 Magna was exporting nearly 60% of its auto parts production to the US, and within a few years had annual revenues of over $1 billion. In 1986, the firm had over 100 factories, 10,000 employees, and each car built in North America contained $73 worth of Magna parts (Anderson and Holmes 1995).

Another example of success in the parts industry is that of Frank Hassenfratz. Another postwar immigrant, Hassenfratz was a Hungarian uprising refugee and former army engineer who came to Canada in 1957. Hassenfratz started Linamar, (named after his daughters Linda, Nancy, and his wife, Margaret) in a Guelph, ON basement in 1966 with one lathe bought with borrowed money. His first contract was making fuel pumps for Ford Motor. By the 1970s Linamar had established itself as a leading manufacturer of close tolerance metal parts and components such as steering columns, axles, or oil pumps in the auto, defence and aerospace fields.

Like Magna, Linamar had a unique organizational structure, with each of its subsidiaries (eleven by the early 1980s, employing nearly 2,000 workers) autonomously-run, usually by managers who had worked their way up from the shop floor. Like Magna, too, the company was non-unionized. Linamar's healthy growth reflected the new opportunities that an integrated auto sector represented following the auto pact: In the 1980s, over 80% of the company's exports were to the US, and the largest single contract Linamar had was with GM in Detroit. Six out of seven of its biggest contracts were North American sole-sourced contracts for auto manufacturers (Ehchin 1991).

Suppliers in newer aspects of the parts-making sector also did well under the auto pact regime. Firms such as the ABC Group, created in 1974, specialized in plastic automotive components, particularly injection moulding. By the 1980s ABC was a major supplier to the Big Three in both Canada and the United States. So too did the Woodbridge Group of Mississauga, ON, founded in 1978. Specializing in foam for seating, Woodbridge's largest customers were Ford and GM in the US and other major American seat suppliers such as the Lear Corporation (ABC, www.abcgroupinc.com/en/default.htm; Romain 1984).

Wescast originally started as the Western Foundry Co. in Brantford, ON, in 1902 building stoves and furnaces for firms such as the T. Eaton Company. In the 1960s the company shifted to auto parts, which eventually became its core business. In 1980, Wescast received a contract to build exhaust manifolds for the Pontiac Firebird and Chevrolet Camaro, assembled at GM plants in Van Nuys, CA, and Norwood, OH. By the 1990s the company had become one of the largest suppliers of exhaust manifolds in the world (Wescast www.wescast.com/en/heritage).

3.3 Benefits of Continentalization: Japanese FDI, FTA and NAFTA

Continentalization helped to spur another major round of inward FDI into Canada, this time from Japan. In the early 1980s, American political pressure led to major Japanese auto investment into the US, including the creation of a GM-Toyota joint venture and plants established by Honda and Toyota. Fearing that US-built Japanese products would flood into Canada through the auto pact, the Canadian government enacted a number of protectionist measures designed to spur Japanese investment into Canada as well, including a port slowdown that stalled Japanese import vehicles, demands for local content requirements and Voluntary Export Restraints. Eventually, Japanese producers decided to also establish facilities in Canada to avoid these difficulties. This would allow them to take advantage of the continentalized Canada–US market for production purposes, one that was further developed by the Canada–US Free Trade (FTA) and North American Free Trade Agreements (NAFTA) in 1989 and 1993 (Anastakis 2001).

Honda, in keeping with the company's philosophy to produce where the company sold its products, announced in 1984 that it would build a

$100 million plant in Alliston, ON, employing about 300 workers to pro-
duce approximately 40,000 vehicles (Mordue 2007). Then, in 1985 Toyota
decided to build plants in both the US and Canada. While the US would get
an $800 million, 200,000 car a year plant with 3,000 workers that would
build the more expensive Camry, the Canadian plant was proportionately
more modest. The Canadian facility, in Cambridge, Ontario, was initially
to be a $150 million investment employing 1,000 workers to build 50,000
Corolla cars annually, the plant's investment quickly escalated to $300 mil-
lion as Toyota confirmed the stamping plant and a paint shop increasing
potential employment to 2,000 workers (Kawahara 1998; Shook 1988).

By the late 1980s, both Honda's and Toyota's Canadian plants had
spurred further Japanese investment and production. Days after Toyota
announced its Cambridge facility, Honda announced that it was expanding
its own Alliston plant. These two initial forays by the Japanese were joined
by a $500 million Suzuki–GM joint venture at Ingersoll, ON, which began
production in 1989 building small cars for the Canadian market. Moreover,
Japanese parts suppliers established in Canada to support the assemblers,
further expanding the Canadian parts sector.

In coming to Canada, not only did the Japanese find that they could
maximize their economies of scale by utilizing their Canadian and American plants together, allowing them to achieve content requirements under
the FTA and NAFTA, but they could also take advantage of the excellent
quality and productivity of their Canadian plants to boost the range and
depth of their output. For instance, Honda's Canadian workers were sent to
the US for their initial training. Yet from the mid-1990s, every new Honda
vehicle launched in North America has been done so in Alliston, before it
has gone into production in the US. At the same time, Honda has utilized
Alliston as its sole global source for its Odyssey minivan production, and
even exported these vehicles back to Japan. Toyota's decision to produce
the Lexus 350 at its Cambridge plant gives the Canadian facility the distinction of being the only site outside of Japan to build the Lexus brand.
Toyota's 2005 decision to build a $1.2 billion new truck plant for North
American production of the RAV4 in Woodstock, ON, (including an electric
version) confirms the confidence of the firm in the Canadian sector and the
benefits of continentalization. The fact that Japanese production in Canada
is usually more than four times the consumption of Japanese cars (the bulk
are exported to the US) indicates clearly that the Japanese investments in
Canada have proven beneficial, not just to Canada, but to the companies
themselves (JAMA Canada 2004, pp. 17–18).

Conclusion: The Future of the Canadian Sector— Canada–Korea, CETA, TPP

Since its peak in the 1990s and early 2000s, the Canadian industry has
declined. In part, this was due to the demise of the auto pact, which had
largely been superseded by the 1989 FTA and the 1993 NAFTA. These

measures effectively rendered the auto pact requirements moot (the auto pact itself was eventually deemed illegal by the World Trade Organization in 2001 because it discriminated against the newer entrants into the Canadian industry, namely Toyota and Honda), and the entry of Mexico fully into the North American industry created a new continental competitor for auto investment dollars (Weintrub and Sands 1998).

Further, the downturn in the industry in 2008–10 resulted in the Canadian and Ontario governments providing billions of dollars in support for GM and Chrysler (and a share of direct ownership of those two firms), but when those companies re-emerged from their difficulties, their footprints in Canada had shrunk. By the 2010s, Canada had lost a number of manufacturing plants, and an increasing Canadian dollar, the loss of the auto pact and the heightened competition for auto investment dollars in the US south and Mexico put the Canadian industry in a precarious position. By then, Canada's global rank as an auto manufacturer had fallen out of the Top 10, and the sector's status going forward became uncertain.

As a consequence, Canadian manufacturers (and the Canadian government) have continued to seek greater market access. This has culminated in the establishment of further trade agreements beyond North America. In 2015, the Canada–Korea Free Trade Agreement (CKFTA) came into force, granting further access to both countries, including auto products. Further trade agreements between Europe and Canada, through the CETA (Comprehensive Economic and Trade Agreement), and nations of the Pacific Rim, through the TPP (the Trans-Pacific Partnership) are pending, and have generated considerable discussion regarding their impact upon the Canadian sector, both in terms of market access and further inward foreign investment.

Nonetheless, the impact of FDI in shaping the Canadian industry, first from US producers in the pre-Second World War period whose proximity to Canada and desire to utilize their Canadian branch plants to access British markets shaped the industry profoundly. The continued search for markets resulted in the continentalization of the industry, which itself ultimately resulted in another round of FDI from Japanese MNEs in the 1980s. While the Canadian assembly sector is completely dominated by foreign MNEs, the Canadian-owned parts sector has been able to take advantage of the significant MNE FDI and access to markets to prosper, as seen through the Magna case study.

Thus, in examining the reasons why Canada's auto industry has remained competitive within the global auto industry for more than a century, there are three compelling lessons that we can learn about this sector. First, while proximity to the United States ultimately led to the demise of an indigenous sector, it also helped to create a vibrant foreign-owned cluster, with a significant Canadian-owned parts sector. Second, foreign ownership and continentalization not only boosted technology transfer, productivity and efficiency, but also helped to shape Canadian branch-plant operations' efforts to penetrate their own foreign markets, particularly in the context of the British Commonwealth. Finally, these factors, and the emergence of additional FDI in the Canadian sector, have historically been significantly impacted by public policy, especially trade policy through periods of both protectionism and regional trade agreements.

References

ABC 2016, Availale from: <www.abcgroupinc.com/en/default.htm>

Anastakis, D. 2001, 'Requiem for a trade agreement: The auto pact at the WTO, 1999–2000', *Canadian Business Law Journal*, vol. 34, no. 1, pp. 313–335.

Anastakis, D. 2004, 'From independence to integration: The corporate evolution of the Ford motor company of Canada, 1904–2004', *Business History Review*, vol. 78, no. 2, pp. 213–253.

Anastakis, D. 2005, *Auto Pact: Creating a Borderless North American Auto Industry, 1960–1971*, University of Toronto Press, Toronto.

Anastakis, D. 2013, *Autonomous State: The Struggle for a Canadian Car Industry From OPEC to Free Trade*, University of Toronto Press, Toronto.

Anderson, M. and Holmes, J. 1995, 'High-skill, low-wage manufacturing in North America: A case study from the automotive parts industry,' *Regional Studies*, vol. 29, no. 7, pp. 655–671.

Ankli, R.E. and Frederiksen, F. 1981, 'The influence of American manufacturers on the Canadian automobile industry', *Business and Economic History*, vol. 9, no. 1, pp. 101–113.

Beigie, C. 1970, *The Canada-U.S. Automotive Agreement*, Private Planning Commission, Montreal.

Bladen, V.W. 1961, *Report of the Royal Commission on the Automotive Industry*, Queen's Printer, Ottawa.

Catherine, Y.C. 2000, 'R&D, foreign direct investment and technology sourcing', *Review of Industrial Organization*, vol. 16, pp. 385–397.

Caves, R.E. 1974, 'Multinational firms, competition, and productivity in host-country markets', *Economica*, vol. 41, no. 162, pp. 176–193.

Chandler, A. 1977, *The Visible Hand: The Managerial Revolution in American Business*, Harvard University Press, Cambridge, MA.

Chrysler Corporation 1967, *Annual Report*, Baker Library, Harvard Business School, Cambridge, MA.

Clarke, S. 2007, *Trust and Power: Consumers, the Modern Corporation and the Making of the United States Automobile Market*, Cambridge University Press, New York.

Davis, D.F. 1990, 'Dependent motorization: Canada and the automobile to the 1930s', in D. McCalla (ed.), *The Development of Canadian Capitalism*, Copp Clark Pitman, Toronto.

Ehchin, H. 1991, 'Limamar marches to a different tune', *Globe & Mail*, 12 October.

Flink, J. 1990, *The Automobile Age*, Harvard University Press, Cambridge, MA.

Ford Motor Company 1965–67, *Annual Reports*, Baker Library, Harvard Business School, Cambridge.

General Motors 1967, *Annual Reports*, Baker Library, Harvard Business School, Cambridge.

Gibb-Clark 1986, 'Magna's main man', *Globe & Mail*, 31 October.

Globerman, S. 1979, 'Foreign direct investment and "Spillover" efficiency benefits in Canadian manufacturing industries', *Canadian Journal of Economics*, vol. 12, no. 1, pp. 42–56.

Halberstam, D. 1986, *The Reckoning*, Morrow, New York.

Holmes, J. 1983, 'Industrial reorganization, capital restructuring and locational change: An analysis of the Canadian automobile industry in the 1960s', *Economic Geography*, vol. 59, no. 1, pp. 251–271.

Holmes, J. 1996, 'Restructuring in a continental production system', in J.N.H. Britton (ed.), *Canada and the Global Economy: The Geography of Structural and Technological Change*, McGill-Queen's University Press, Montreal.

Hyde, C. 2003, *Riding the Roller Coaster: A History of the Chrysler Corporation*, Wayne State University Press, Detroit.

JAMA Canada (Japanese Automotive Manufacturers Association of Canada) 2004, *A short history of the Japanese Auto Industry in Canada*. Available from: <www.jama.ca.industry/history>

Kawahara, A. 1998, *The Origin of Competitive Strength: Fifty Years of the Auto Industry in Japan and the U.S*, Springer, New York.

Keeley, J.F. 1983, 'Cast in concrete for all time? The negotiation of the auto pact', *Canadian Journal of Political Science*, vol. 16, no. 2, pp. 281–298.

Klier, T., and j. Rubenstein, 2008. *Who Really Made Your Car? Restructuring and Geographic Change in the Auto Industry*, Upjohn Institute, Kalamazoo, MI.

Lewchuk, W. and Wells, D. 2006, 'When corporations substitute for adversarial unions: Labour markets and human resource management at Magna', *Relations Industrielles/Industrial Relations*, vol. 61, no. 4, pp. 639–665.

Lilley, W. 2008, *Magna Cum Laude: How Frank Stronach Became Canada's Best-Paid Man*, Douglas Gibson Books, Toronto.

Mays, J. 2004, *Ford and Canada; 100 Years Together*, Syam Publishing, Montreal.

McDiarmid, J. 1940, 'Some aspects of the Canadian automobile industry,' *The Canadian Journal of Economics and Political Science*, vol. 6, no. 2, pp. 258–274.

Molot, M.A. (ed.) 1993, *Driving Continentally: National Policies and the North American Auto Industry*, Carleton University Press, Ottawa.

Mom, G. 2015, *Atlantic Automobilism: Emergence and Persistence of the Car, 1895–1940*, Berghahn Books, New York and London.

Mordue, G. 2007, 'Government foreign direct investment and the Canadian Automotive Industry, 1977–1987', PhD. thesis, University of Strathclyde.

Moritz, M and B. Seaman. 1981, *Going for Broke: Lee Iacocca's Battle to Save Chrysler*, Doubleday, New York.

Perry, R. 1982, *The Future of Canada's Auto Industry: The Big Three and the Japanese Challenge*, James Lorimer, Toronto.

Porter, M. 1990, *The Competitive Advantage of Nations*, Free Press, New York.

Reisman, S. 1978, *The Canadian Automotive Industry: Performance and Proposals for Progress*, Queen's Printer, Ottawa.

Report on Business Magazine 1986, *Life in the Fast Lane*, vol. 12, no. 1, Globe Publishing, Toronto.

Roberts, C. 2002, 'Harnessing competition? The UAW and competitiveness in the Canadian Auto Industry, 1945–1990', Ph.D. Dissertation, York University.

Roberts, D. 2006, *In the Shadow of Detroit: Gordon M. McGregor, Ford of Canada, and Motoropolis*, Wayne State University Press, Detroit.

Robertson, H. 1995, *Driving Force: The McLaughlin Family and the Age of the Car*, McClelland and Stewart, Toronto.

Romain, K. 1984, 'Woodbridge foam succeeding after spin-off from Monsanto', *Globe & Mail*, 17 September.

Shook, T.L. 1988, *Honda: An American Success Story*, Prentice Hall, New York.

Statistics Canada n.d., Catalogue 42–210, *Motor Vehicle Parts and Accessories Manufacturers*, various years, various pages.

Thomas, K.P. 1996, *Capital Beyond Borders: States and Firms in the Auto Industry, 1960–1994*, Palgrave Macmillan, New York.

Traves, T. 1987, 'The development of the Ontario automobile industry to 1939,' in I. Drummond (ed.), *Progress Without Planning: The Economic History of Ontario From Confederation to the Second World War*, University of Toronto Press, Toronto.

Weintrub, S. and Sands, C. (eds.) 1998, *The North American Auto Industry Under NAFTA*, Centre for Strategic and International Studies, Washington, DC.

Westcast 2006, Available from: <www.wescast.com/en/heritage>

Wilkins, M. and Hill, F.E.H. 1964, *American Business Abroad: Ford on Six Continents*, Wayne State University Press, Detroit.

3 Different Ways to the Global Market

The Dynamics of Japan's Electrical Equipment Companies

Shigehiro Nishimura

Introduction

Since the late 19th century, the electrical equipment industry has maintained a constant global structure that had two main characteristics. First, the industry has continued producing essentially the same systems for more than a century. Since the invention of the Edison system—a combination of a steam turbine, steam engine, and generator installed on Pearl Street in Manhattan—the centralized generation system comprising a central power plant and distribution system has remained fundamentally unchanged (Hughes 1996), even though in-system devices and their levels of efficiency have continually developed under changing political and economic conditions. Second, because of the nature of the products, which represent an aggregation of know-how and require handcrafted precision work, the global suppliers and manufacturing sites have also remained basically identical over time. The leading electrical manufacturers include General Electric (GE; the United States), which was consolidated in 1892, Siemens (Germany), established in 1847, Alstom (France), established in 1928, Toshiba (Japan), established in 1904, Hitachi (Japan), established in 1920, Mitsubishi Electric (Japan), established in 1923, and Mitsubishi Heavy Industries (MHI; Japan), established in 1934.

From the 1990s onward, however, the electrical equipment industry underwent global reorganization and changed its long-term industrial structure as electric power businesses around the world underwent privatization and liberalization beginning in the 1970s and markets—especially in emerging economies such as China and India—expanded (Table 3.1). Electrical companies increased their output of key devices and provided them to expanding markets. At the same time, they had to reinforce their manufacturing and marketing capabilities to cope with rigorous global competition by reorganizing both their manufacturing bases and alliances. In 2014, MHI and Hitachi consolidated their thermal power generation businesses into a joint venture named Mitsubishi Hitachi Power Systems Limited. In the same year, GE and Siemens also competed for the acquisition of Alstom's energy business; in the end, GE bought Alstom's electrical equipment

Table 3.1 Net Installed Capacity of Electric Power Plants

				(MW)
	United States	Japan	China	India
1970	360,327	68,262	24,180	16,271
1975	527,346	112,285	41,000	22,249
1980	630,782	144,780	67,000	33,675
1985	701,875	169,528	82,200	51,180
1990	733,589	194,730	137,891	74,700
1995	776,112	227,517	204,100	95,081
2000	811,349	260,490	319,330	117,783
2005	978,539	277,324	559,510	145,755
2010	1,041,000	287,027	1,032,150	206,526

Source: UN. *Energy Statistical Yearbook*. Several issues.

Note: The data for Japan in 1970 excluded Ryukyu Islands.

business, which turned the global structure of the industry into a 'big three' arrangement.

While global manufacturers competed with each other over the same expanding markets, devices crucial to the competitiveness of an electrical company emerged. The gas turbine combined cycle (GTCC) generating system,[1] which combines a steam turbine and a gas turbine to maximize efficiency, became the focal point of global competition. Electric power companies demanded that producers provide efficient systems capable of delivering minimal costs—namely, energy that could produce more electricity with less fuel. Of all the items in the system, gas turbines are particularly crucial to the efficiency of generating systems.

The strategies of electrical equipment companies, however, have varied between countries as well as between individual companies. While GE has produced competitive, high-efficiency turbines in its home country and exported them to China and India—where it holds partner companies responsible for inspections and maintenance—Japanese companies have established local manufacturing joint venture companies with local producers and contracted out portions of the production. In China, Japanese companies have started manufacturing turbines through technological contracts with major Chinese makers. In India, meanwhile, they have established joint ventures to produce turbines for Indian and other markets. It is notable that MHI has begun manufacturing high-efficiency gas turbines in the United States, which is one of the world's biggest markets of electrical equipment.

Why did global producers of electrical equipment choose different strategies? Why did Japanese companies make foreign direct investments (FDI) in China and India, while GE did not? This chapter sheds light on the strategies of Japanese companies in comparison with GE and examines the path dependency of Japanese companies forced to move manufacturing facilities beyond their borders in order to stay competitive in the expanding markets. Furthermore, this chapter explores the reasons why Japanese companies' global strategies vary from company to company. Analyzing Japanese companies' strategies can be helpful in comprehending the industry's global structural changes.

1 Global Competition and Strategies

1.1 Market Share and International Trade

First, one needs to review the competitiveness of US and Japanese companies through global market-share data and international trade statistics. Table 3.2 shows the global market share of the industry from 2002 to 2010. The biggest portion of the world electrical equipment market, as of 2010, goes to GE at about 32%, followed by Alstom at about 19%, and then Siemens and MHI at about 13%. In short, a small group of just four manufacturers accounts for three-quarters of the world production. It is also clear that because MHI is ranked among the top four companies, the Japanese electrical industry has a certain degree of global competitiveness.

Table 3.2 shows the global share of electrical equipment; however, it would be best to break the figures down into gas and steam turbine devices and then evaluate their competitiveness. Table 3.3 shows the trends of gas turbine exports—export of large-sized gas turbines other than turbojets and turbo-propellers—of the United States and Japan from 1996 to 2015. Across the whole period, US exports amounted to about $39.4 billion, while those of Japan amounted to about $7.8 billion. Considering that the US exports were about five times larger than the corresponding Japanese exports, US companies clearly hold a competitive edge over Japanese firms in the gas turbine field—an advantage that extends into China and India. During the same period, US gas turbine exports to China were more than $1,080 million in value, while Japanese exports to China totaled just $314 million, or one-third of the US export volume. In the Indian market, US exports amounted to $1,114 million, whereas Japanese exports were of about $109 million—less than one-tenth of the American total. Thus, gas turbines from US companies demonstrate overwhelming competitiveness over those from Japanese companies in both the global and emerging markets.

On the other hand, Japanese companies have competitiveness in the steam turbine field. Table 3.4 shows the trends in large-sized steam turbine exports of the United States and Japan from 1996 to 2015. The total Japanese exports across the entire period had a value $5.3 billion, while US exports came in at $1.3 billion. Steam turbine exports from Japan to China amounted to $356 million, whereas those from the United States to China totaled $14 million. Furthermore, Japan topped the United States in exports

Table 3.2 Heavy Electrical Equipment Market Share by Value

(%)

	2002	2003	2004	2005	2006	2007	2008	2009	2010
1	GE 24.40	GE 32.30	GE 33.60	GE 33.20	GE 33.20	GE 34.40	GE 32.70	GE 28.80	GE 31.90
2	ABB 12.00	ABB-Alstom 18.90	ABB 24.20	Siemens 16.30	Siemens 16.30	Siemens 16.90	ABB 21.90	Alstom 11.00	Alstom 19.30
3	Siemens 10.40	Siemens 10.00	Siemens 16.10	ABB 11.20	ABB 11.20	ABB 11.60	Siemens 20.40	MHI 9.40	Siemens 12.80
4	WH 8.60	WH 9.00	MHI 9.00	MHI 9.50	MHI 9.50	MHI 9.80	MHI 11.70	Siemens 7.40	MHI 12.50
5	Alstom 8.20	MHI 8.00		Alstom 8.60				Vestas 7.30	
6	MHI 8.00								
Other	28.40	21.80	17.10	21.20	29.80	27.30	13.30	36.20	23.50

Source: Datamonitor. Global Heavy Electrical Equipment. 2003–2011.

Table 3.3 Export of Gas Turbines

(1,000 US dollars)

From the US to	World		Japan		China		India	
	(Value)	(%)	(Value)	(%)	(Value)	(%)	(Value)	(%)
1996–2000	5,018,938	100.0	405,096	8.1	112,843	2.2	176,151	3.5
2001–2005	7,523,412	100.0	230,449	3.1	180,821	2.4	87,739	1.2
2006–2010	12,067,985	100.0	517,029	4.3	316,059	2.6	522,218	4.3
2011–2015	14,788,154	100.0	766,002	5.2	470,846	3.2	328,441	2.2
Total	39,398,490	100.0	1,918,576	4.9	1,080,568	2.7	1,114,548	2.8

From Japan to	World		US		China		India	
	(Value)	(%)	(Value)	(%)	(Value)	(%)	(Value)	(%)
1996–2000	1,356,972	100.0	245,366	18.1	0	0.0	47,792	3.5
2001–2005	2,194,479	100.0	623,968	28.4	95,338	4.3	4,761	0.2
2006–2010	2,233,021	100.0	276,362	12.4	172,809	7.7	29,874	1.3
2011–2015	1,993,623	100.0	4,779	0.2	45,538	2.3	27,523	1.4
Total	7,778,095	100.0	1,150,475	14.8	313,686	4.0	109,950	1.4

Note: The data refer to HS841182 Gas Turbines, except Turbojets and Turbopropellers, of a power exceeding 5,000 KW.

Table 3.4 Export of Steam Turbines

From the US to	World		Japan		China		India	
	(Value)	(%)	(Value)	(%)	(Value)	(%)	(Value)	(%)
1996–2000	309,732	100.0	2,195	0.7	6,039	1.9	511	0.2
2001–2005	83,467	100.0	1,540	1.8	729	0.9	321	0.4
2006–2010	193,114	100.0	4,382	2.3	2,054	1.1	1,656	0.9
2011–2015	699,343	100.0	0	0.0	5,542	0.8	18,539	2.7
Total	1,285,656	100.0	8,117	0.6	14,364	1.1	21,026	1.6

From Japan to	World		USA		China		India	
	(Value)	(%)	(Value)	(%)	(Value)	(%)	(Value)	(%)
1996–2000	1,061,316	100.0	96,643	9.1	134,890	12.7	80,638	7.6
2001–2005	1,248,598	100.0	689,254	55.2	87,521	7.0	2,346	0.2
2006–2010	1,658,938	100.0	539,080	32.5	125,172	7.5	70,530	4.3
2011–2015	1,374,088	100.0	298,318	21.7	8,844	0.6	39,252	2.9
Total	5,342,941	100.0	1,623,296	30.4	356,427	6.7	192,766	3.6

Note: The data refer to HS840681 Turbines—steam and other vapor types—of an output exceeding 40 MW, except for marine propulsion.

to India by a whopping margin—$193 million from Japan compared with only $21 million from the United States. Although Japanese companies held a competitive edge in the steam turbine export market, the scale of the business as a whole was much smaller than that of gas turbines; the value of US gas turbine export was a comparatively massive $39.4 billion over the same period.

According to foreign trade statistics, as a whole, it is notable that US companies hold an overwhelming competitive advantage in the field of gas turbines—the essential device for competitiveness. Although Japanese companies hold a greater share than their US counterparts in the steam turbine field, the scale of the sector amounts to just a fraction of that of the gas turbine business. Another point worth noting is that the US market is essential for Japanese companies in both the steam turbine and gas turbine fields.

1.2 Different Strategies of US and Japanese Companies

From the trade statistics, it is obvious that US turbine companies exported their products from their home country. GE, a leading gas turbine company, manufactures high-efficiency, large-scale gas turbines at its factory in Greenville, South Carolina, where it has the largest gas turbine validation facilities (GE n.d.). Although the company has also run a gas turbine manufacturing plant in Belfort, France, since 1959, almost all of its exports from the US are likely from the Greenville plant. Furthermore, GE has facilities for repair and maintenance all over the world; in China, GE has a site in Qinhuangdao, while the company has also established a joint venture named BHEL-GE Gas Turbines Service with a local manufacturer in Hyderabad, India (GE n.d.).

While GE exports turbines from the United States, Japanese companies have utilized another strategy. In hopes of securing a substantial share of the growing markets in which GE holds a leading share and competing with GE and local manufacturers, Japanese companies have established several local manufacturing facilities for steam and gas turbines via technological tie-ups and joint ventures. They have also relocated their manufacturing processes with the aim of taking advantage of the lower cost of labor and economies of scale.

MHI is the most aggressive company among the Japanese manufacturers. MHI has two joint-venture partners in China. The first partner is Harbin Turbine Company Limited, to which MHI provided the main components of its advanced-type steam turbines in June 2002 (MHI 2002). According to the terms of the contract, MHI was to provide high- and medium-pressure turbine blades, rotors, and other important parts. In December of the following year, MHI received an order from the Harbin Turbine Company for 12 sets of main components for 600-MW steam turbines. These components were assembled with other parts and accessories at Harbin and then delivered to Chinese power companies (MHI 2003). The second partner is

Qingdao Jieneng Steam Turbine Group, with which MHI set up Mitsubishi Heavy Industries Jieneng (Qingdao) Steam Turbine Company in 2013. The aim of this joint venture is to design and market medium- and small-sized turbines and marine turbines. Through the venture, MHI provides manufacturing licenses with Qingdao Jieneng Steam Turbine Group and sells turbines made by the Group (MHI 2013).

In India, MHI also formed a joint venture, L&H-MHI Turbine Generators Private Limited, with the Indian company Larsen & Toubro Limited in 2007. The establishment of local manufacturing was required by the Indian government's industrial development policy. Having launched operations in 2010, the company now produces and sells steam turbines and generators in the Indian market with a workforce of more than 1,000 employees. MHI receives turbines through L&H-MHI Turbine Generators Private Limited and then exports some components to the company. In this manner, MHI expanded both its local production and exports from Japan (Japan Bank for International Cooperation 2012; MHI 2011a, 2011b).

During the 2000s, Mitsubishi commenced technology transfer activities and the local production of gas turbines. In 2004, Mitsubishi jointly created the Mitsubishi Heavy Industries Dongfang Gas Turbine (Guangzhou) Co., Ltd., to which it transferred advanced gas turbine technology and then began manufacturing and mending high-temperature modules there. This joint company provides its counterpart, the Dongfang Electric Group, with parts for gas turbines (MHI 2014a). In addition to China, Mitsubishi began manufacturing locally in the United States: the large-scale 'Project USA' led by Mitsubishi Power Systems Americas, Inc. began in 2009. Through the project, in 2013, Mitsubishi established a manufacturing facility capable of producing 12 gas turbines a year in the United States (MHI 2014b). Together with the facilities of the original Takasago Works in Japan, which can produce 36 units annually, Mitsubishi had the resources to provide the global market with competitive gas turbines.

While MHI aggressively expanded its manufacturing base across borders, other Japanese companies—Toshiba and Hitachi, which, as will be described in the following section, are essential electrical equipment companies producing a wide range of equipment and appliances, including turbines—also entered into agreements with Chinese and Indian companies to set up local manufacturing organizations.

In 1991, Hitachi teamed up with Dongfang Electric Corporation to produce a steam turbine for thermal power plants in China. The alliance was, to some extent, forced by global competition over China's huge market. At the time, the Harbin Power Equipment Company, a major electrical equipment manufacturer, joined forces with Westinghouse Electric Corporation (United States), whereas fellow major manufacturer Shanghai Electric Group tied up with Siemens (Germany). If Hitachi had not tied up with Dongfang Electric, observers say, it could have gotten off to a very slow start in China's emerging market. However, Hitachi successfully entered the Chinese market through the alliance and obtained orders of more than 100 billion by 2008. In addition, Hitachi and Dongfang Electric jointly expanded their thermal power plant business outside of China. After receiving an order for steam turbines from Libya, the two companies jointly set out to produce and deliver eight steam turbines after 2009 (Satō 2008).

In India in 2010, Hitachi joined BGR Energy Systems Limited in establishing BGR Turbines Company Private Limited to conduct steam turbine business. In 2013, the joint venture received an order from the Indian national power company for two sets of 800-MW, supercritical, pressure-type steam turbines (Hitachi Limited 2013).

In 2008, Toshiba established Toshiba JSW Turbine and Generator Private Limited in India as a joint venture with a local company and installed a manufacturing facility for advanced-type steam turbines that ranged from 600 to 1,000 MW (this factory was completed in 2012; Toshiba 2012). Toshiba regards its Indian facility as one of its global manufacturing sites for steam turbines and steam turbine generators for thermal power plants, second only to its Keihin complex in Yokohama, Japan. The East Asian electrical equipment market will develop by expanding into the major Asian region.

As described above, in the latter half of the first decade of the 21st century, Japanese electrical equipment companies began establishing and securing manufacturing facilities in China and India. Why did Japanese companies choose an FDI strategy instead of the export business? The next section examines the history of the Japanese steam and gas turbine industry in order to deduce the answers to this question.

2 Development of the Japanese Steam and Gas Turbine Industry

2.1 Steam Turbines: From Introduction to Original Technology

Just after World War II, the Japanese electrical equipment industry lagged behind its American and European counterparts in terms of technology, especially that for steam turbines. In order to rebuild their businesses, electrical companies tied up with Western companies and introduced advanced foreign technology. In 1952, Toshiba restored its technological partnership with GE, which the two first concluded in 1905, while Mitsubishi Electric and Fuji Electric restored their alliances with Westinghouse Electric and Siemens, respectively. Hitachi, which had no pre-war technological affiliations with any foreign companies, signed patent licensing and technological contracts relating to steam turbines and generators with GE in 1953, and thereby it began introducing advanced technology. The number of electrical-equipment-related technology introduction contracts between Japanese electrical companies and foreign firms reached 25 during the period from 1952 to 1960 (Hasegawa 2006).

Since the thermal efficiency of thermal power systems grows proportionally with capacity, steam temperature, and pressure levels, power companies called for the installation of efficient, large-scale systems. In order to meet these demands, Japanese manufacturers continued introducing technology for the larger steam turbine, but they also constructed giant factories for large turbines in order to realize economies of scale and scope: Toshiba constructed the Tsurumi complex and Hitachi built the Hitachi complex (Takeuchi 1966). Being low on technological capabilities at the time, electric power companies preferred to import GE or Westinghouse equipment with high thermal and economic efficiency rather than buy items from domestic manufacturers. Hoping to spur the development of a stronger electrical industry, the Japanese government responded by devising a 'first unit for import, second unit for domestic' formula through administrative guidance (Kikkawa 2004). While electric power companies imported the first unit in each size from GE or Westinghouse, electrical manufacturers endeavored to produce larger steam turbines by themselves and eventually accumulated manufacturing capabilities and experience. As a result, the technological skills of Japanese manufacturers 'reached the levels of companies abroad—at least on the hardware side—in the 1980s' (Hasegawa 2006, p. 28).

For 20 years, starting in the 1950s, Japan's manufacturers pursued the development of larger-capacity steam turbines and succeeded in the domestic production of 1,000-MW units in 1969 (Hasegawa 2006). During this period, however, steam conditions such as temperature and pressure of steam were basically unchanged, and there was no rapid growth. Steam turbines using steam conditions over the critical point of water (22.064 MPa and 374.2°C) are 'supercritical-pressure' (SC) units, which originated in the United States and first appeared in Japan in the second half of the 1960s. SC units became the standard and remained that way for about 20 years until the 1980s (Ogino and Iwasaki 2012).

Steam conditions improved in Japan from the late 1980s and 1990s onward. Steam turbines using steam temperature of over 593°C under supercritical pressure are 'ultra-supercritical-pressure' (USC) units, which were successfully completed in 1993. After that, higher-pressure and higher-temperature units were developed in succession. USC technology was 'a technology that developed in Japan, where fuel cost was relatively high, and aimed to reduce amount of fuel consumption and generating cost by enhancing efficiency from the higher steam conditions' (Fukuda 2014, p. 15). USC technology thus became a foundation of Japanese competitiveness in the global market.

2.2 Struggles For Original Technology: Gas Turbine

Japanese companies had accumulated gas turbine technologies to a certain extent before the end of World War II. However, technical tie-ups with American and European companies and the introduction of foreign technology are what enabled Japanese companies to accumulate technological skills in gas turbines and retain global competitiveness in the field (Table 3.5). In 1958, Toshiba entered into a contract with Brown Boveri & Cie (Switzerland) to introduce gas turbine technology to Japan. Toshiba manufactured gas turbines designed by Brown Boveri under license and shipped them to coal mines and gas plants in Japan as well as to power plants in South Korea. From 1970 to 1976, Toshiba and Brown Boveri carried out joint research and development on cooled blades, which are essential parts of gas turbines, and eventually constructed an experimental unit (Itō, Honma and Satō 2008). MHI partnered with Westinghouse Electric Corporation to introduce gas turbine technologies in 1961 and proceeded to manufacture gas turbines under Westinghouse licenses. By manufacturing Westinghouse's types of gas turbines, Mitsubishi could accumulate 'technical skills by analyzing and improving the causes of problems that they had experienced over long-term operations' (Tsukagoshi 2008, p. 74). In the early 1970s, Mitsubishi had enough prowess to develop a turbine for machine driving together with Westinghouse. Hitachi teamed up with GE on gas turbines for land use in 1964 and accumulated technical skills by manufacturing gas turbines of standard, GE-designed type as part of an international division of labor (Gotō et al. 2012).

Gas turbines manufactured during the 1960s were mainly small sized, and companies started manufacturing medium-sized and large-sized gas turbines in the 1970s. The manufacturing of large-sized gas turbines began in the first half of the 1970s, and 137 units were made from 1974 to 1978

Table 3.5 Gas Turbine Technology Introduction

Major actors	Alliance partners	Terms	Technology—gas temperature
Toshiba	Brown, Boveri	1958–1981	650°C (1961)
			760°C (1969)
			945°C (1976)
	GE	1982–	1,100°C (1982)
			1,300°C (1990s)
			1,500°C (2000s)
MHI	Westinghouse	1961–1998	700°C (1960s)
			900°C (1970s)
			1,000°C (1976)
			1,150°C (1980s)
			1,350°C (1989)
Hitachi	GE	1964–	800°C (1964)
			1,100°C (1980s)
			1,300°C (1990s)

(Tōkei Sakusei Iinkai 1979). However, the output of large-sized gas turbines decreased to 82 units during the next five years (1979–1983) and then decreased further to 59 units over the ensuing five-year period. This was due to the low efficiency of gas turbines at that time. During the 1970s, a GTCC plant—combining a gas turbine and a steam turbine—could not exceed the thermal efficiency of a conventional thermal plant (Ikegami 2009). The inlet gas temperature, which determines the thermal efficiency of the unit, was insufficient (around 700°C to 1,000°C), and the capacity of each single unit was not only relatively small but also uneconomical.

In the 1980s, a GTCC with high-efficiency gas turbines attracted attention as a means of meeting social needs such as energy conservation and reduced emissions. During this period, the thermal efficiency of gas turbines increased to enable efficient operations of GTCC with steam turbines. Gas turbines used liquefied natural gas (LNG) as fuel, and the inlet gas temperature rose to 1,100°C; as a result, the thermal efficiency of GTCC plants could surpass that of conventional thermal plants. However, such high-efficiency gas turbine technologies were introduced mainly through US companies and then shifted to domestic production.

Hitachi tied up with GE to share the 1,100°C-class gas turbine technology and manufactured the devices under license. Hitachi completed a type of gas turbine and installed it at the Kawasaki Thermal Power Plant of Japan National Railways in 1981. This unit was 'the first combined cycle power unit of the exhaust heat recovery type in Japan' (Gotō et al. 2012, p. 21).

Toshiba canceled its technological tie-ups with Brown Boveri and concluded a new contract with GE pertaining to large-sized gas turbines in 1982. Toshiba acquired patent licenses and technological assistance from GE, using its new assets to produce a GTCC system. The system, which comprised a high-efficiency gas turbine (1,100°C) and a steam turbine, was installed at a Tokyo Electric Company power plant. Furthermore, in 1987, Toshiba completed five units of another GTCC system and installed the units at a Chubu Electric Company thermal power plant (Itō, Honma and Satō 2008).

For GTCC applications, a gas turbine had to achieve an inlet gas temperature of 1,150°C. Under its technological contracts with Westinghouse, MHI commenced the development of this class of gas turbines in 1980, and it realized and installed a 1,150°C-class gas turbine at a Tohoku Electric Company power plant in 1984. This was not only the first gas turbine to be produced purely domestically but also a device that adopted Mitsubishi's unique technologies, such as the premix combustion system for gas burners (MHI 2014a). The level of efficiency of this plant was about 10% higher than that of conventional thermal power plants (Tsukagoshi 2008).

As described above, high-efficiency gas turbine technology was established in Japan during the 1980s, albeit based on introduced foreign technology. During the first half of the 1990s, as GTCC became feasible both technologically and economically, the Japanese electrical equipment industry entered a stage at which it could manufacture efficient, large-sized gas turbines under licenses and enlarge the industry as a whole.

While Japanese electrical companies introduced high-efficiency gas turbine technology from US companies, they also endeavored to develop original technologies by joining national research and development projects. The 'advanced gas turbine project' (the Moonlight Project)—carried out by the Agency of Industrial Science and Technology of the Ministry of International Trade and Industry (MITI) for ten years (1978–1988)—set a go-ahead technological target and pushed gas turbine-related companies' technological capabilities upward dramatically (Hori 1981). The project—budgeted at ¥21 billion for research and development—aimed to develop high-efficiency gas turbines that could realize GTCC systems with a total thermal efficiency of 55% (lower heating value [LHV]) and function on 20–30% less fuel than existing systems. Fourteen companies (Asahi Glass, Central Research Institute of Electric Power Industry, Daido Steel, Hitachi, Hitachi Materials, Ishikawajima-Harima Heavy Industries [now IHI], Kawasaki Heavy Industries, Kobe Steel, Kyocera, MHI, Mitsui Engineering and Shipbuilding, Mitsui Mining & Smelting R&D Centre, NGK Insulators, and Toshiba) joined the project through the Advanced Gas Turbine Research Consortium, which they organized (Hori 1981).

The significance of the advanced gas turbine project is that—triggered by the project—gas turbine production in Japan 'grew out of foreign technologies and brought forth any number of models developed and designed with original technology' and those gas turbines 'successfully entered the world market and appreciated in reliability' (Ikegami 2009, p. 113). Taking advantage of the project, Japanese gas turbine manufacturers made dramatic leaps in technological prowess: from the stage of introducing advanced technology and licenses from US companies to the stage of producing turbines with their own technologies.

2.3 Growth of Domestic Production

In the 1990s, the Japanese electrical equipment industry shifted the emphasis of production from steam turbines to gas turbines in accordance with the evolution of power systems. While Japanese manufacturers once introduced advanced technologies from their foreign tie-up companies and absorbed them, now they began developing original technologies. Figure 3.1 shows trends in the domestic output of steam turbines and gas turbines since the 1970s. The output of steam turbines increased up to the first half of the 1990s and peaked at about ¥870 billion (over the five years from 1990 to 1994). On the other hand, the output of gas turbines during the first half of the 1980s amounted to ¥40 billion, which was much smaller than that of steam turbines over the same period (approximately ¥730 billion). Gas turbine manufacturing gradually grew, however, with the output of gas

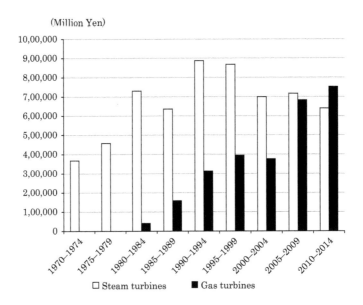

Figure 3.1 Production of Steam and Gas Turbines in Japan

Source: MITI, *Yearbook of Machinery Statistics*.

turbines reaching about ¥750 billion within the five-year period from 2010 to 2014—a figure that topped the steam turbine total.

The competitiveness that USC technology yielded in the export market is evident in the trade statistics for steam turbines. Table 3.6 shows the output, exports and imports, balance, and export ratio to production in Japan since the 1970s. The output of steam turbines grew steadily starting in the 1970s and peaked at about ¥890 billion during the five years from 1990 to 1994. After that, the output decreased to about ¥640 billion during the five years from 2010 to 2013. Export volume expanded to about ¥200 billion in the first half of the 1980s, while the export ratio of production rose to 35.6% during the same period. Although the export volume and export ratio declined, exports began increasing again around 2000 and reached ¥232 billion in spite of a decrease in domestic output, and the ratio climbed to about 40%. On the other hand, steam turbine imports have remained low since the 1970s; therefore, the balance has continuously been a surplus of more than ¥100 billion. Based on these trends, one can recognize that electrical equipment companies simultaneously decreased domestic production and expanded exports around 2000, with the products becoming increasingly competitive in the global market.

Table 3.6 also shows the trade balance of gas turbines. The figures in this table represent amounts of money, include all gas turbine capacities, and cover not only finished products but also partial products. The export of gas turbines increased in tandem with domestic production; particularly, exports began soaring in 2000 and the export ratio hovered around 30%, except for the period from 2000 to 2004, when it was 77.1%. On the other hand, it is distinctive that, unlike the imports of steam turbines, the imports of gas turbines were so high that the trade balance sometimes went into a deficit in the first half of the 1980s and late 1990s. Since 2000, however, the balance has been a substantial surplus, albeit with some fluctuation. As the next section will explain, the large number of gas turbine imports came from the fact that some companies imported advanced US-made gas turbines and combined them with their own competitive steam turbines to create highly efficient GTCC systems for power plants.

While the output of gas turbines increased, making the turbines the main products, the production has been markedly export oriented. Table 3.7 shows exports and imports of large-sized land and marine gas turbines (with more than 22,065 kW of capacity). The export ratios (units) of large-sized gas turbines averaged 78.1% over the entire period stretching from 1948

Table 3.6 Production, Exports, and Imports of Steam and Gas Turbines (Japan)

(Million Yen)

	Output	*Exports*	*Imports*	*Balance*	*Export ratio*
Steam turbines					
1970–1974	367,562	43,300	3,723	39,577	11.8
1975–1979	457,840	162,964	1,396	161,567	35.6
1980–1984	729,752	194,490	17,508	176,982	26.7
1985–1989	636,746	105,341	3,049	102,291	16.5
1990–1994	886,692	164,594	3,502	161,092	18.6
1995–1999	867,888	162,736	17,030	145,706	18.8
2000–2004	699,261	198,466	4,350	194,116	28.4
2005–2009	716,251	252,396	8,350	244,046	35.2
2010–2014	640,052	252,039	11,536	240,503	39.4
Gas turbines					
1970–1974		39,448	4,448	35,000	
1975–1979		85,637	14,245	71,393	
1980–1984	40,463	53,867	60,938	-7,072	
1985–1989	158,195	51,278	37,085	14,193	32.4
1990–1994	312,736	111,914	72,508	39,407	35.8
1995–1999	393,842	112,181	138,896	-26,715	28.5
2000–2004	375,877	289,697	73,613	216,083	77.1
2005–2009	682,242	247,594	88,997	158,596	36.3
2010–2014	751,675	187,866	101,223	86,642	25.0

Source: Ministry of International Trade and Industry, Yearbook of machinery statistics; Ministry of Finance, Trade statistics of Japan.

Table 3.7 Export Ratio of Land and Marine Gas Turbines (Japan)

(number of units, MW, %)

	Installed in Japan		Exports		Total production		Export ratio	
	Units	Capacity	Units	Capacity	Units	Capacity	Units	Capacity
Large-sized gas turbines								
1948–1978	20	923	166	5,500	186	6,422	89.2	85.6
1979–1983	8	919	74	2,388	82	3,308	90.2	72.2
1984–1988	12	843	47	2,275	59	3,118	79.7	73.0
1989–1993	40	3,891	80	7,942	120	11,833	66.7	67.1
1994–1998	56	8,017	92	11,401	134	17,038	68.7	66.9
1999–2003	24	2,648	116	16,399	140	19,046	82.9	86.1
2004–2008	33	4,632	134	15,643	167	20,275	80.2	77.2
2009–2013	55	9,162	126	20,182	181	29,343	69.6	68.8
Sum	248	31,033	835	81,730	1,069	110,383	78.1	74.0

Source: Gas Turbine Society of Japan, *Production statistics for gas turbines & superchargers in Japan.*

to 2013. It is worth noting that the export ratio of large-sized gas turbines was high and that, from the beginning of the gas turbine industry in Japan, companies exported the products to foreign markets to compete globally rather than in the domestic market. The likely reason why the export ratio of large-sized gas turbines (units) was as high as about 90% before 1983 is that there were few chances to install lower-efficiency gas turbines that were inferior to conventional thermal power plants in Japan. The ratio then dropped to about 70% in the latter part of the 1990s and rose to more than 80% after 1999. This upswing in the ratio underlines the competitiveness of high-efficiency gas turbines developed in Japan.

In the world market, however, as mentioned above (Table 3.3), the competitiveness of Japan-made gas turbines is comparatively weaker than that of US-made products—particularly those from GE, which holds an overwhelming share of the market. GE can produce so many highly advanced, effective gas turbines and export them to the market that they possess significant competitive advantages in terms of both quality and cost. In order to cope with GE, Japanese companies have to simultaneously realize high efficiency, quality, and price competitiveness. One way to meet these needs is to establish local manufacturing facilities through technological partnerships and joint ventures and relocate manufacturing processes in order to take advantage of the lower costs of labor and economies of scale. The reasons why Japanese companies made FDI in China and India arise from the Japanese companies' competitive disadvantages in the scale of business and, in part, the backwardness of the gas turbine technology.

3 Different Strategies within Japanese Companies

A company's technological capability in gas turbines plays a role in shaping its overall strategy. Each company's strategy to compete within the global market varies depending on the characteristics and levels of its own technology: MHI successfully developed competitive gas turbines on the basis of independent technology; Hitachi developed and commercialized gas turbines for co-generation systems in the forms of its own products, and Toshiba completed its own gas turbine technology but could not commercialize it.

3.1 MHI's Global Strategy

In 1986, MHI completed a 1,250°C-class gas turbine that was designed and manufactured domestically without any Westinghouse-licensed technologies. This type of gas turbine adopted a turbine blade cooling technology (air cooling blades), which was the result of the Moonlight Project and mainly served the co-generation market (MHI 2014a; Tsukagoshi 2013). In 1989, Mitsubishi developed a 1,350°C-class gas turbine and installed units in Florida (United States) in 1991. This gas turbine was extremely efficient, with an inlet gas temperature of 1,350°C. The development of this type was a Mitsubishi initiative, with assistance from Westinghouse, and it created an opportunity for the dissolution of the technological alliance between the two firms (Tsukagoshi 2008). In 1997, Mitsubishi successfully developed a 1,500°C-class gas turbine. Over the course of developing this class—with the technological relationship with Westinghouse completely eliminated—Mitsubishi began navigating 'a road of sovereign independence' (MHI 2014a). The 1,500°C-class gas turbine incorporated a steam cooling system for the burner combined with the company's original premix combustion system (Tsukagoshi 2008). Furthermore, in 2011, Mitsubishi completed a 1,600°C-class gas turbine and installed it at a Kansai Electric power plant. The 1,600°C-class gas turbine utilized the fruits of the 'Technological development of 1,700°C-class gas turbine elements' national project, which commenced in 2004 (Tsukagoshi 2013).

During the development process, Mitsubishi was able to cancel its technological alliance with Westinghouse, from which it had introduced advanced technologies since the 1920s. Mitsubishi proceeded with the cancellation of its technological alliances with Westinghouse from the 1980s to the 1990s in a step-by-step fashion (Mizuho Bank Ltd. Industry Research Division 2014). Although Mitsubishi and Westinghouse concluded their technological partnership contracts for steam turbines and gas turbines one after the other in the 1960s, the relationship between the two companies evolved into an equal partnership when they revised the contract for steam turbines in 1989 and that for gas turbines in 1991. Furthermore, the relationship was completely dissolved when Westinghouse sold its thermal power business to Siemens in 1998. Mitsubishi achieved technological independence from foreign companies because 1) Westinghouse permitted Mitsubishi to take an initiative in development in the advanced domain, which led Mitsubishi to complete and establish its own technological base and 2) Mitsubishi developed its own technologies by taking advantage of two national projects: the Moonlight Project (beginning in 1968) and the project aiming at the development of 1,700°C-class advanced gas turbines (beginning in 2004; Mizuho Bank Ltd. Industry Research Division 2014). The most significant point is that the cancellation of contracts with Westinghouse in 1998 gave Mitsubishi the ability 'to sell gas turbines and steam turbines all over the world, including the United States' (MHI 2014a, p. 335).

3.2 Hitachi and Toshiba

Hitachi jointly developed and improved gas turbines with GE. In 1990, Hitachi developed a dry burner with low NOx output as an original technology, which was then incorporated into GE-designed gas turbines. In 2000, Hitachi took steps to develop a 1,300°C-class gas turbine jointly with GE. Meanwhile, Hitachi endeavored to develop original gas turbines independent of GE technology. In 1988, Hitachi produced an original gas turbine that 'was designed and manufactured completely with in-house original technologies for the first time' (Inoue 2008, p. 67). Hitachi developed the turbine—with an inlet gas temperature of 1,260°C—by targeting the most popular type among the licensed products. Although this type was initially delivered to domestic petrochemical companies to serve as components of co-generation systems, they were exported to Korea's power companies for power generation after 2000 and later delivered to countries all over the world. Furthermore, Hitachi developed another type of gas turbine with more capacity via its own technology and installed the unit at a Kyushu Electric power plant in 2010 (Gotō et al. 2012).

Hitachi, however, could not develop a large-scale, competitive gas turbine for GTCC systems independently. Hitachi's decision sheds light on the structure of global competition today. Hitachi consolidated its thermal power equipment businesses with those of MHI to set up Mitsubishi Hitachi Power Systems in 2014. This joint venture has a wide variety of product lines, ranging from GTCC to conventional thermal plants, integrated gasification combined cycle power plants, geothermal power plants, fuel cells, and so on (Mitsubishi Hitachi Power Systems n.d.). It was obvious that this transaction aimed to realize economics of scale and scope and help Hitachi cope with GE and Siemens in the global market.

Toshiba, also unable to develop an efficient gas turbine for GTCC systems, decided to conclude a strategic alliance with GE. Toshiba also aimed to develop a gas turbine with its own technology, while introducing advanced technology from GE. In 1986, Toshiba developed a gas turbine for a driving test compressor. The combustion gas temperature was 1,000°C. In 1991,

Toshiba independently developed an efficient 1,300°C-class gas turbine, which supplied peak load power to Tokyo Electric for two years as an independent power plant (Itō, Honma and Satō 2008). However, this Toshiba-developed gas turbine never went on the market because of technological inferiority; today, Toshiba does not manufacture any gas turbines by itself. Toshiba's strategy differed from the two companies mentioned above. In January 2013, Toshiba created a strategic alliance with GE under which the two companies would jointly provide the global market with highly efficient GTCC power plants by combining GE's advanced gas turbines and Toshiba's efficient steam turbines. Practically, Toshiba and GE commercialized their GTCC system using GE's 1,600°C-class gas turbine (the most highly advanced unit available; Hattori and Hyōmori 2013). Although GE had once tied up with Hitachi as well, GE limited the alliance to Toshiba and did not contract with Hitachi regarding anything other than the 1,500°C-class gas turbine.

Conclusion

MHI (Mitsubishi Hitachi Power System) is now one of three global major electrical equipment manufacturers and able to compete with GE and Siemens in the global market. The competitiveness of MHI is backed by a different strategy: It not only exports turbines but has also established local manufacturing facilities in China and India via technological tie-ups and FDI, while GE continues to produce high-efficiency gas turbines domestically. Like MHI, Hitachi (before the consolidation of its thermal power equipment business into the joint venture) and Toshiba have moved their steam and gas turbine manufacturing facilities beyond Japanese borders.

The FDI strategy of Japanese companies arises from their path of industrial development. From the aftermath of World War II to the 1980s, manufacturers tied up with foreign companies to introduce advanced technologies for both steam and gas turbines and endeavored to domesticate technologies. At the same time, however, the contracts contained market regulations that limited the export markets of the Japanese counterparts. In order to circumnavigate the limitations, Japanese companies had to develop their own technologies to compete with global manufacturers. In the steam turbine field, Japanese companies successfully developed the USC unit in the 1990s and acquired technological advantages in the global market. FDI by Japanese companies aimed to compete with global manufacturers in expanding markets by taking advantage of the lower cost of local labor.

In the gas turbine field, Japanese companies began working to develop original technologies in the latter part of the 1980s. Of the Japanese manufacturers, Mitsubishi successfully developed independent technology that liberated the company from its dependence on foreign technology and made it 'one of a few makers that could develop large-sized gas turbine based on its own independent technology' (MHI 2014a, p. 328). As a result, MHI revised and eventually dissolved its subordinate contract with Westinghouse and acquired the right to make and sell its own gas turbines freely all over the world. However, despite stamping its ticket to the world GTCC market, MHI saw GE secure a large portion of this market. Thus, in this field, MHI made FDI in China and India by taking advantage of the lower cost of local labor.

On the other hand, two other Japanese companies were unable to develop efficient gas turbines for GTCC applications. Hitachi combined its thermal power plant business with that of Mitsubishi to become a joint venture that could better handle global competition. In possession of high-efficiency steam turbine technology, Toshiba allied with GE, which had the ability to produce high-efficiency gas turbines, to compete with global giants. Over the course of this global industrial reorganization, Japanese companies extended their manufacturing businesses beyond their borders.

Note

1 A GTCC system comprises steam and gas turbines: first, the gas turbine generates rotating energy by burning LNG or gasified coal; the steam turbine then generates rotating energy via steam fluid from a boiler heated by the exhaust gas from the gas turbine. The thermal efficiency of a GTCC is much higher than that of a single steam or gas turbine. GTCC systems are the primary components of the main systems that are newly installed today.

References

Fukuda, M. 2014, 'Senshin chō-chōrinkaiatsu karyoku hatsuden (Advanced-USC) yōso kaihatsu project' [Advanced USC technology development project], *Nihon Gas Turbine Gakkai Shi* [Journal of Gas Turbine Society of Japan], vol. 42, no. 4, pp. 275–280.

GE n.d., *GE power generation: Service and repair centers*. Available from: <https://powergen.gepower.com/services/repair-and-maintenance.html> [13 October 2016].

Gotō, J., Kuba, S., Teranishi, M., Kamino, K. and Hirose, F. 2012, 'Hitachi gas turbine no ayumi to series tenkai' [Hitachi's gas turbine product range and development background], *Hitachi Hyōron* [Hitachi Review], vol. 94, no. 11, pp. 758–763.

Hasegawa, S. 2006, 'Jūdenki kōgyō no hatten to hatsudensetubi nōryoku no keisei: Sengofukkō kara 1980 nen dai made o chūshin ni' [The formation of the ability to supply generation plants in postwar Japan], *Aoyama Keiei Ronshū* [Aoyama Journal of Business], vol. 41, no. 1, pp. 1–31.

Hattori, Y. and Hyōmori, K. 2013, 'Kō-kōritsu combined cycle hatsuden system no saishin gijutsu' [State-of-the-art technologies for high-efficiency combined-cycle power generation systems], *Toshiba Review*, vol. 68, no. 11, pp. 8–11.

Hitachi Limited 2013, *News release*. Available from: <www.hitachi.co.jp/New/cnews/month/2013/01/0123.html> [23 January 2013].

Hori, A. 1981, 'Kō-kōritsu gas turbine no kenkyū kaihatsu ni tsuite' [Research and development of advanced gas turbines], *Nihon Kikai Gakkai Shi* [Journal of the Japan Society of Mechanical Engineers], vol. 84, no. 747, pp. 129–133.

Hughes, T.P. 1996, *Networks of Power: Electrification in Western Society, 1880–1930*, The Johns Hopkins University Press, Baltimore, MD.

Ikegami, T. 2009, 'Sangyō-yō ōgata gas turbine no gijutsu keitōka chōsa' [Historical development of industrial large gas turbine], in The National Museum of Nature and Science (ed.), *Gijutu keitōka chōsa hōkoku* [Report on historical development of technologies], vol. 13, The National Museum of Nature and Science, Tokyo, pp. 77–146.

Inoue, H. 2008, 'Hitachi ni okeru gas turbine kaihatsu no ayumi' [The history of gas turbine development at Hitachi Ltd.], *Nihon Gas Turbine Gakkai Shi* [Journal of Gas Turbine Society of Japan], vol. 36, no. 3, pp. 199–205.

Itō, M., Honma, T. and Satō I. 2008, 'Tōshiba gas turbine kaihatsu no rekishi' [Gas turbine development footprints of Toshiba Corporation], *Nihon Gas Turbine Gakkai Shi* [Journal of Gas Turbine Society of Japan], vol. 36, no. 3, pp. 193–198.

Japan Bank for International Cooperation 2012, *Mitsubishi Jūkō, India no denryoku busoku kanwa no tame turbine, boiler o genchi seisan* [To ease shortage of electricity of India, MHI produced turbines and boilers locally]. Available from: <www.jbic.go.jp/wp-content/uploads/reference_ja/2012/12/2870/jbic_RRJ_2012076.pdf> [18 December 2012].

Kikkawa, T. 2004, *Nihon denryokugyō hatten no dynamism* [A Dynamism of Japan's Electric Power Industry], Nagoya University Press, Nagoya.

Mitsubishi Heavy Industries 2002, *News release*, No. 917. Available from: <www.mhi-global.com/news/sec1/e_0917.html> [23 July 2002].

Mitsubishi Heavy Industries 2003, *News release*, No. 973. Available from: <www.mhi-global.com/news/sec1/e_0973.html> [19 December 2003].

Mitsubishi Heavy Industries 2011a, *Press information*, No. 1396. Available from: <www.mhi-global.com/news/story/1101111396.html> [11 January 2011].

Mitsubishi Heavy Industries 2011b, *Press information*, No. 1404. Available from: <www.mhi-global.com/news/story/1102021404.html> [2 February 2011].

Mitsubishi Heavy Industries 2013, *Press information*, No. 1613. Available from: <www.mhi-global.com/news/story/1301151613.html> [15 January 2013].

Mitsubishi Heavy Industries 2014a, *Umi ni riku ni soshite uchū e 2: Enkaku—Showa kara Heisei e* [To Sea, Land, and Universe 2: A History—From Showa to Heisei Era], MHI, Tokyo.

Mitsubishi Heavy Industries 2014b, *Umi ni riku ni soshite uchū e 2: gijutsu, seihin jigyō hen/ shiryō hen* [To Sea, Land, and Universe 2: Technology and Product Edition/ Data Edition], MHI, Tokyo.

Mitsubishi Hitachi Power Systems n.d., *Corporate overview*. Available from: <www.mhps.com/en/company/outline/index.html> [6 February 2015].

Mizuho Bank, Ltd. Industry Research Division 2014, 'GE jūdenjigyō ni miru innovation senryaku' [Innovation strategy of GE's heavy electrical equipment business], *Mizuho Industry Research*, vol. 45, no. 2, pp. 100–108.

Ogino, R. and Iwasaki, Y. 2012, 'Hatsudenyō Jōki turbine gijutsu no hensen' [History of steam turbine technology for power generation], *The Journal of the Institute of Electrical Engineers of Japan*, vol. 132, no. 12, pp. 836–839.

Satō, N. 2008, *Hitachi, hatsuden setsubi de teikei o kakudai* [Hitachi expanded alliance in electric generating equipment]. Available from: <http://business.nikkeibp.co.jp/article/topics/20080623/163420/>. [June 25 2008].

Takeuchi, H. 1966, *Denki kikai kōgyō* [Electrical equipment industry], Toyokeizai Shimposha, Tokyo.

Tōkei Sakusei Iinkai [Statistics Committee of GTSJ] 1979, *Kokusan gas turbine shiryō shū* [Data book on gas turbine made in Japan], Gas Turbine Society of Japan, Tokyo.

Toshiba 2012, *Press release*. Available from: <www.toshiba.co.jp/about/press/2012_02/pr1201.htm>. [12 February 2012].

Tsukagoshi, K. 2008, 'Mitsubishi sangyō-yō gas turbine no kaihatsu no rekishi' [Development history of Mitsubishi industrial gas turbine], *Nihon Gas Turbine Gakkai Shi* [*Journal of Gas Turbine Society of Japan*], vol. 36, no. 3, pp. 206–212.

Tsukagoshi, K. 2013, 'Hatsudenyō gas turbine no kō-on, kō-kōritsuka no shinten to shōrai tenbō' [Progress and future development of advanced gas turbine for power generation], *Nihon Gas Turbine Gakkai Shi* [Journal of Gas Turbine Society of Japan], vol. 41, no. 1, pp. 53–58.

4 Exploring the Rise of Big Pharma

A French-Inspired Model for the Global Vaccine Industry

Julia Yongue

Introduction

Vaccines, a Distinctive Product and Industry

Medical historian Jean-Paul Gaudillière wrote that pharmaceuticals are *not ordinary goods* ("une marchandise pas comme les autres") (Gaudillière 2005, p. 115). One could argue that vaccines, one type of pharmaceutical used primarily to prevent rather than cure disease, possess many features distinguishing them from all other medicines. Whether due to these particularities or others, business historians, with a few but notable exceptions, have tended to devote less attention to this sector of the pharmaceutical industry than others. Vaccine production—perhaps because it was not an outgrowth of the chemical industry—received only brief mention in Alfred Chandler's study of the evolution of the chemical and pharmaceutical industries (Chandler 2005). Thanks, however, to the seminal work of Louis Galambos, Jonathan Liebenau, and others, much is now known about the development of the U.S. vaccine industry, though less research has been done on others, namely the French vaccine industry (Galambos 1995; Liebenau 1987).

Perhaps the most salient feature of vaccines is their fundamental nature as products: Because they trigger an immune response in the body, they necessarily entail a certain degree of risk. Indeed, vaccines have even been referred to by the Institute of Medicine as "unavoidably unsafe" (Institute of Medicine 1985, p. 86). Thus for public health authorities, whose mandate it is to protect society from infectious disease as well as vaccine-induced side effects, implementing a strong regulatory framework to ensure an adequate level of safety has always been a priority. As the principal, if not the sole purchaser of vaccines, governments are also tasked with implementing measures to guarantee a sufficient stock of vaccines from various producers. By implementing policies and regulations to respond to changing circumstances and needs, the state has guided and in some cases shaped the development of the vaccine industry through its dual role of public health and industrial policy-maker.

Another feature is that despite a global consensus among health authorities regarding the importance of vaccination, there are no universal standards—even among European Union member states—regarding the 'correct' dosage, strain, or optimal age at which an infant or adolescent should be immunized (WHO Vaccine-Preventable Disease Monitoring System 2015). Given this global patchwork of national policies, developing products that can be exported and administered in any market worldwide has been a challenging task for multinationals. For this reason and others, vaccine production remained for most of its long history a predominantly *local* industry comprised mainly of institute and laboratory producers shielded from competition through government policy rather than a *global* one dominated by multinationals.

France's "Pasteurian Model" in a Global Context

Like the diseases that scientists since Louis Pasteur have sought to prevent, France's industry, in contrast to those of many other nations, has always in a sense been global. The Pasteur Institute, founded in 1888, produced vaccines for use in France, parts of Europe, and French colonies across Africa and Asia. The first overseas Pasteur Institutes were located in Saigon (1891), Tunis (1893), and Algiers (1894), and were established for the purpose of vaccinating local populations and conducting research on diseases endemic to those regions (Institut Pasteur International Network 2015).

The production of vaccines was one of the founding branches of the pharmaceutical industry, and with their commercialization, the notion of what might today be called a 'business model' began to take shape. As Jonathan Simon and Axel Hüntelmann (2010, p. 60) described in their excellent study on the early vaccine industry, France and Germany became its first movers. From these operations, a system integrating research, development, treatment, and production took root in Europe, particularly in France, which is often referred to today as the *Pasteurian* (or Pastorian) *model*. According to this pragmatic model, scientists undertook research on a specific disease with the clear goal of developing a vaccine to prevent it (Stokes 1997; Mérieux 1997, p. 19, 313). It was also self-supporting, as scientific activities could be financed thanks to earnings from commercial activities. From the time of its inception, the model 'travelled' all over the world, including to Japan, whose importer was a physician, bacteriologist, and founder of the Kitasato Institute, Kitasato Shibasaburō (1853–1931). While the Pasteurian operating model was embraced globally, most of the actual production and use of vaccines took place locally. Some reasons why vaccine production remained a local undertaking can be traced to practical issues relating to transportation (e.g., the need to maintain the cold chain for certain vaccines), national public health policies designed to minimise risk (e.g., regulations prohibiting imports so as to prevent foreign sources of contamination), the special status of vaccines in most healthcare systems as a type of public good, and so on.

The main question to be addressed in this chapter is: What factors enabled the French to secure a dominant position in the global vaccine industry? To offer an answer, comparing the French case to that of the Japanese—whose production model is French inspired, yet whose vaccine industry has remained small and locally focused—is particularly useful. To explore these differences, this chapter comprises three sections. The first section, *Vaccine Industry Dynamics: The Transition From a National to a Global Operation* traces the principal drivers for the evolution of the industry's structure as a whole. The purpose of the second section, *The Re-emergence of the French Vaccine Industry*, is to examine the process by which the French, in particular, were able to attain a leading position in the global vaccine industry by the mid-2000s. Charles Mérieux, whose enterprise, through numerous mergers and acquisitions has become Sanofi Pasteur, played a central role in building the foundations for a strong French vaccine industry after World War II while also transforming it from a local to a global operation. Due to a lack of space, the role of the state, which was of vital importance in this transformation, receives only a brief mention in this chapter devoted to the development of the vaccine industry and the factors for its competitiveness.

To further elucidate why the points made in the two previous sections were of utmost importance to the French rise to global dominance, *Japan's French Connection to the Global Vaccine Industry* examines the French entry into the world's second largest single market for pharmaceuticals, Japan. Japan's industry—the antipode to the French—merits careful examination, as it provides, by virtue of its many differences, a key to answering the question posed above as well as identifying the major influences on the development of the global vaccine industry. Japan's case is distinctive for a number of reasons. First, health authorities, until only recently, rejected a form of vaccination that has become the standard in most nations, combination vaccines, in favour of single-dose injections. Second, until 2006, no new-generation paediatric vaccines had been approved, including the Hib vaccine (*haemophilus influenzae type B*), which by March 2006 had already been introduced in some 106 countries, 90 of which had added it to their routine schedules (WHO Fact Sheets 2005). Another particularity, one that makes Japan's case vital to the understanding of the industry's overall evolution since the 1980s, is its institute-based production model, which as mentioned above, is ironically French inspired. By examining Japan's recent connection to the French vaccine industry, this section also sheds light on the impact of new technologies, namely combination vaccines as well as the importance of the operating model on the vaccine industry's transformation from a small, local business to a large-scale operation spanning the globe.

1 Vaccine Industry Dynamics: The Transition From a National to a Global Operation

While the vast majority of infants and adolescents worldwide receive at least some form of vaccination during their lifetime, the global vaccine industry is tiny in comparison to mainstream pharmaceuticals in terms of earnings. According to a European Vaccine Manufacturers survey, vaccine sales made up only 1.5 percent of the total pharmaceutical market in 2002 (European Vaccine Manufacturers 2004; Scherer 2007). Thus, although the vaccine industry is vital to public health, it has generally not yielded returns commensurate with other pharmaceuticals. According to an historian of science and medicine, Stuart Blume, "they have never been a commercially attractive activity" (Blume 2005, 60). This assertion can be supported by numerous factors. First, unlike most pharmaceuticals, vaccines are subject to tiered pricing, meaning that the same vaccine is sold in different markets at substantially different prices, an aspect that multinationals carefully take into consideration when formulating global marketing strategies. Second, because discoveries relating to biologicals are difficult to patent, significant innovations do not always translate into higher corporate returns. Third, while higher entry barriers linked to a substantial initial investment in plants and equipment do indeed deter new competitors, existing vaccine producers are at a disadvantage due to higher running costs and more frequent and rigorous quality control and monitoring inspections than pharmaceuticals (Dupuy and Friedel 1990). Finally, until the application of robotic technologies in the 1990s, new vaccine development took enterprises on the average much longer than other pharmaceuticals (Hawthorne 2003). Given these features coupled with prices that tend to decrease over time and profitability dependent on the degree to which the manufacturer can achieve economies of scale, the vaccine industry has, through much of its modern history, tended to have more in common with generic drugs than mainstream pharmaceuticals.

1.1 From Golden Age to Crisis (1950s to early 1980s)

The outlook for the vaccines industry was once less bleak. From World War II to the mid-1970s, vaccines enjoyed a golden age thanks to the discovery and dissemination of life-saving products, perhaps the most remarkable example being the polio vaccine. By the early 1980s, however, producers in many countries faced a crisis. Their public image became tainted by the rise in vaccine-induced injuries. In the United States, expensive litigation along with public policies to reduce healthcare costs had a negative impact on the industry's operations. According to David Mowery and Violaine Mitchell,

> Between 1966 and 1977, one-half of all U.S. commercial vaccine manufacturers stopped producing and distributing vaccines. This trend

continued through the 1980s as Eli Lilly, Pfizer, Glaxo, Wellcome Dow Chemical, and Merrell-National Laboratories exited vaccine production, in some cases selling their operations to other firms.
(Mowery and Michell 1995, p. 975; US Congress 1986)

The threat of vaccine shortages loomed. Some companies were forced to halt production following refusals by insurers to provide litigation insurance (Institute of Medicine 1985, p. 11). Large-scale pharmaceutical firms responded by channelling research funds away from vaccines into more promising areas such as antibiotics, which were considered less risky and more lucrative (Temin 1980, pp. 58–87). The government finally stepped in by implementing measures such as the 1986 National Vaccine Injury Compensation Program, which helped to reduce the burden of litigation; however, legal loopholes and falling prices deterred producers that had already left the industry from returning (Offit 2005).

In Europe, a more favourable regulatory environment over the same period allowed its vaccine producers to avert a similar crisis (Galambos 2008, pp. 12–14)—one reason why they were spared is protectionism. As underlined in one of Louis Galambos's pioneering studies on Merck,

> Overseas markets [in the late 1970s] were difficult . . . to crack. A number of the European companies were looked on by their governments as "national institutions": Pasteur and Mérieux, both in France, and Behringwerke in Germany were the Big Three. . . . Though Merck . . . was much larger than any of these firms, they had the support of their national governments, as did Sclavo in Italy, RIT in Belgium and Holland, and Burroughs Wellcome and Glaxo in the United Kingdom. As a result, MSDI was making no vaccine sales in France, Germany, Britain, Italy, and Spain.
> (Galambos and Sewell 1995, pp. 146–147)

In addition to protectionism, European governments' decision not to exert pressure on producers to lower prices fostered a more industry-friendly environment, which in the long term has had a beneficial effect on their overall competitiveness: Although the United States still offers the largest market gains, Europe produces most of the world's vaccines—89.4 percent of the total by the early 2000s (European Vaccines Manufacturers 2004, p. 10).

1.2 From Crisis to Consolidation (late 1980s and 1990s)

In the midst of this relative decline were some hopeful developments. New conjugate or combination vaccines, containing multiple vaccines in a single injection, were a promising technological and marketing innovation for the vaccine industry and served as a major catalyst for the first wave of consolidation in the mid-1980s and 1990s. Of note is that though novel in form and composition, combination vaccines were not entirely new products. Early combination vaccines, launched in the 1950s and 1960s incorporated two and in some cases three vaccines. The new-generation combination vaccines that proliferated in the late 1980s, however, offered genuinely innovative features that made a more substantial contribution to public health than their precursors by reducing risk and guaranteeing wider coverage. One example is the DTP vaccine (diphtheria-tetanus-pertussis), a first-generation combination vaccine. By substituting the whole-cell pertussis vaccine with the much safer acellular version, developed in Japan in 1981, manufacturers were able to virtually eliminate pertussis vaccine-induced adverse events, a major cause of litigation (Geier and Geier 2002). In addition to safety enhancements, new products incorporated components that had not previously been combinable. Entirely new paediatric vaccines such as Hib (*haemophilus influenzae* type B vaccine) were added as well as hepatitis A and recombinant hepatitis B. Through these innovations, combination vaccines have become increasingly more complex and sophisticated.

The rise in the demand worldwide for these new-generation combination vaccines triggered a change in the market structure. Before their widespread use, *adult vaccines* comprised mainly of the seasonal influenza vaccine dominated the market as the most lucrative vaccine segment. However, this category was surpassed in most markets by *new paediatric vaccines* both in terms of size and returns by the early 1990s. The rise in the demand for new combination vaccines offers a clear illustration of a point made in the introduction, which is the significance of the state in guiding and shaping the development of the vaccine industry. Thanks to their wide coverage against diseases and alleviation of the need to stockpile single-dose vaccines, public health authorities in Europe and the United States have fully endorsed them by making them their vaccination standard. In the backdrop of this change was the sharp rise in the number of new routine vaccines, which has nearly doubled in some countries since the early 1980s. Consequently, other stakeholders, namely parents and guardians, have backed the use of combination vaccines due to their convenience in reducing both the number of trips to medical institutions and injections for their children.

Viewed in the long term, new-generation combination vaccines proved to be radical innovations that have made single-dose vaccines virtually obsolete in many countries. For multinationals, particularly those with strong marketing divisions and the capacity to scale up production, they provided a boon to vaccine manufacturing, a waning sector of the pharmaceutical industry. New products were launched, as firms cooperated and competed to expand products lines and global market share. As noted by Ronald Ellis and Douglas Gordon, the creation of new combination vaccines radically altered the relationships *between* firms, and more notably to the purposes of this chapter, the overall composition of the vaccine industry:

> Given the number and complexity of potential combination vaccines . . .
> there may be no single manufacturer that would develop all of the

component vaccines itself. Consequently, alliances between manufacturers would be required to share their respective component vaccines for the creation of the ultimate combination products.

(Ellis and Gordon 1994, p. 46)

An increasing number of inter-company alliances and company-institute arrangements formed in the 1980s and early 1990s. One example is the alliance between Mérieux and Merck, which enabled the latter to enter more of Europe's once-closed markets. In this way, combination vaccines also provided a catalyst for a fundamental change in the business environment and new opportunities for globalization.

As relationships between large producers and types of products evolved, smaller vaccine manufacturers found it increasingly difficult to compete and many closed. Their disappearance from the production landscape coupled by moves to consolidate and/or cooperate heralded further changes in the composition of the industry from one comprised of numerous locally focused operations to one increasingly dominated by multinationals. Some examples include Ciba Geigy's acquisition of 50 percent of Sclavo (Italy) in 1991 and new agreements between both Merck and Commonwealth Serum Laboratories (Australia) in 1992 and SmithKline Beecham and Behringwerke (Germany) in 1993.

1.3 Towards a Global Vaccine Industry Dominated by Multinationals (since 2000)

New-generation combination vaccines served as the major catalysts for a change in the first phase of the industry's consolidation; however, by the late 1990s, other factors came into play. First, the development of more new vaccines such as HPV (human papillomavirus vaccine), designed to prevent cervical cancer brought unprecedented profits to the vaccine industry making it resemble more closely mainstream pharmaceuticals than generic drugs in terms of earnings, disease targets (e.g., cancer), and even advertising strategies. The Institute of Medicine reported that in 1982 the entire American vaccine industry was valued at $170 million (Institute of Medicine 1985). According to Kalorama Information (2014), a market research organization, by 2009, the world vaccine market had grown to US$22.1 billion with growth rates of 10 percent per annum.

Second, was a change in the global operating environment. As mentioned above, cross-border alliances such as the one between Merck and Mérieux opened national markets to international competition. Thus with more choices of suppliers for national governments to consider, price competition intensified. As firms sought to strengthen their competitiveness by increasing global market share, further acquisitions ensued, this time on an even larger scale than in the 1980s and 1990s. In 2005, Novartis acquired Chiron, while Pfizer acquired Wyeth (2009) and later Baxter (2014). By 2008, multinationals based in just four nations, Great Britain, France, the United States,

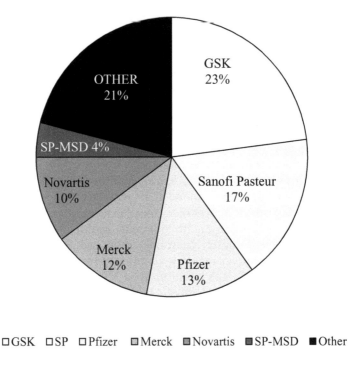

☐GSK   ☐SP   ☐Pfizer   ▣Merck   ▪Novartis   ▪SP-MSD   ■Other

Figure 4.1   Market Share of Major Vaccine Producers, 2008

and Switzerland, became the principal producers of approximately 80 percent of the world's vaccines (Kaddar 2008). In Figure 4.1 below, "Other," while significant in percentage terms is comprised mainly of small- and medium-sized manufacturers in populous emerging markets such as India and China, niche producers (start-ups), Japan, and so on.

2 The Re-emergence of the French Vaccine Industry

2.1 From Artisanal to Industrial Production

The origins of vaccine research in France can be traced to the Pasteur Institute in Paris; however, the roots of its modern vaccine industry are in Lyon, where it is still situated today. The industry's point of departure was the establishment of the Mérieux Biological Institute in 1897, which produced both human and animal vaccines. Marcel Mérieux, its founder, looked upon the Pasteur Institute where he had studied as the model for his own operations, which were by comparison still 'artisanal' in scale (Dumons 1992, p. 333). It was not until after his death in 1937 when his second son, Charles (1907–2001), who had also studied at the Pasteur Institute, took up the reins of the operation that it would begin to transform from a relatively small Europe-focused business into a global corporation.

Key to setting this process in motion was Charles Mérieux's early realization of the need to revolutionize his approach to production. Requisite to effecting this radical change was the scaling up of his operations so as to reduce per unit cost. The idea to do so originated in 1944 when the French government sent him to the United States on a special assignment to study the organization of blood transfusion activities. During Mérieux's tour of numerous public and private facilities, he observed that American producers were already manufacturing on a massive scale unknown in France at that time, which he called "industrial biology." He believed that by implementing a similar system at his own enterprise, France, and in later years, Europe, could achieve self-sufficiency and no longer have to depend on U.S. imports of vaccine/serum products.

In the 1950s, Mérieux set about equipping his factory at Marcy-Étoile to attain a comparable production capacity as in the U.S. while also incorporating new techniques such as lyophilization (Mérieux 1997). To achieve this aim, he strove to turn his laboratory into a full-fledged business, installed high-capacity tanks specially designed for use in his factory, and began a global search for innovative technologies to further increase vaccine output and safety. New scientific and manufacturing technologies developed in the United States would have a particularly strong influence on Mérieux's strategy choices throughout his lifetime. During his frequent travels, he cultivated personal and professional ties with leaders in the scientific, public health, and business fields, including an especially close relationship with Jonas Salk, best known for his discovery of the polio vaccine.

2.2 Foundations for a Post-war French Comeback

As mentioned in the introduction, the regulatory regime for vaccines differs significantly across nations. Thus to facilitate the exportability of his products while enhancing safety, in 1955 Mérieux organised the first of many major international conferences, one of whose goals was to create universal manufacturing standards (Mérieux 1997). He also became a leading proponent of the standardization of routine vaccine schedules particularly across the African continent so as to improve disease coverage and contain infection. Of particular note is that Mérieux's interests were not simply in the improvement of vaccines themselves but also in the ways that they could be administered. From an early date, his company became not only a producer of vaccines but also syringes. This interest in finding novel ways to administer vaccines would translate into innovations made in the 1950s and early 1960s, when he began collaborating with an American syringe manufacturer to develop a double-chambered syringe designed to inject multiple vaccines. Each syringe contained a "by-pass" allowing the vaccines to remain unmixed until the time of injection (Galy 2006). The early syringe he helped to develop would become a prototype for the more complex and sophisticated new-generation combination vaccines described above.

In addition to the expansion of production capacity and product lines, Mérieux also aspired to increase the scope of his operations beyond the borders of Europe. Given his careful observations of the U.S. industry since his first visit in 1944, he was aware of the mass withdrawals in the 1970s and early 1980s. However, unlike his counterparts, he saw the exodus not as a sign of decline but as an opportunity for a French comeback (Mr. L. Friedel, pers. comm., 2012). In 1968, in preparation for full-scale, global expansion, which would require considerable capital, he consolidated his own operations before selling off 51 percent of his shares to Rhône-Poulenc and listing the company. Then in 1978, Mérieux made the first of several major overseas acquisitions, Merrell-National Laboratories, an attractive purchase due to its advancements in the development of a new, safer pertussis vaccine. Moreover, the purchase would provide the French industry with its first major foothold in the North American market.

In 1989, he made another major purchase, Connaught Laboratories, established in the University of Toronto, whose operating model closely resembled that of the Pasteur Institute (Rutty 2008). Connaught was Canada's largest and most innovative producer, whose 1954 field trial had contributed to the launch of Salk's polio vaccine. The purchase enabled Mérieux to secure a 30 percent share in the global market for human vaccines and gain full entry into the North American region (Blondeau 1999). To further solidify the company's stake, a strategic alliance was negotiated in 1994 with Merck, the key player in the U.S. vaccine industry. This arrangement gradually evolved into a joint venture for vaccine marketing and co-development that by 2008 had secured a four percent share of the world vaccine market (see Figure 4.1). Through this relationship, the French gained access to some of Merck's highly innovative vaccine components, which could be used in new-generation combination vaccines in exchange for better access for Merck into Europe's once-closed national vaccine markets.

2.3 Changes in Ownership and Further Consolidation

Consolidation fundamentally changed not only the structure of the global industry but also that of the French domestic industry. In 1985, a partnership formed between Mérieux and the Pasteur Institute for the production of human and veterinary vaccines, which would eventually lead to a full acquisition of the latter's vaccine production division in 1992. With this purchase, the company's name was changed to Pasteur-Mérieux Serums and Vaccines with Alain Mérieux, the son of Charles Mérieux as the first president. Though the new entity bore the name *Pasteur*, the acquisition terminated the Pasteur Institute's commercial activities; i.e., the production and sale of vaccines. Following the acquisition, the institute would no longer operate according to the self-supporting model introduced by its founder,

Louis Pasteur, who combined research to develop new vaccines with patient treatment, production, and sales. Though Charles Mérieux always considered himself a Pasteurian, whose work was a form of public service, the scale that he was able to achieve through *industrial biology* and marketing of novel products brought an entirely new dimension to Pasteur's initial model, one that was essential to the French in securing a major stake in the global vaccine industry.

In 1994, two years after the acquisition of the Pasteur Institute's manufacturing division, the remaining shares of the company were sold to Rhône-Poulenc, whose management changed the firm's name to Pasteur Mérieux Connaught (PMC). A final wave of consolidation in the French vaccine industry occurred in the 2000s after Charles Mérieux's death. In 1999, Synthélabo and Sanofi merged to become Sanofi-Synthélabo, followed by the 2004 hostile takeover of Aventis, which formed after a merger between Rhône–Poulenc and Hoechst.[1] Though not discussed at length in this chapter, it should be noted that in addition to business interests, politics continued to play a significant role in guiding the creation of a strong French vaccine industry from the days of Mérieux (Ruffat 1996; Müller-Stewens and Alsher 2006). In 2004, Sanofi Pasteur became the world's largest company solely devoted to the production of human vaccines, which currently manufactures one billion doses annually, shipped to some 500 million people worldwide (Sanofi Pasteur 2016). While Charles Mérieux would not live long enough to witness all of the large-scale, cross-border mergers that would eventually lead to the full consolidation of the French vaccine (and pharmaceutical) industry, he played a crucial role in building the necessary foundations to achieve it.

3 Japan's French Connection to the Global Vaccine Industry

3.1 Establishing a Foothold in the Japanese Market

By the late 1990s, the French industry had expanded into all the major vaccine markets, save one, Japan. According to an interview with Louis Freidel, founder of PMC's (Pasteur Mérieux Connaught) joint venture in Japan, the idea to enter the Japanese market occurred to him by chance. In a 1996 article he happened to read in *Le Monde*, it was reported that a Japanese infant had died of the measles. Freidel found the news unusual since infants in France are vaccinated against such diseases, and decided to propose the idea of investing in Japan to the company's chairman, Michel Greco (Monin and Friedel 1996). Another consideration was price. Japan's vaccine prices are the highest in the world, the second being the United States (Mr. Friedel, L. pers. comm. 2011).

Finding a suitable joint venture partner was a major hurdle, as all the manufacturers Freidel approached showed no interest. In 1987, Connaught had co-founded a company called CD Vac with Daiichi Pharmaceutical Company (which became Daiichi Sankyo Pharmaceutical Company in 2005) to sell blood derivatives in Japan. At that time, PMC had already withdrawn from this sector; however, CD Vac was still registered as a company. Friedel approached Daiichi, and a joint venture was formed in 1997, which following numerous mergers, became *PMC-Daiichi Sankyo Vaccine Company Limited*. He decided that the new company's first launch would be the Hib (*haemophilus influenzae type B*) vaccine or ©ACTHib. In addition to its novelty, ACTHib had no competitors—domestic or foreign—and offered long-term marketing potential since it could be used in various combination vaccines, which had not yet been launched in Japan.

3.2 Features of the Japanese Vaccine Industry

Though Kitasato Shibasaburō, founder of Japan's first commercial vaccine (sera) production operation, was a contemporary of Louis Pasteur, the differences between the French and Japanese industries today are stark. As shown below, the first difference is that private institutes and laboratories dominate the industry as the country's principal suppliers (MHLW 2007, p. 23; Japanese Association of Vaccine Industries 2008 and 2009). As of 2008, there are two foreign multinationals operating in Japan: GSK and MSDI. The latter markets vaccines and other pharmaceuticals through Banyu, its fully owned subsidiary. In both cases, however, their presence is negligible; 2008 profits from sales accounted for less than one percent of total domestic sales.

Second, in order to ensure the safety, stable supply, and traceability of vaccines in use in Japan, regulators have aimed since 1947 to maintain a policy of full self-sufficiency. According to the Ministry of Health, Labour and Welfare (MHLW), in 2008, 98.5 percent were domestically produced (MHLW 2007). Third, litigation has had a more profound effect on regulators' views of risk. From 1989 to 2006 amidst a series of rulings against the Japanese government, regulators approved only one new product, the hepatitis A vaccine. Related to the third is the fourth difference, the dearth of combination vaccines one example being the MMR vaccine (measles-mumps-rubella) (Andreae, Freed and Katz 2004). Following adverse reactions to the mumps vaccine, health officials officially removed it from the market, despite intense criticism from vaccine experts (Plotkin 2009). Officials replaced it in 1988 with the MR vaccine (measles-rubella), a modified version of the MMR vaccine, the standard in most countries. New-generation combination vaccines could not be found in Japan until 2012. Finally, the *adult vaccines* segment, comprised mainly of the influenza vaccine, has long been the largest and the most lucrative category in Japan. As mentioned above, *paediatric vaccines* surpassed the *adult vaccines* category in many countries in the 1990s.

Table 4.1 Domestic Vaccine Manufacturers Operating in Japan in 2008

Manufacturer (1)	Legal Status	Annual domestic sales (mil yen)	Vaccines (ratio of total sales, 2003)
Kaketsuken (2)	Incorporated Foundation	31,902	34%
Denka Seiken	Joint-stock Company	11,692	33%
Biken (Institute for Microbial Diseases, Osaka University)	Incorporated Foundation	9,100	96%
Kitasato Institute	University	8,800	100%
Japan BCG Laboratory	Joint-stock company	2,700	100%
JPRI (Japan Poliomyelitis Research Institute)	Incorporated Foundation	938	100%
Takeda Pharmaceutical Co.	Joint-stock Company	1,086,431	Less than 2%

(1) Meiji Dairies (Meiji Nyūgyō) also engaged in the small-scale production of the hepatitis B vaccine (less than one percent of total sales) in 2008 but withdrew from the industry in 2009.
(2) "Ken" is an abbreviation for "institute" or "laboratory" in Japanese. The Japanese name of the Kitasato Institute is Kitasato *Ken*kyūsho.

3.3 Inventing a "New" Disease

According to a 2005 WHO Fact Sheet, Hib is a bacterial disease that strikes children under the age of five, though infants between four and 18 months are the most susceptible (WHO 2005). An estimated three million children worldwide contract the disease annually. The most common symptoms include pneumonia and meningitis, which may result in permanent damage including deafness and mental retardation in 15 to 35 percent of those who contract it. Although the Hib vaccine has become routine in most developed countries, it was relatively unknown to the average Japanese until the 2000s. Thus in order to successfully market it, PMC had in effect to *create* a new disease. This was no easy task given that many health experts believed that Japan had a much lower incidence than other countries, a perception that was reinforced by existing medical practices: Japanese paediatricians generally respond to infections by administering antibiotics, making the virus more difficult to detect. To verify its presence with absolute certainty, analyses of blood samples (for pneumonia) or spinal fluid (for meningitis), which are not routine at Japanese medical institutions, must be performed. To challenge the long-standing perception of a lower incidence, Kamiya et al. conducted a study in 1998 at 876 hospitals in six prefectures, revealing it to be the most common cause of meningitis (Kamiya et al. 1998). French representatives submitted these results along with ample international clinical data to Japanese officials at the time of their approval request.

3.4 Japanese Approval and Marketing Problems

Of note is that PMC was not the first multinational vaccine producer to attempt to enter Japan's vaccine industry. Though only recently, GSK has begun to make more substantial inroads thanks to the approval of Ceravix (cervical cancer) in 2009 and the formation of a joint venture with Dai-ichi Sankyo in 2012, Japan Vaccine KK. From a much earlier date, MSDI (Merck) has endeavoured to penetrate Japan's domestic vaccine market for many years with mixed results. As mentioned above, the MMR vaccine was officially removed from the routine vaccine schedule and replaced with the MR vaccine (measles-rubella), making it unfeasible to contemplate market-ing its innovative mumps vaccine in Japan's domestic market. Nonetheless, among Merck's overseas targets, Japan was particularly attractive. This was due not only to market size but also a high incidence of certain dis-eases including hepatitis B, once referred to as a national disease (Sugawara 2009, p. 2).

In the mid-1980s, Merck submitted an application to market its recom-binant hepatitis B product, Recombivax HB. However, because regulators refused to accept any foreign clinical data at that time, Merck had no choice but to begin new trials. In 1987, researchers from a domestic manufacturer Kaketsuken, who had developed a similar product, submitted their appli-cation with trial data for some 2,300 Japanese volunteers, while Merck, working with Banyu, submitted a new set of data from a comparable cohort (Mr. K Matsuyama, pers. comm. 29 May 2012). In 1988, following exami-nations of both sets of data, officials granted approval to Kaketsuken and Merck on the same day. In the end, Merck did succeed in launching its vaccine candidate; however, because the hepatitis B vaccine was not made routine, sales would never reach the levels seen in other overseas markets.

In a similar way, Japanese regulators refused to accept PMC's applica-tion on the grounds that the data submitted was insufficient. Their deci-sion to reject the company's large pool of foreign data came as a surprise to the French given the vaccine's positive safety record and widespread use worldwide (Mr. L. Freidel L., pers. comm. 2012). As in the previous case, new trials got underway, which took approximately two years. The French perceived the approval process as being longer and more extensive than in other major markets. However, according to an interview with a min-istry official, the time the evaluation necessitated was average by Japanese standards (Ms. Imai M 2011 pers. comm., 18 Nov 2011). Delays are often longer than in other countries, particularly for vaccines, due in part to a much smaller number of examiners than in other countries (Yongue 2008, pp. 166–191; Shimazawa and Ikeda 2012, pp. 312–317; Nakayama 2003).

In 2007, ten years after establishing the joint venture with Daiichi, PMC became the first foreign company ever to receive approval for a paediatric vaccine in Japan. However, the first shipments did not reach most medical institutions until nearly two years later in December 2008. Even three years after its approval, there was still a two-month waiting period due to shortages. The delays were not caused by safety concerns. ACTHib had received a favourable endorsement from the Japan Medical Association and was gaining wider recognition among parents. Medical institutions as well as some of those who were the most knowledgeable of ACTHib were eagerly awaiting the vaccine. According to a 9 March 2009 article in AERA, Japan's equivalent of Newsweek or Time, an infant, whose parents—a gynaecologist and a paediatrician—were on a waiting list for the vaccine, died from Hib-induced meningitis (AERA 2009, p. 76). Packaging issues, not the vaccine itself, were the main cause of the problems (Freidel, L. 2012 pers. comm). A solution was found: The introduction of a special inspection system at the Marcy-Étoile plant, which required workers to check each and every vial by hand before packaging and shipment to Japan.

Since ACTHib's 2007 launch, the policy environment in Japan has changed dramatically as witnessed by measures to promote wider use of preventive vaccination and an unprecedented number of new foreign vaccine approvals (Akazawa et al. 2014). In response, the Japanese vaccine industry has begun to evolve via consolidation, alliances, and new-to-Japan vaccine products. In 2013, Biken announced a merger with JPRI, a combination vaccine launch, and the opening of a state-of-the-art plant designed to increase production capacity and boost overseas sales. The Kitasato Institute, whose model was from its founding inspired by that of the French, spun off its production division in 2011 in a similar way, though at a much early date, as the Pasteur Institute. The new entity is known as *Kitasato Daiichi Sankyo Vaccine*. Recent vaccine policy revisions combined with an increasing multinational presence are also having a noticeable effect on the domestic industry strategies as some large-scale Japanese pharmaceutical manufacturers are entering the vaccine industry through agreements with institutes. Nonetheless, given public health authorities' fundamental policy stance of maintaining full self-sufficiency in vaccines while encouraging coordination and cooperation among producers so as to ensure a sufficient supply, the Japanese vaccine industry is more likely to retain many of its specificities at least in the short term by adapting its French-inspired production model to the changing domestic circumstances than by abandoning it completely.

Conclusions

Through the French case, this chapter identified the specificities of the vaccine industry and explored its evolution from a local to a global business. It also assessed the importance of the French industry's (1) operating model, including its shift from institute to multinational-based production, (2) introduction of technological and marketing innovations, namely combination vaccines, (3) consolidation, (4) entrepreneurship, and (5) scaling up of production capacity through industrial biology as the major drivers for globalization. These five factors along with the state's support for the development of a strong national industry has enabled the French to secure and maintain their competitiveness in the long term.

To elucidate the overall significance of these factors in a broader context, the third section examined the French connection to the Japanese vaccine industry and compared some of their most salient differences. Despite the similarities in their early roots, their development paths diverged, particularly in the 1980s and 1990s. Unlike the French, the Japanese have retained their own version of the self-supporting, institute-based Pasteurian model rather than shift to one whose production and marketing are carried out by multinational pharmaceutical enterprises. Two historical factors: Japan's institute-centred production model and its distinctive national vaccine policies including regulators' preference for single-dose vaccines and reluctance to approve any new vaccines for over a decade have had a considerable impact on its industry's size, competitiveness, and global presence in the long term. By comparing the French and Japanese vaccine industries, the final section of this chapter provided some important implications for other vaccine-producing nations, namely the connections one can make between national industry structure, operating model, and global competitiveness.

Note

1 Synthélabo underwent considerable consolidation with other small firms before merging with Sanofi. Synthélabo, which became part of L'Oréal in 1973, formed through mergers with five laboratories: Dausse, Delagrange, Delalande, Métabio-Joullié, and Robert & Carrière.

References

Akazawa, M., Yongue, J., Ikeda, S. and Sato, T. 2014, 'Considering economic analyses in the revision of the preventive vaccine law: A new direction for health policy-making in Japan?', *Health Policy*, vol. 118, pp. 127–128.

Andreae, M.C., Freed, G.L. and Katz, S.L. 2004, 'Safety concern regarding combination vaccines: Experience in Japan', *Vaccine*, vol. 22, pp. 3911–3916.

Blondeau, A. 1999, *Histoire des Laboratoires pharmaceutiques en France et leurs médicaments* (History of Pharmaceutical Laboratories in France and Their Medicines), Collection Santé, p. 181.

Blume, S. 2005, 'Lock in, the state and vaccine development: Lessons from the history of the polio vaccines', Research Policy 34, Elsevier, 160.

Chandler, A.D. 2005, *Shaping the Industrial Century: The Remarkable Story of the Evolution of the Modern Chemical and Pharmaceuticals Industries*, Harvard University Press, Cambridge, MA.

Dumons, B. 1992, 'Marcel Mérieux (1870–1937) l'émergence de la bactériologie industrielle entre Saône et Rhône (Marcel Mérieux (1870–1937) the emergence of industrial bacteriology between the Saone and the Rhone)', *Cahiers d'histoire*, vol. 3/4, pp. 327–335.

Dupuy, J.M. and Freidel, L. 1990, 'Viewpoint: The lag between discovery and production of new vaccines for the developing world', *Lancet*, vol. 336, pp. 773–774.

Ellis, R.J. and Gordon, R.D. 1994, 'Combination Vaccines', Ronald J. Ellis and R. Douglas Gordon, *International Journal of Technology Assessment in Healthcare*, vol. 10, no. 1, pp. 185–192.

European Vaccines Manufacturers 2004, *Worldwide vaccine manufacturers in figures*, Edition, p. 10. 7. Available from: <http://vaccineseurope.eu/wp-content/uploads/2012/12/Worldwide-Major-Vaccine-Manufacturers-in-Figures-2004.pdf>

Friedel, Louis, former head of Pasteur Mérieux Connaught Daiichi, 19 May, 17 June, 2 October, 2011.

Galambos, L. 2008, 'What are the prospects for a new golden era in vaccines?', *Eurohealth*, vol. 14, no. 1, pp. 12–14. Available from <www.lse.ac.uk/LSEHealthAndSocialCare/pdf/eurohealth/VOL14No1/Galambos.pdf> [16 June 2016]

Galambos, L. and Sewell, J.E. 1995, *Networks of Innovation: Vaccine Development at Merck, Sharp & Dohme, Mulford, 1895–1995*, Cambridge University Press, Cambridge.

Galy, M. 2006, 'Le Docteur Mérieux et la mise sous forme pharmaceutique' (Doctor Mérieux and the formulation and filing of vaccines), in *Témoignages Sans Frontière entre 2 médecines* (Testimonies Without Borders between medicines), Museum of Biological Sciences Doctor Mérieux, 28–29.

Gaudillière, J.P. 2005, 'Une marchandise pas comme les autres Historiographie du médicament et de l'industrie pharmaceutique en France au XXe siècle', in C. Bonah and A. Rasmussen (eds.), *Histoire et Médicament aux XIXe et XXe siècles*, Editions Glyphe, Paris, p. 115.

Geier, D. and Geier, M. 2002, 'The true story of the pertussis vaccine: A sordid legacy?', *Journal of the History of Medicine*, Oxford University Press, vol. 57, pp. 249–284.

Hawthorne, F. 2003, *The Merck Druggernaut: The Inside Story of a Pharmaceutical Giant*, Wiley, Hoboken, NJ.

Imai, M. 2011, Tuberculosis and infectious disease division of the Health Service Bureau, MHLW, Tokyo, interview, 18 November.

Institut Pasteur 2015, *History*. Available from: <www.pasteur.fr/en/international/institut-pasteur-international-network/history> [7 March 2016].

Institute of Medicine Division of Health Promotion and Disease Prevention (eds.) 1985, *Vaccine Supply and Innovation*, National Academy Press, Washington, DC.

Japanese Association of Vaccine Industries (Association of Biologicals Manufacturers of Japan) 2008 and 2009 Yearbooks, *Wakuchin no Kiso: Wakuchinrui no Seizo kara Ryūtsū* (Vaccine Basics: From Production to Distribution).

Kaddar, M. 2008, World Health Organization, EPI Seminar 2008. Available from: <www.who.int/influenza_vaccines_plan/resources/session_10_kaddar.pdf>

Kalorama Information 2010, Press release 'Global vaccine market exceeds $20 billion', 12 August. Available from: www.kaloramainformation.com/about/release.asp?id=1693 [14 July 2014].

Kamiya, H., Uehara, S., Kato, T., Shiraki, K., Togashi, T., Morishima, T., Goto, Y., Sato, O. and Standaert, S. 1998, 'Childhood bacterial meningitis policy in Japan', *Paediatric Infectious Disease Journal*, vol. 17, no. 9, pp. S183–S185.

Liebenau, J. 1987, *Medical Science and Medical Industry, the Formation of the American Pharmaceutical Industry*, Johns Hopkins University Press, Baltimore, MD.

Matsuyama, K., former Banyu executive and researchers, who wished to remain anonymous, who were directly involved in the hepatitis B vaccine trials in Japan, pers. Comm., [29 May 2012].

Mérieux, C. 1997, *Virus Passion* (Virus Passion), Robert Lafont, Paris.

Ministry of Health, Labour and Welfare 2007, *Wakuchin Sangyō Bijon Kanseishō Taisaku wo sasae, shakaiteki kitai ni kotaeru sangyōzō wo mezashite* (Vaccine Industry Vision: Supporting Measures to Prevent Infection While Aiming to Respond to Societal Expectations of Industry), March.

Monin, P. and Freidel, L., 'École de Management de Lyon', Programme ESC Lyon, International Strategies of firms: Pasteur Mérieux Connaught (PMC) in Japan-1996.

Mowery, D.C. and Mitchell, V. 1995, 'Improving the reliability of the US vaccine supply: An evaluation of alternatives', *Journal of Health Policy, Politics and Law*, vol. 20, no. 4, pp. 973–1000.

Müller-Stewens, G. and Alsher, A. 2006, 'A The acquisition of Aventis by Sanofi', University of St Gallen, Case Study 306-238-1.

Nakayama, T. 2003, 'Nihon no Wakuchin Seisaku wa naze sekai kara tachiokuretekita noka' (Why do Japan's vaccine policies lag behind others in the world?), *Iyaku Medicine and Drug Journal*, vol. 24, no. 3. Available at https://iyaku-j.com/iyakuj/system/dc8/index.php?trgid=8386

Offit, P.A. 2005, 'Why are pharmaceutical companies gradually abandoning vaccines?', *Health Affairs*, vol. 24, no. 3, pp. 622–630.

Plotkin, S.A. 2009, 'Commentary: Is Japan deaf to the mumps vaccination?', *Paediatric Infectitious Disease Journal*, vol. 28, p. 176.

Ruffat, M. 1996, *175 ans d'industrie pharmaceutique française: histoire de Synthélabo* (175 Years of the French Pharmaceutical Industry: History of Synthélabo), Editions de la Découverte, Paris.

Rutty, C.J. 2008, 'Personality, politics, and public health: The origins of Connaught Medical Research Laboratories (1888–1917)', in E.A. Heaman, A. Li and S. McKellar (eds.), *Figuring the Social: Essays in Honour of Michael Bliss*, University of Toronto Press, Toronto.

Sanofi Pasteur 2016, Available from: <www.sanofipasteur.com/en/about_us/> [3 March 2016].

Scherer, M. 2007, 'An industrial organization perspective on the influenza vaccine', *Managerial and Decision Economics*, vol. 28, pp. 393–405.

Shimazawa, R. and Ikeda, M. 2012, 'The vaccine gap between Japan and the UK', *Health Policy*, vol. 107, pp. 312–317.

Shūkan AERA 2009, 'Nikagetsu machi to jibara no kabe: yatto kaikin sareta hib wakuchin' [The two-month wait and cost burden barriers: Ban on the Hib Vaccine finally lifted], 9 March, p. 76.

Simon, J. and Hüntelmann, A.C. 2010, 'Two models for production and regulation: The diphtheria serum in Germany and France', in V. Quirke and J. Slinn (eds.), *Perspectives on 20th Century Pharmaceuticals*, Peter Lang, Frankfurt/Main, pp. 37–61.

Stokes, D. 1997, *Pasteur's Quadrant: Basic Science and Technological Innovation*, The Brookings Institute, Washington, DC.

Sugawara, Y. 2009, 'B-gata Kan'en wakuchin' (Hepatitis B Vaccine), *Scientific Reports of the Chemo-Sero-Therapeutic Research Institute Renmei*, vol. 18, pp. 1–20.

Temin, P. 1980, *Taking Your Medicine: Drug Regulations in the United States*, Harvard, Cambridge, MA.

Tesuka, Y. 2010, *Sengyō Gyōsei no Kozō to Direnma* [The Structure of Postwar Policy and Dilemma], Fujiwara Shobō, Tokyo.

US Congress House of Representatives, Subcommittee on Health and the Environment, Committee on Energy and Commerce 1986, *Childhood Immunizations*, Government Printing Office, Washington, DC.

World Health OrganisationVaccine-Preventable Diseases Monitoring System 2015, Available from: <http://apps.who.int/immunization_monitoring/en/globalsummary/ScheduleResult.cfm> [7 March 2016].

World Health Organisation Fact Sheets, Available from: <www.who.int/mediacentre/factsheets/fs294/en/> [14 May 2015].

Yongue, J. 2008, 'Shin'yaku Kaihatsu wo meguru kigyō to gyōsei' [Corporate Development of New Drugs and Drug Policy], in A. Kudō and M. Ihara (eds.), *Kigyō to Gendai no Shihonshugi* [Enterprises and Modern Capitalism], Minerva Shobō, Kyoto, pp. 166–191.

Part II

Localized Knowledge as a Lasting Competitive Advantage

5 Longevity in Regional Specialization
The Dutch Water Construction Industry

Bram Bouwens

Writing about industrial districts and regional clusters in the *Handbook of Business History*, Jonathan Zeitlin calls for more historical research into the sustainability of industrial districts. After they had been created, how did industrial districts or local productive systems survive for an extended period of time? How did they respond to periodic shifts in markets and technologies and to the usual ups and downs of the economic cycle? (Zeitlin 2008).

This chapter about the Dutch water construction industry, focusing on dredging, draining and reclaiming activities, will explore these questions about long-term continuity. The companies in this industry are nowadays requested worldwide for land reclamation projects, maintenance of canals and rivers and the construction of ports. This industry evolved from simple movers of sand to the prime contractors that use high-tech equipment and are also responsible for embankments and infrastructure on land. Figures on this industry should be conceived with some consideration.[1] In 2015, this industry in the Netherlands contained about 75 companies, employed 6000 people and had a turnover of 1,83 billion euros. Most of these firms incorporated a wide variety of maritime services and integrated many links of the value chain. The largest company, Royal Boskalis Westminster, provided and still provides all kind of services related to maritime infrastructure. In 2015, this company employed about 8300 people and had a turnover of 3,2 billion euros. About half of the revenues were earned by dredging activities and inland infrastructure. The rest was earned by offshore and energy activities and towage and salvage eliminations. The company operated in 90 countries around the world with a versatile fleet of 900 vessels and floating equipment (annual report RBW 2015).

In a historical perspective, the industry was geographically highly concentrated. In the 19th century, Sliedrecht and to a lesser extent also Werkendam were small villages, not that far from Rotterdam, that housed many entrepreneurs engaged in water construction activities. Nowadays, many firms in this industry are still located in this area. First, this chapter will analyze why this region in the Netherlands developed into the most important centre of this industry during the 19th century, and how the people and their firms from this relative backward region succeeded in acquiring international commissions, ranging from Russia, China, the Dutch East and South America. It turns out that the features of the Industrial District, as formulated by the 'father' of this concept, Alfred Marshall, really fitted to this region. Second, this chapter discusses how the relatively small scale dredging firms that constructed and maintained waterways and harbours and protected populated areas against flooding and erosion developed into global leaders in large-scale and complex water construction projects during the 20th century. While the initial advantages seem to have been located in networks and close family relationships, during the second half of the 20th century the sector became more and more concentrated in a few large companies, that diversified their activities into related maritime engineering and worked increasingly outside their home country. Which competitive advantages enabled these companies to create such a dominant position in the international market for dredging, draining and reclaiming, and to what extent did regional characteristics play an important part in their success story? What is the impact of multinational enterprises on the structure and competitiveness of the district and the role of the small and medium-sized companies? This issue is highly discussed in the Industrial District literature (Zeitlin 2008; MacKinnon, Cumbers and Chapman 2002; Malmberg and Maskell 2002). This chapter will show that the concept of Industrial District is not a static one, but a feature that in its conception changes over time towards a more dynamic interpretation. In looking for explanations, this chapter will explore the whole cluster of firms that operated in the field of maritime infrastructure and the position of that cluster within the Dutch industry. This cluster went beyond the boundaries of the rather small geographical concentration of the initial Industrial District. The keys to success of this industry were the huge infrastructural projects launched by the government as well as the link between the Dutch companies and other Dutch multinational companies, in particular, the oil industry, the offshore industry and the shipping industry.

1 Rise of the Dredging Industry in the Netherlands during the 19th Century

The Netherlands is a country that historically is associated with water management. The traditional coexistence of low-lying areas, rivers and sea in combination with an economy largely related to transport, navigation and ports, made the Netherlands into a natural environment for developing dredging and reclamation techniques. These activities took place in many areas in the Netherlands. Yet, Sliedrecht and to a lesser extent Werkendam, relatively small towns on the river Merwede, about 30 kilometers east of Rotterdam, stood out. From the 16th century, men from Sliedrecht had a strong reputation in using spades and wheelbarrows to dig canals, deepen harbours, keep waterways navigable and to protect the fragile banks

Table 5.1 Home Town of Dredging Firms Working on Improvements of the River Waal, 1830–1912

Home town	Number of firms	Percentage of total
Sliedrecht	83	21
Hardinxveld	35	9
Pannerden	34	9
Nijmegen	21	5
Giessendam	14	4
Zaltbommel	11	3
Werkendam	8	2
Elsewhere	186	47
Total number of firms	392	100

Calculations based on: Van Heiningen, Diepers en delvers, annex 3, 384–390.

of drainage canals. In the 19th century, most men in the Sliedrecht area worked in this industry and combined this heavy manual labour with small-scale agricultural activities. They travelled to other parts of the country and even across the border to do their relatively unskilled work. Table 5.1 shows the whereabouts of the contractors involved in the maintenance of the river Waal that served both the flow of ships and the safety of villages situated on the river. The table thus gives an indication of the importance of the small town Sliedrecht during the 19th century.[2]

It is a fascinating question why this region became the core of the Dutch industry of water construction. Several factors can be mentioned. The geographical conditions of the area promoted excavation, reclamation and other maritime construction activities. The location, close to the river and the important harbours of Rotterdam, was a natural breeding ground for these activities. The fact that the occupational substitutes were limited encouraged men to travel to distant parts of the Netherlands to dredge, drain and reclaim. In terms of discipline, every man that was able to handle a spade and could persevere long working hours, was suited for the job. This profession fitted the Calvinistic hard-working sober type of people that dominated this area (Bos 1969, 1974; Vandersmissen 1985; Bouwens and Sluyterman 2010). The techniques of the industry were rather simple and 'on the job training' was common practice. At this time the area thus showed the first features of what Alfred Marshall, who 'discovered' the concept, called Industrial District. The business structure was comprised of small locally owned firms that made investment decisions locally and scale economies rather low. The trade was transmitted from one generation to another, the skills were recognized outside the area and employers did not have any problems attracting sufficient labour on the local market. These features created the Industrial District (Marshall 1920; Belussi and Caldari 2008).

The government played a crucial role in the development of this industry by initiating huge infrastructural projects. During the 19th century many canals were constructed, important rivers deepened and new land created. The organization was very clear. The engineers of the Ministry took the lead and were responsible for design, planning, organization and management of the projects. Initially, the contractors didn't have any say in the projects. The engineers not only defined the technical specifications, but also the working hours, the housing of the personnel and the other labour conditions (Bouwens and Sluyterman 2010). Over the century this unilateral relation gradually changed, because of the governmental decision *not* to invest in equipment that was needed for water construction operations.

During this century the technology of dredging changed fundamentally. Steam powered dredgers replaced human power and horse- and wind-driven engines. Steam power enabled other inventions such as the centrifugal pump and the rotating cutter head. The innovations increased the productivity of the industry enormously (Van Heiningen 1991; Bos 1974). The government pushed the industry to invest in the new technology. Initially, when the state engineers required that steam engines should be used in their projects, foreign dredging companies took the place of the national firms. In reaction, several Dutch companies from the traditional dredging area around Sliedrecht joined forces to be able to compete with the foreigners. From the 1860s the firms organized themselves in—rather unstable—associations that brought together enough capital to enable them to invest in steam technology and related innovations. The associations that were built around existing local and regional networks and family ties greatly contributed to the professionalism of the sector and can be seen as an institutional prerequisite for the transformation of the industry. The coherent spatial scope and the rather narrow specialization profile strengthened this transformation and kept the knowledge regional. The Industrial District, where both market and non-market mechanisms played a role, was consolidated. At the same time the central position of the government was not called into question, but the modernization of the industry had a long term impact on the relations between government and industry.

The relation between the authorities and the contractors also changed because of the entrance of engineers as company directors. Many entrepreneurs now decided to send their sons to the Technical University of Delft (Lintsen 1995). As the new generation of directors entered the industry during the late 19th century, the firms not only had more technological knowledge, but also important connections with the engineers of the government. The dredging companies were able to discuss and negotiate with the government on a more equal footing. The industrialization and professionalization of this sector also resulted in a reinforcement of the cooperation with other industries in the area. The 'men of Sliedrecht' did a growing appeal to the shipbuilding companies in the region that gradually specialized in the design and construction of modern dredging equipment and machines for landfill operations. Because they were now educated at the same academic level as the shipbuilders, communication and cooperation improved from the second half of the 19th century. Being co-located was a major advantage for this industry (Boschma and Ter Wal 2007; Lintsen 1995; Korteweg 2014). These linkages were diagonally organized, typical for a situation where service processes were involved (Goodman and Bamford 1989).

The personal links among the Dutch engineers from both water construction firms, government and shipbuilding industry helped the Dutch companies that focused on maritime infrastructure projects in acquiring international commissions. The Dutch state employed engineers who had a strong international reputation and were often consulted by foreign governments in matters of land reclamation, drainage and hydrology, the construction of canals, harbours and the creation of sluice gates (Van der Ven 2003; Fockema Andrea 1951). In the slipstream of the state engineers, the dredging companies obtained many foreign commissions. During the 19th century and first half of the 20th century, this internationalization did not have a structural impact on the traditional dredging area. In contrast to Industrial Districts with manufacturing industries, the competitive advantages of this service industry were not diluted by internationalization (Pla-Barber and Puig 2009). Knowledge or skills were not transferred on a large scale. The equipment and the people that controlled the machines were only temporarily at the location of the construction project and moved 'home' or to another commission as soon as the project was completed.

The activities in colonial Indonesia offered the contractors a stepping stone to other areas in Asia. Again, networks were crucial. The Dutch contractor J.A. Kalis travelled to Yodo to instruct Japanese labourers, after he was recommended by engineers of the Dutch government (De Neve 2000). Businessmen, politicians and diplomats were active in promoting the abilities of the Dutch industry and their comparative advantage in knowledge and efficiency. In the late 19th century, the banker E.D. van Welree and the director of the Holland-China-Trading Company, F.B. s'Jacob, successfully lobbied with the Chinese authorities. The East Asiatic Dredging Company, in which several Dutch contractors were associated, got the commission to participate in deepening the Huangpu river. Through their networks, the Dutch dredging firms acquired many commissions in all parts of the world, from Asia to Latin-America. Sometimes it was evident that these companies from small nations had advantages in acquiring foreign state commissions, because they were not seen as threatening to the power of those states (Bouwens and Sluyterman 2010).

The First World War interrupted the international expansion of the industry, but new opportunities opened in the Netherlands soon afterward. Again, huge public projects stimulated the expansion and consolidation of the industry. The construction of an enclosing dam in the Zuiderzee, a sea arm that covered about 5000 square kilometres, made the reclamation of large areas possible. Dikes were constructed within the new freshwater lake and water was pumped out (Van der Ham 1999; Van der Ven 2003). The scale of the projects required close cooperation between the leading dredging companies. Most businessmen knew each other and occasionally they were even related. The larger companies—most of them concentrated in the traditional area—established a joint venture to engage in the huge projects related to the Zuiderzee land reclamation. Soon, the smaller companies joint forces to compete with the first association. Obviously, the state was happy to have two competing groups of contractors. Joining forces was the answer of the industry to meet the challenges of the infrastructural projects. More equipment was involved as ever before, but the cooperation did not stimulate innovation and thus created a risk to individual firms and the industry as a whole at the time the major assignments dried up (Bouwens and Sluyterman 2010).

During the 1930s overcapacity and fierce competition caused serious problems for most companies. The government reduced the number of commissions, while the contracts related to the huge Zuiderzee-project came to an end. Most companies had to survive through maintenance-work. Profitability deteriorated. The industry set up a business interest organization and reached a cartel agreement, but all that was not enough in the face of the huge overcapacity in the industry. The alternatives were limited. A few companies from the Sliedrecht region succeeded in setting up foreign subsidiaries. Boskalis, that established the Westminster Dredging Company in the UK, was one of them. A commission from the Anglo-Dutch company Unilever to dredge the Bromborough Docks was the starting point of a successful extension of their activities on the other side of the North Sea (Bouwens and Sluyterman 2010). Again, the impact of the internationalization strategies on the Industrial District were limited and only gradually changed the paradigm. The internationalization of this industry put pressure on the existing framework with its close cooperation of small and medium-sized companies in the area, but equipment and also personnel were exported from the Netherlands to the UK. This strengthened the socio-cultural identity of the dredging area, where women had to live without their husbands for a longer time period.

2 The Creation of a Dominant Position in the International Dredging Industry during the Second Half of the Twentieth Century

After the Second World War Dutch companies that specialized in water construction activities were in high demand because of the need to repair the war damage. Harbours and bridges were destroyed and land inundated. This was in particular true for the island of Walcheren, after the dikes had been bombed in 1944 by the Allied Forces to drive out the German troops. Repairing the dikes in Walcheren was challenging, because it took nearly a year before the work could be started and all that time the sea had moved in and out through the gaps, making them larger and deeper. It was impossible to close the gaps in the traditional way by simply protecting the sea bottom with fascine mattresses and dumping boulder clay in the gap. Desperate measures were needed, and these included the sinking of old ships and the use of caissons left over from the D-Day invasion. The use of caissons had been considered when the Zuiderzee dike was built in the late 1920s, but at that point in time the traditional methods had been preferred, and with success. In 1945, however, the caissons proved their usefulness and from then on became part of the arsenal for building sea protection (Van der Ham 1999; Den Doolaard 2001).

In 1953, a combination of high spring tides and a storm surge broke many dikes in the provinces of Zealand, North Brabant and South Holland. Over 1800 people lost their lives, 800 kilometres of dikes were damaged and 2000 square kilometres of land were flooded, mostly with salt water. The extent of the damage called for drastic measures. After the repair work had been done, the government presented an extensive plan for a new flood protection system called The Delta Plan. The plan involved damming the tidal estuaries to create a stronger barrier at the coast. It included the construction of many dams, several storm surge barriers, locks that separated salt and fresh water and higher sea dikes (Van der Ven 2003). Initially, the dredging companies were hardly involved in the designing process, but gradually the importance of their expertise was acknowledged.

The plan as a whole was huge, but most of the individual projects were large as well, and often moved into new territories that required organizational and technical innovation. For that reason, the government was not prepared to commission individual contractors, not even the larger ones, but insisted on contractors forming alliances. Thus the larger Dutch dredging companies had to share the work between them. As a consequence, they were all involved in the learning process. Other sectors also profited. Dutch shipbuilders responded to the demand for equipment that was needed to carry out the commissions and the government also ordered some special purpose vehicles for the more experimental parts of the Delta Project. The Delta Project started in 1954 with the Storm Surge Barrier on the Hollandse IJssel and formally came to an end with the completion of the Oosterschelde Barrier in 1988, though work on dikes and new dams continued after that date (Van der Ven 2003; Van Heezik and Toussaint 1996; Van der Ham 1999).

The Delta Project meant a huge boost for the Dutch dredging companies. Especially the larger firms benefitted greatly from the large and lucrative projects. They now invested heavily in new technologies, organized special research and development departments and tried through acquisitions to gain a first foothold in related industries like shipbuilding. This allowed them to express an increasingly clear mark on the projects. To illustrate the expansion of the six leading Dutch companies in this field, Figure 5.1

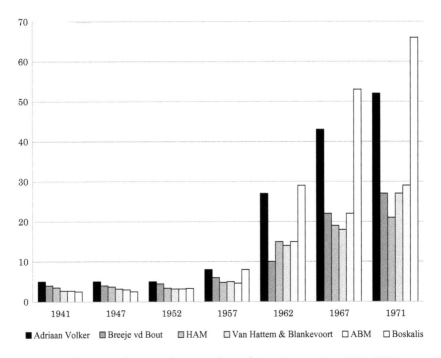

Figure 5.1 Fleet Size of Six Leading Dutch Dredging Companies, 1941–1971

Source: Nationaal Baggermuseum Sliedrecht (NBS), Archive Centrale Baggerbedrijf: Measured is the size of the fleet in age value. The age value is the construction value minus depreciation with 1.5% point per year.

shows the increase in the value of their dredging equipment between 1941 and 1971.[3]

Developments in the home market offered the Dutch dredging companies interesting work with innovative elements that added to their competitive strength, apart from the traditional work in building and extending harbours and creating urban spaces.

3 Linkages with the Off Shore Industry: The Case of Boskalis

The creation of a dominant position in the international dredging industry during the second half of the twentieth century was not only a result of the impressive construction projects on the home market. Another feature that highly contributed to the expansion of the industry was the expansion of the oil industry that was stimulated by the fast post-war economic growth. The exploration and production of oil demanded a lot of work in the field of water construction, and the same was true for the transport of oil that took place in increasingly larger tankers. Most of these activities took place abroad, but that formed no hindrance for the Dutch dredging companies. They benefited from the fact that one of the big international oil companies, Royal Dutch Shell, happened to be located in the Netherlands and Britain (Sluyterman 2007).

To illustrate the links between the dredging and oil companies, this section will also focus on the dredging company Royal Boskalis Westminster that was already mentioned above. This firm was founded in 1910 by three families from the traditional dredging area. These families already cooperated since the late 19th century in different associations, but now decided to bring together their equipment (capital), expertise and networks in order to acquire larger commissions. During the first decades the company focused on projects on the home market, but as we have seen, Boskalis founded a British subsidiary, the Westminster Dredging Company, in the 1930s. Via this subsidiary the first forays in the oil business took place. In 1953, Boskalis became one of the four partners in the Overseas Dredging Company (ODC), existing of two Dutch and two English partners. The ODC worked in Kuwait, Iran and Doha for oil related projects. With the latter two projects, there was also a link with Shell. Because the financial results were disappointing, the ODC was dissolved. The partners went their own way. Boskalis continued in the Middle East, and through Shell subsidiaries in the area found a new niche in operating oil terminals. This work included maintenance of offshore mooring buoys and the provision of tugs for the birthing and un-birthing of vessels. From the Middle East Boskalis moved to Africa where the operation of oil terminals was taken in hand in Nigeria and South Africa. Apart from this specialized activity, Boskalis found plenty of work in Nigeria for the oil operations of Shell. This included the construction of canals to bring the drilling equipment to the drilling site and land reclamation to build up the drilling rigs. The Dutch dredging companies were also contracted by the Nigerian government for extending harbours and preparing building sites (Sluyterman 2009).

Before the Second World War the colony Indonesia had been a focal point for Dutch companies working abroad. This ended when in 1957 the Republic of Indonesia nationalized all Dutch companies. Instead, new clusters of Dutch companies developed in other parts of the world. One such cluster was around the Lake of Maracaibo, where Shell rapidly extended its oil production and set up a refinery in the 1950s. The Dutch bank HBU opened an office in Maracaibo, Van Leer, producer of oil barrels, established a factory and the dredging company HAM constructed a canal. A similar cluster arose in Nigeria. Unilever, through its subsidiary UAC, was already active in this country. Van Leer opened a factory in 1939. In the 1950s, other corporations followed, like the Dutch trading company Hagemeyer and the oil company Shell. The oil production brought the dredging companies HAM and Boskalis, followed by the shipping company Damen, who set up a joint venture for the maintenance of the dredging vessels. Thus the presence of one Dutch company stimulated the arrival of others. In the European communities abroad, they regularly met at receptions and parties, no doubt also discussing future projects and commissions (Sluyterman and Wubs 2009).

During the 1960s, oil production took off in the North Sea, bringing the oil-related activities much closer to home. The larger Dutch dredging companies became involved with the exploration of oil through a joint venture, Netherlands Offshore Company (NOC), in which five companies participated. NOC was involved in the construction of seagoing drilling rigs. They did not intend to take on the actual drilling, but left that to the company Sedneth, a joint venture between NOC and the American company Sedco. The costs for the first rig were for 80 percent covered by the contract from Shell. It was built to the design of Shell engineers. In addition, NOC decided to play a role in the offshore industry by building its own crane barges. Tankers were converted to special vessels for the offshore laying of pipelines and performing heavy duty lifting. Finding sufficient work for these vessels after the building boom of the early 1970s turned out to be the bottleneck. In 1979, NOC sold their ships. Shell was a particularly interesting client for Boskalis, and a source of information for future developments. When Boskalis became a listed company in 1969, it invited a just retired board member of Shell to become its first chairman of the supervisory board. When he stepped down, another retired board member of Shell took over until 1985.

The Dutch organization of dredging companies made a world ranking of dredging companies in 1979, measured in investment in their fleets. Table 5.2 shows that the top-ten companies included four from the Netherlands, and one from Belgium.[4]

Table 5.2 World's Largest Dredging Companies in 1979

Ranking	Company	Country	Value of the dredging fleet, in millions of guilders
1	Boskalis	Netherlands	467
2	State company	China	448
3	Volker Stevin	Netherlands	408
4	State company	Soviet Union	234
5	HAM	Netherlands	218
6	Dredging International	Belgium	193
7	Penta Ocean Construction	Japan	171
8	US Army Corps of Engineers	US	163
9	BAM	Nederland	155
10	State organization of Iraqi Ports	Irak	154

Source: Nationaal Baggermuseum (NBS), Archive Centrale Baggermaatbedrijf, 3.03, figures about the world dredging market.

The recession of the 1970s did not hit the dredging companies immediately because of the oil boom in the Middle East. Dutch dredging companies and building companies signed huge contracts for constructing harbours, roads and industrial sites. The recession did hit the shipbuilding industry, though one of the few companies that survived and later grew into prominence was IHC, specialized in the building of dredging vessels such as the trailing suction hopper dredgers and the cutter suction dredgers. When the oil prices started to go down in the early 1980s, the dredging industry felt the impact heavily. This was particularly true for Boskalis because it had diversified in the 1970s and found many of the new activities that were not directly related to maritime engineering, loss making. The Dutch dredging companies were discussing a new round of consolidation and expected Boskalis to disappear from the market (Bouwens and Sluyterman 2010). However, Boskalis succeeded in convincing the banks that a reconstruction and a return to the core dredging activities would be preferable. The Dutch AMRO bank, later to form part of ABN AMRO, was instrumental in saving the company from bankruptcy, underlining the importance of the Dutch network of international operating companies. The company did not disappoint its bankers. In 1988, a small version of Boskalis was able to regain the trust of the market and then start on a new course of expansion (Bouwens and Sluyterman 2010). After the restart of the company, a further consolidation of the industry took place, but Boskalis was not one of its victims.

4 Global Expansion after 1985

Figure 5.2 illustrates the expansion of Dutch dredging companies in foreign markets between 1985 and 2000 (Annual Reports Centrale Baggermaatschappij, 1985–2000). Not until 1988 did they succeed in increasing their turnover. The increase after 1988 was overwhelmingly achieved in foreign markets. The Dutch market remained sluggish and only picked up modestly after 1995.

The new growth area of the 1990s was Asia. One of the largest projects for the global industry of dredging, draining and reclaiming was the construction of an airport off the coast of Hong Kong. Two islands were merged into one to create Chek Lap Kok airport. 14 trailing suction hopper dredgers, 4 cutter suction dredgers, 3 booster pump stations, 7 grab dredgers and some 20 hopper barges were deployed from all over the world. Dutch and Belgian dredging companies participated in the consortia that were formed to execute the work. Contracts were signed in 1992 and the airport was ready in 1998. During the project, so many Dutch employees were present in Hong Kong that a Dutch primary school was opened.[5] Other large land reclamation projects in Asia followed. But the economic growth in Asia also led to the demand for newer and larger harbour facilities. In the meantime, maintaining harbours and canals remained a core business for the dredging companies.

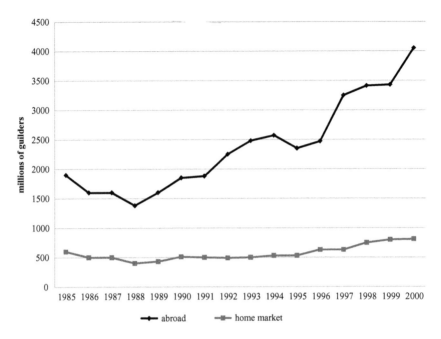

Figure 5.2 National and International Dredging Production of Dutch Companies, 1985–2000

Source: Annual Report Centrale Baggermaatschappij, 1985–2000.

The large land reclamation projects pushed the companies to increase the size of their vessels. To compare, in 1968 Boskalis introduced the then largest trailing suction hopper dredger in the world with a hopper capacity of 9000 cubic metres. In 1997, it launched the jumbo trailer W.D. Fairway with a capacity of 23,000 cubic metres, again the largest trailer in the world at the moment of its launching. But size was not the only relevant aspect of the new trailers, and in fact, smaller trailers were also added to the fleet, for specific purposes. The modern ships contained far more computer aided instruments to make the dredging process more accurate. The innovation of the dredging fleet took place in close collaboration between the dredging and shipbuilding companies, that in most cases still came from the same area. The Dutch shipbuilder IHC was much in demand and established a prominent position in this field (Vandersmissen and Stam 1993; Korteweg 2014).

The modernization of the fleet also brought changes in the traditional conception of the Industrial District. The demand for highly trained personnel to use the technologically advanced equipment increased, but this was not always available in the region. Due to this and to the increasing internationalization large companies like Boskalis developed from a company with local people into—what they called—an international work community. As a consequence, the socio-cultural identity of the industry changed and was no longer synonymous with a specific geographical area. On the other hand, the main enterprises still stayed at the traditional area, making use of the closely located small and medium sized companies to deliver specific products and services. The globalization process challenged the Industrial District. One of the solutions was a closer and more formalized cooperation. Mergers and acquisitions, both horizontal and vertical, were the order of the day. The number of participants in the cluster decreased, while at the same time the sourcing increasingly came from outside the district and the multinationals like Boskalis determined the organization. One could argue that the Industrial District changed in its cohesion where the multinationals now were the binding element.

In the 1990s, new competitors appeared from close by. Two Belgian dredging companies, DEME and De Nul showed rapid growth in the new markets that developed during this decade (Vanderostyne 1994). Sustaining competitive advantage was clearly difficult. How were those Belgian competitors able to become such serious competitors? In this case, one could argue that the Flemish dredging companies were, in fact, part of the same area. One of the two main companies had its roots in the Netherlands. In 1993, inspired by the publications of Michael Porter (Porter 1980, 1985, 1990), the Dutch study centre for technology and policy TNO analyzed the economic strength of the Dutch and Belgian dredging sectors as part of one cluster. How could the strength be explained? First: modern dredging companies required expensive ships and other expensive equipment that made it difficult for newcomers to enter the sector. Moreover, the network of personal links between clients and contractors as well as between contractors, subcontractors and suppliers was dense. As far as dredging activities were concerned, substitution was practically non-existent. The power of the companies towards their suppliers of dredging equipment was not particularly strong, because of the dominant position of IHC. However, dredging companies tried to avoid complete dependence on one source of supply. The power of dredging companies towards the clients was limited, because clients were mostly governments. On the other hand, governments didn't have too much choice if the work was highly specialized. In short, the TNO study concluded that power relations were fairly balanced (Jacobs et al. 1993).

In 2001, Boskalis estimated the annual turnover of the world dredging market at around 7 billion euros, half of which, approximately 3.5 billion euros, was achieved on free markets. These markets that were assessable to firms from foreign countries have been dominated by the large West-European dredging companies. Their share accounted for an estimated 60 percent. With a share of 20 percent of the free market, Boskalis considered itself market leader from the beginning of the new millennium (Annual Report Boskalis 2001). Competing for this prime position were one other Dutch company, Van Oord, and two Belgian companies, DEME and Jan de Nul.

Together these four dredging companies can lay claim to a very competitive position on the world market.

Conclusion

After more than hundred years, Sliedrecht and its neighboring towns are still the prime location for companies that are specialized in water construction projects, containing activities in the field of maritime infrastructure. The largest Dutch company Boskalis, and the dominant shipbuilder of dredging vessels, IHC Merwede, has its headquarters in Sliedrecht. The other large Dutch dredging company has its headquarters in Rotterdam, less than thirty kilometres from Sliedrecht. When the industry transformed from labour-intense to capital-intense during the second half of the 19th century this area remained the centre of this industry. At the same time, it is fair to say that the sustaining cluster of dredging and supporting companies has become wider and includes Dutch companies in other regions as well as part of Belgium. Still, on a world market one could easily define the Netherlands and Belgium as one region.

The Dutch companies have profited from the fact that the natural location of the region and the country required extensive protection against rivers and sea. At the same time, the water was put to good use by constructing and maintaining harbours and canals. For that reason, there was continuous work to do. For the sector, it was of vital importance that the 19th century government decided that the companies had to purchase their own equipment. This strengthened the Industrial District through a process of integration and an increase in the inter-industrial relations. It enabled the more entrepreneurial companies among them to grow in size and capital investment and made the government dependent on their capabilities.

Also on the long run, the competitive strength of the industry was the demanding home market that forced the companies to innovate. Huge infrastructural projects in the 20th century, such as the Zuiderzee project and the Delta project added to the size and capabilities of the Dutch dredging companies. Competition and cooperation between firms from the same area were well balanced and institutionalized. These features also contributed to the success of the industry on the international market. On this market, the Dutch companies undeniably had an advantage due to the fact that one of the largest oil companies, Royal Dutch Shell, was established in the Netherlands (and England). The dredging companies could therefore negotiate their foreign contracts in the Netherlands (and England). Market leader Boskalis encouraged access to the personal network deliberately by inviting retired Shell executives to sit on their supervisory board. It is clear that the Dutch companies that maintained and constructed maritime infrastructure thanked their strong international competitiveness not just to their location by the sea and the technically challenging Zuiderzee and Delta Project. The fact that the Netherlands was home to one of the world's largest oil companies stimulated the dredging companies to explore new paths, both geographically and technologically.

Once established as the leading international companies with an impressive fleet of expensive state of the art ships, it was difficult for newcomers to enter the market. The Belgium dredging companies succeeded in challenging them, but it could be argued that they had formed part of the same cluster and had easy access to the same group of supportive suppliers. A more recent threat comes from the Chinese state-owned companies, who may have enough access to funding to overcome the entrance barrier. So far, Dutch companies have responded to this challenge by extending their services to the early stages of the design process and by investing in the newest technology.

It is interesting to see that that the major Dutch companies still came from the area where the dredge, drain and reclaim activities once started. The headquarters of these companies are still located at the same place. The increasing scale and scope of the firms gave the companies in the district an edge on the international markets. Nevertheless, some changes occurred. No longer do all employees come from the same area, and though transmission from one generation to another still happen and the Marshallian 'atmosphere' is still sensible, many specialized academics from other parts of the country, and even from outside the Netherlands, entered these firms. Vertical integration and the creation of conglomerates also transformed the image of the industry. The features of the Industrial District changed over time, especially after 1945 when multinational enterprises, with strong linkages to firms inside, but also outside the district, took the lead. The success of these large corporations also strengthened the small and medium-sized corporations in the region that specialized in maritime services. While the large corporations tended to integrate more linkages and put pressure on the existence of the local providers, they also developed into a kind of catalyst that brought in new opportunities for small and medium-sized companies. They opened the district for new markets, bringing in innovative challenges and a dissemination of new practices. With the dominance of the multinational corporations, the location-specific institutional setting of the Industrial District altered its nature. The regional embeddedness was not completely lost, but the evolution of these large corporations created new challenges for the small- and medium-sized companies in the region that had to compete with firms outside the area.

Notes

1 The maritime cluster in the Netherlands contains 12 sectors, ranging from shipbuilding and dredging to harbor management and maritime supply industry. These 12 sectors of the maritime cluster realized a total added value of 23,5 billion euros in 2015. This is about 3,5% of Dutch GDP. The cluster accounts for about 265.000 jobs. Figures from the Dutch business association 'Maritiem Nederland.'

2 Calculations based on: Van Heiningen, *Diepers en delvers*, annex 3, 384–390.
3 Source: Nationaal Baggermuseum Sliedrecht (NBS), Archive Centrale Baggerbedrijf: Measured is the size of the fleet in age value. The age value is the construction value minus depreciation with 1.5% point per year.
4 Source: Dredging Museum Sliedrecht, Archive Centrale Baggermaatschappij, 3.03, figures about the world dredging market.
5 *Cohesie (company magazine Boskalis)*, June 1994; *Terra et Aqua*, no. 100, September 2005: Forty years of maritime solutions that changed the world; interview with B. van der Zwaan, 13 Aug. 2009.

References

Annual reports Boskalis, 1965–2015.
Belussi, F. and Caldari, K. 2008, 'Alfred Marshall and industrial districts', *Cambridge Journal of Economics*, vol. 33, no. 2, pp. 335–355.
Bos, W. 1969, *Sliedrecht: dorp van wereldvermaardheid*, Zaltbommel, Europese Bibliotheek.
Bos, W. 1974, *Van baggerbeugel tot sleepzuiger: een overzicht van de ontwikkeling in de Nederlandse baggerindustrie*, Sliedrecht, Van Wijngaarden.
Boschma, R.A. and Ter Wal, A.L.J. 2007, 'Knowledge networks and innovative performance in an industrial district; the case of a footwear district in the South of Italy', *Industry and Innovation*, vol. 14, no. 2, pp. 177–199.
Bouwens, B. and Sluyterman, K. 2010, *Verdiept verleden: een eeuw Koninklijke Boskalis Westminster en de Nederlandse baggerindustrie*, Amsterdam, Boom.
Doolaard, A. 2001, *Het verjaagde water. Geannoteerde uitgave door K. d' Angremond en G.J. Schiereck*, Delft.
Fockema, A.S.J. 1951, 'Waterschapsorganisatie in Nederland en in den vreemde', *Mededelingen der Koninklijke Nederlandse Academie van Wetenschappen: afdeling letterkunde, nieuwe reeks*, vol. 14, no. 9, pp. 309–330.
Goodman, E. and Bamford, J. 1989, *Small Firms and Industrial Districts in Italy*, London/New York, Routledge.
Ham, W. van der 1999, *Heersen en beheersen: Rijkswaterstaat in de twintigste eeuw*, Zaltbommel, Europese Bibliotheek.
Heezik, A. van and Toussaint, B. 1996, *Van spelbepaler tot medespeler: een verkennend onderzoek naar het opdrachtgeverschap van Rijkswaterstaat in de negentiende en twintigste eeuw*, Den Haag, RWS.
Heiningen, H. van 1991, *Diepers en delvers: geschiedenis van de zand- en grindbaggeraars*, Zutphen, Walburg Pers.
Jacobs, D., Limpens, I., Kuijper, and Ven. B. van de, 1993, *De economische kracht van de baggerindustrie: clusterstudie met behulp van de 'methode Porter'*, Apeldoorn, TNO.
Korteweg, J. 2014, *70 Years of IHC Merwede*, Hoog Keppel, IHC.
Lintsen, H.W. (ed.) 1995, *Geschiedenis van de Techniek in Nederland, De Wording van een moderne samenleving 1800–1890. Deel IV*, Zutphen.
MacKinnon, D., Cumbers, A. and Chapman, K. 2002, 'Learning, innovation and regional development; a critical appraisal of recent debates', *Progress in Human Geography*, vol. 26, no. 3, pp. 293–311.
Malmberg, A. and Maskell, P. 2002, 'The elusive concept of localization economies; towards a knowledge-based theory of spatial clustering', *Environmental and Planning*, vol. 34, no. 3, pp. 429–449.

Marshall, A. 1920, *Principles of Economics* (8th ed.), London, MacMillan.

Neve, R. de 2000, 'De Hollandse methode in Japan', in L.A. van Gasteren and H. Beukers (eds.), *In een Japanse stroomversnelling: berichten van Nederlandse watermannen—rijswerkers, ingenieurs, werkbazen—1872–1903*, Amsterdam, Euro Book Productions.

Pla-Barber, J. and Puig, F. 2009, 'Ís the influence of the industrial district in international activities being eroded by globalization? Evidence from a traditional manufacturing industry', *International Business Review*, vol. 18, no. 5, pp. 435–445.

Porter, M.E. 1980, *Competitive Strategy: Techniques for Analyzing Industries and Competitors*, New York, Free Press.

Porter, M.E. 1985, *Competitive Advantage: Creating and Sustaining Superior Performance*, New York, Free Press.

Porter, M.E. 1990, *The Competitive Advantage of Nations*, New York, Free Press.

Sluyterman, K. 2007, *Concurreren in turbulente markten, 1973–2007. Geschiedenis van Koninklijke Shell*, Amsterdam, Boom.

Sluyterman, K. 2009, 'Boskalis in het kielzog van de olieindustrie, 1950–1980', in H. Greefs and I. Van Damme (eds.), *In behouden haven: Liber Amicorum Greta Devos. Reflecties over maritieme regio's*, Tielt, Lannoo, pp. 165–184.

Sluyterman, K. and Wubs, B. 2009, *Over grenzen: multinationals en de Nederlandse markteconomie. Bedrijfsleven in Nederland in de twintigste eeuw*, Amsterdam, Boom.

Vanderostyne, M. 1994, *Waterbouwers: de wereldwijde expansie van de Vlaamse waterbouw na 1945*, Tielt, Lannoo.

Vandersmissen, H. 1985, *Ophogen en uitdiepen; uitgegeven ter gelegenheid van het 50-jarig jubileum van de Vereniging "Centrale Baggerbedrijf,"* Den Haag, Centrale Baggerbedrijf.

Vandersmissen, H. and Stam, J. 1993, '50 jaar IHC', *Ports and Dredging*, Speciale editie—50 jaar IHC.

Ven, G.P. van de (ed.) 2003, *Leefbaar laagland: geschiedenis van de waterbeheersing en landaanwinning in Nederland*, Utrecht, Matrijs.

Zeitlin, J. 2008, 'Industrial districts and regional clusters', in G. Jones and J. Zeitlin (eds.), *The Oxford Handbook of Business History*, Oxford, Oxford University Press, pp. 219–243.

6   Going Global in Fragmented Markets

The European Publishing Industry Since the Second Postwar Period

Nuria Puig and María Fernández-Moya

Introduction

Publishing is one of the few industries in which old Europe retains much of its historical leadership and allure. Since the 19th century, European companies have figured among the elite of the international publishing sector, a position they have maintained despite the dominance of US publishers and expansion of the Chinese market. Moreover, publishing constitutes the primary cultural industry in Europe. In 2013, European publishers reported annual sales of 22.3 billion euros, 560,000 new titles, and around 130,000 full-time employees (Federation of European Publishers 2013). A global map of publishing markets created by the International Publishers Association (IPA) in 2013 shows Europe's hegemony in both aggregate and relative terms. Interestingly, the book industry is the only knowledge and entertainment sector in which Europe remains a world leader. Indeed, most of the world's largest publishing conglomerates are European, and the three major international book fairs—Frankfurt, London, and Bologna—all take place in Europe. Finally, 'The Global 56 Largest Book Publishers' (*Publishers Weekly* 27 June 2014) reveals that, in 2013, seven of the top ten, 11 of the top 20, and 31 of the top 56 publishing groups were based in Europe.[1] Outside the European Union, the largest publishers were in the United States (9), Japan (7), China (2), Korea (2), Brazil (2), and Russia (1).

How has Europe managed to hold on to its competitive edge in this industry? To answer this question, in this chapter, we will reconstruct the evolution of the publishing sector since the end of World War II, with a special focus on the period of 1950–1980. The pertinence of the period selected is clearly justified, as these middle decades of the 20th century are crucial to understanding the sector's current configuration. During these years, the book industry underwent a profound transformation, one upon which the leadership of North American and European publishers would be built and the internationalization of European publishing groups initiated.

The basic hypothesis behind the title is a 'paradox.' American firms enjoy the world's largest homogenous market and economies of scale; however, European firms, from the fragmented national markets, successfully became dominant in the worldwide industry. Why? The main argument of this chapter is that the success of European publishers has stemmed from the flexibility in their approach to the internationalization process. This strategy has enabled them to grow and globalize while also maintaining and developing their competitive strengths, overcoming the great cultural barriers that characterize the activity of publishing, and continuing to operate from their European headquarters. In this chapter, we will also highlight the abilities of these European publishers to innovate. Many of the commercial innovations that revolutionized the sector in the middle decades of the 20th century originated in Europe (even if they reached their maximum expression in the American market). What is more, European publishers have shown a remarkable capability to innovate and cooperate within the institutional sphere, both inside and outside their borders.

Our focus, then, will be on the growth and internationalization strategies, ever more inseparable, which have been employed by the publishing sector. The formation of multinational companies has been one of most fertile areas of research in recent years (see *Business History Review* 2015). Although some influential hypotheses are trying to explain these internationalization strategies, it is important to note that the strategies are clearly influenced by the industry in which a firm operates. Much less research has been done in this area, which is central to understanding the reasons behind the decisions that companies make regarding the location of their activities. In this sense, the special nature of the publishing industry—and its strong presence in Europe—provides a perfect example for exploring how and whether the specificities of certain industries affect (or even determine) their location and competitiveness in the global economy.

The chapter is organized as follows. Section 1 provides a brief overview of the specifics of the book publishing industry. Section 2 examines the *revolution in books* that took place between the 1950s and 1980s, looking closely at the role of European publishers through the mirror of the fast-growing American industry. Section 3 presents a description and analysis of the decisive elements that have enabled the competitiveness of European firms and their transformation over time. We address the strategic responses of European publishers at the sectoral level in comparison with North American publishers. Section 4 offers detailed descriptions of the German publisher Bertelsmann, Spanish publisher Salvat, and British company Pearson. We conclude with some broad observations and directions for future research.

1 Publishing: The Basic Nature of a Unique Industry

No industry illustrates the transition from the industrial to the digital age as powerfully as the manufacturing of books. Publishing has been defined as the coordination of the various processes needed to bring a book from an idea in the mind of the author to a printed (or digital) product available for distribution to a relevant audience (Federation of European Publishers

2014). As publishers manage and disseminate content, publishing is also a marketing activity in which finance is the critical tool. The publisher provides the finance necessary to transform a writer's work into a manufactured book (or digital product).

Book publishing is an extraordinarily diverse industry, with a huge variety in type, size, scope, focus, and orientation. According to the North American Industry Classification System (NAICS), the publishing industry (code 511) includes establishments engaged in the publishing of newspapers, magazines, other periodicals, and books, as well as directories, mailing lists, and software. In economic terms, although book publishing is not more important than these other segments, its cultural and educational relevance is immense. The book industry forms the core of the publishing industry, and it is its most representative division. This industry is also a key player in the knowledge society and economy that is emerging in the post-industrial world.

The structural feature, core, and stable characteristic of the publishing industry is the duality of the business. Publishing is a both cultural and creative industry. What constitutes the singular truth of industrial culture? According to the Australian economist David Throsby (2001), one of the most important scholars in the field of cultural economy, cultural goods and services share several parameters: Their productive process is marked by creativity; they represent a form of intellectual property; and they communicate a value or symbolic meaning that gives an emotional element to their consumption.

Nevertheless, the sector is dynamic, and publishers have to adapt to its continuous evolution. Indeed, the impact of technological change on publishing has been unrivaled ever since the first industrial revolution transformed the composition and printing of books and permitted a mass market for books to emerge. Simultaneously, as literacy rates in Europe and North America rose and incomes increased, an unprecedented market for books was created. This combination of factors resulted in the strengthening of copyrights and the expansion of bookstores and public libraries. Since the end of the 20th century, publishing has been undergoing a similarly profound transformation. Technology (photo reproduction and computer-based composition) is now changing the industry even more radically. Economic changes, including the multi-nationalization of major publishing companies and linking of publishing to other knowledge and entertainment industries, are also altering the landscape of books and publishing. This traditional industry—a 'profession of gentlemen'—is becoming a highly competitive, commercial, and technology-based activity. There is a clear trend toward consolidation in the industry (as large publishing firms acquire smaller ones and media corporations move into publishing) and toward the emergence of large multinational firms (whose financial management determines their nature and direction).

What are the key explanatory variables in the internationalization process of the publishing industry? Despite the crucial role played by the publishing industry in the modern knowledge economy as well as its two-century-long contribution to both the rise of an increasingly educated and informed society and the overall process of globalization, publishing has received little attention by historians and international business scholars (a few exceptions are Berghoff 2010, pp. 8–83, 2013, pp. 169–190; Hall 2014; Fernández-Moya 2009, 2012; Van Lente and De Goey 2008).

In general terms, do publishers develop a process analogous to other economic sectors, or is this internationalization process conditioned by the duality of the publishing business? Jose Manuel Lara Bosch, former president of Planeta, the eighth largest international publishing company, explained the difficulties of this industry:

> The book and everything surrounding it corresponds to an area which is very intimate and personal for the residents of a particular country, whose habits are heavily marked by their customs and traditions. These create an area of interest, a type of literature or non-fiction with characteristic local themes, and this is very difficult to design or create from within some other country. The cultural industry is one which is very national, even regional.
>
> (Lara 2002, p. 221)

In this sense, the internationalization of publishing companies has been different from that of other strictly economic sectors. Most of its peculiarities stem from the role of cultural distance in the process. This is the central variable, the main obstacle in the process of crossing borders, and one that carries much more weight in the design of internationalization strategies in publishing than in any other sector. In sum, the internationalization process of the publishing industry does not seek to overcome national borders (a conventional element for 'internationalization' in general), but the cultural and linguistic borders.

This fact has led respected authors such as Philip Altbach to describe the global publishing industry in terms of center and periphery (Altbach 1997, p. 320). Population, literacy rates, the use of a 'world language,' income levels, the existence of publishing infrastructures, and a history of active publishing all help to determine the strength of the publishing industry. Patterns of worldwide ownership of publishing companies and other knowledge-based firms, government policy, and flows of international trade may also contribute to the success of a publishing enterprise in a given country. 'Centers and peripheries exist in publishing, and these relationships help to determine the place of a nation in the world of knowledge creation, distribution and use' (Altbach 1997, p. 321). In the end, this particular structure leads to geographical concentration. Most of the books that are sold and read around the world are actually produced in a small number of countries, and some of these are European. In order to understand this, in the next section, we shall focus on the remarkable concentration process that took place after the second postwar period.

2 Transformations of the World Publishing Industry Since World War II

The Golden Age, namely the post-World War II economic boom years, marked a turning point in the worldwide publishing industry. This was a period of change in the world patterns of book production and consumption. A number of advances in printing, publishing, and distribution techniques would make it possible to produce low-priced, good-quality books on a vast scale. To unravel the various factors that explain the new publishing paradigm, we will examine the quantitative and qualitative changes the industry underwent during this period.

2.1 The European Preeminence: Quantitative Data

The evolution of the number of titles published between 1950 and 1975 reveals a spectacular growth in publishing output, as shown in Table 6.1.[2] While this was true of almost all countries, the growth was particularly intense in the United States and Europe.

Table 6.1 Leading Publishing Countries, by Number of Book Titles (1950–1973)

	1950	1955	1960	1965	1970	1973	Growth ratio 1973/1950
Five European nations	51,329	60,580	70,736	96,981	132,621	145,645	283
1 United States	11,022	12,589	15,012	54,378	85,287	83,724	759
2 Soviet Union	43,100	54,732	76,064	76,101	78,899	80,196	186
3 Germany, Federal Republic	14,094	16,66	21,103	25,994	45,369	48,034	340
4 Japan	13,009	21,653	23,682	24,203	31,249	35,857	275
5 United Kingdom	17,072	19,962	23,783	26,314	33,441	35,177	206
6 France	9,993	11,793	11,872	17,138	22,935	27,186	272
7 Spain	3,633	4,812	6,085	17,342	19,717	23,608	649
8 India	18,769	18,559	10,741	13,094	14,145	14,064	74
9 Netherlands	6,537	7,353	7,893	10,193	11,159	11,640	178
10 Poland	5,218	7,199	7,305	8,509	10,038	10,744	205
11 Yugoslavia	4,371	5,105	5,355	7,980	8,119	10,110	231
12 Romania	2,700	5,182	6,335	6,090	7,681	10,100	374
13 Brazil	3,718	3,385	5,377	4,975	8,579	9,948	267
14 Belgium	4,573	4,212	3,645	3,748	4,414	8,953	195
15 Czechoslovakia	4,990	4,399	7,93	9,043	9,041	8,567	171
16 Sweden	3,719	4,756	5,825	6,666	7,709	8,242	221
17 Italy	8,904	6,494	8,111	10,385	8,615	8,122	91
18 Switzerland	3,527	3,829	4,899	6,367	8,321	7,942	225
19 Hungary	3,071	5,206	5,205	4,528	5,238	7,581	246
20 Turkey	2,100	3,250	3,447	5,442	5,854	7,479	356

Source: Division of Statistics on Culture and Communication, Office of Statistics, UNESCO.

The size of print runs, a figure not included in the preceding table, also varied from country to country. Nations with large populations, high literacy rates, strong domestic and foreign demand, and high production capabilities, such as the Federal Republic of Germany and the United Kingdom, were printing an average of 10,000 copies of fiction books and 5,000 copies of non-fiction work in each run. The average run in Australia and Italy was between 5,000 and 7,000 copies. Other countries, such as Canada and Switzerland, were printing runs of 4,000–5,000 copies. Average runs in Spain, Norway, Denmark, and Sweden were around 3,000 copies (Barker 1956, p. 23). In terms of publishing output—that is, the number of titles plus the number of copies per run—the country position did not vary greatly from what is reflected in Table 6.1. By the mid-1960s, the total annual world production of titles had reached 400,000 (*Courier* September 1965, p. 15). English, French, German, and Spanish titles continued to lead, while the combined production of socialist countries totaled 36% of the world output of book titles. Twelve countries alone were producing two-thirds of the world's books: the Soviet Union, the United States, the United Kingdom, France, Germany, Japan, China, France, India, Spain, Italy, the Netherlands and Czechoslovakia; however, figures are probably overstated in the cases of the Soviet Union, China, and India where pamphlets counted as books. The chief exporters of books were the United Kingdom, the Netherlands, the United States, France, Switzerland, and West Germany.

The book industry indeed developed at a fast pace over the next two decades, and European publishers were able to maintain their preeminence at a time of relative industrial decline. Although the figures in the preceding section show that the United States and the Soviet Union independently led the rankings of publishing powers, the great center of world publishing was Europe. This is particularly true if we consider the proportion of titles published to number of inhabitants. Table 6.2 sheds additional light on this phenomenon.

Table 6.2 Book Production by Number of Titles per Million Inhabitants (1955–1977)

	1955	1960	1965	1970	1975	1977
World	131	144	168	187	185	187
Africa	13	19	23	23	27	26
Asia	64	53	57	62	65	68
North America	66	82	219	280	288	281
South America	72	90	79	79	101	107
Europe	320	383	450	535	558	588
Oceania	68	121	286	361	235	245
Soviet Union	279	355	329	329	310	328

Source: Division of Statistics on Culture and Communication, Office of Statistics, UNESCO.

In 1955, of the 270,000 titles published worldwide, Europe contributed 48.7%. This percentage is relatively high if we consider that the inhabitants of continental Europe comprised barely 15.2% of the total world population. In 1977, 46.3% of the 607,000 books produced worldwide would come from the Old Continent.

Europe not only stood out by the standard measure of number of book titles per million inhabitants, but it also consolidated its advantage over time, with figures considerably higher than its strongest competitors, the Soviet Union and North America. By country, the United States, the Soviet Union, West Germany, Japan, and the United Kingdom led the world market in the early 1970s, but the fastest growth was registered by the United States, Spain, and West Germany, where the number of book titles multiplied by 7.5, 6.5, and 3.4 times, respectively. These figures and those shown in Table 1 reflect the productive capacity of the European publishing sector, an industry designed not only to cover its own domestic markets but also to satisfy demands from abroad. Both tables suggest, therefore, that European publishers were able to meet the challenges of technological change and mass production/consumption by developing innovative or adaptive strategies that helped many of them to succeed. In the next section, we will examine these strategies more closely.

The quantitative data we have just mentioned illustrate two parallel phenomena recorded in the period of 1950–1970: an increase in international publishing output and its progressive geographical concentration. Which variables explain these phenomena? First, the increase in publishing output clearly had as an incentive a spectacular increase in demand. Angus Maddison estimated per capita income in 1950 at $2,024. In 1960, this figure had risen to $2,665, and in 1973, to $3,941, which is practically double that of 1950.[3] In addition, the growth of public spending and an improvement in educational level would help to create a middle class with both purchasing ability and an interest in culture. From a business perspective, these figures stimulated the creation of a market with dimensions never before imagined. We are thus witnessing here a process of the democratization of culture. The diffusion of books came to be quantified on a new scale (see Barker and Escarpit 1973; Escarpit 1965; Miller 2006; Rak 2013).

2.2 Changes in the Publishing Industry (1950–1980): A Qualitative Approach

We must look beyond the abovementioned figures, however, to understand the changes experienced by the publishing sector in this period. The entire dynamic of the sector was profoundly altered. The appearance of the mass-circulation book has probably been one of the most important cultural developments in the second half of the 20th century (Escarpit 1965, p. 4). Viewed as manufactured items, books caught up with other products of the modern industry, simultaneously adapting to the demands of mass production and modern design. To achieve its objective, the mass book had to meet an important requirement, which was to widen its distribution channels and thereby multiply its diffusion. During the middle decades of the 20th century, a new reading public with its own tastes, habits of consumption, and specific needs was emerging. This was a broad public, not particularly erudite, which did not frequent bookshops, and so it was the book that had to seek out its reader and not vice-versa. In this context, the range of sales outlets for books expanded beyond the exclusivity of the bookshop.

One new format that would revolutionize the sector was that of the pocket book.[4] Why did the pocket book trigger a revolution? This was because it built a bridge between the cultural and the lighter, more ephemeral books. The origin of the pocket book is most associated with the British publishing house Penguin (Stevenson 2010). In reality, cheap reprints had appeared on the market on earlier occasions from Oxford, Collins, and MacMillan. What made this initiative different was the creation of a brand that combined quality and affordability: in effect, reprints of good modern books, attractively designed and shockingly cheap (for six pence, the price of a packet of cigarettes). Allen Lane, Penguin's owner, envisioned a market outside that of the traditional book market and knew how to approach it with new forms of distribution. Books would be sold in drugstores and supermarket chains such as Boots, Woolworth's, and Timothy White's. Pocket books were an instant success both within and outside the United Kingdom. In the United Kingdom, the publication of pocket books went from 20 million copies in 1961 to 87.5 million in 1971, comprising 15.5% of the annual production in titles and 28.3% in copies. In 1939, Lane's idea crossed the Atlantic with the creation of Pocket Book, the first American company to publish pocket books. In Germany, the advancement of the pocket book was swift in the 1960s. While in 1961, 1,070 titles were published in this format, by 1971, that figure had risen to 3,550 (*El Libro Español* April 1974, p. 175–182). In Italy, the pocket book was launched in the market by the publisher Mondadori in 1963, but without much success.

Another publishing product that rose strongly in this period was the fascicle format, a series of thematically related books published in installments. The sale of books in fascicles, distributed through newspaper kiosks, was introduced in Italy in 1959 by the publisher De Agostini. After its success there, the innovation spread quickly through the publishing markets of Germany, England, Spain, and finally France. In the Soviet bloc, however, the lack of a free market economy conditioned the evolution of distribution systems. Books were sold, for example, in offices or factories. As a result, of all of these factors, distribution itself acquired a central position within the publishing business. This led many publishing companies to merge both its lines of business within a single company, giving rise to vertical integration.

3 Strategic Responses of European Publishers

What were the decisive elements that enabled the competitiveness of European firms? On the eve of the industrial crisis of the 1970s, the European book industry was still highly fragmented and diverse, not only because of its linguistic and cultural diversity, but also because inherited institutions and regulation played important roles. This deserves some attention.

3.1 A Fragmented Market

In most of continental Europe, public administration influenced the book market through the educational market and fixed prices. The educational system is clearly different in each European country, and publishers can only adapt to these systems if they hope to participate in foreign markets. However, the debate over fixed prices, a system under which the publisher establishes retail prices that booksellers are obliged to respect, has been a constant point of contention in the European publishing sector since the 1970s. Switzerland, Finland, Ireland, and the United Kingdom all had fixed price laws, but these were abolished in the 1960s in the first two cases and in the 1990s in the last two. Spain has always had a law of fixed prices. France temporarily lifted its fixed price law at the end of the 1970s, but re-introduced it in 1982 with a law promoted by socialist minister Jack Lang. Currently, among the great publishing powers, Germany, France, and Spain maintain the fixed price regulation, while the United States and the United Kingdom have no regulation of this kind. To justify such a law, its defenders cite reasons of written culture diffusion, protection of literary activity and production, and of course, position of small retailers in relation to department stores and chains. In an attempt to consolidate these practices and defend the rights and interests of publishers at a transnational level, European publishers and booksellers (usually under a common umbrella) became highly organized and mobilized at the national and transnational levels. National associations to this effect were created in most countries. The Federation of European Publishers, now a Brussels-based lobby, was founded in 1967 (Federation of European Publishers 2014), even though the first meetings of French, German, Italian, Belgian, and Dutch publishers to 'monitor European matters' had taken place as early as 1958.

The linguistic, cultural, and institutional diversity of European markets contrasted with the homogeneity of the American market, which was in full expansion and extremely attractive to publishers. In 1967, the senior vice-president of the McGraw-Hill Book Company, Dan Lacy, described the dramatic changes experienced by the American book publishing industry since the end of World War II. He argued that the baby boom, combined with the democratization, intensification, and sophistication of public education, had created a vast educational market that determined existing as well as forthcoming changes (Lacy 1967, pp. 1–6).

Another major influence on US publishing was the growing importance of the school and library markets. The institutional market came to absorb some 80% of the output of children's books and as well as a large share of adult non-fiction books (Tebbel 1987).

Before World War II, no book had sold more than 100,000 copies, while around 1950, that figure regularly rose to one million (*Courier* September 1965, p. 11). In 1963, the number of publishing houses with headquarters in the United States was 993; by 1977, this number had risen to 1,745. The output value for the sector as a whole increased even faster, from $1.53 billion to $4.79 billion (Lipscomb 2001). These data reflect the position of the United States as a great producer of books. The enormous size of its market would also enable it to become one of the principal importers of foreign books, mostly from Europe, as we will see later.

3.2 Foreign Markets and Competitiveness

How were the fragmented European markets able to challenge the publishing power of the United States? In the United States, publishing growth depended not only on internal growth but also on the country's international cultural influence, which was then at its zenith. In response, European publishers would use their own respective language areas and former empires to build an intense exporting business. This was the general trend, at least. For their export operations, European publishers focused their activities on three fronts: their former colonies, strong intra-European trade, and exports to the United States, whose enormous demand made it a prime customer.

The United Kingdom provides the best example of this export activity. Indeed, it was one of the world's leading exporters of published material. In the 1970s, of the total European publishing exports, 38% came from the United Kingdom. Meanwhile, seen from inside the country, approximately 40% of the combined business of British publishers was in foreign markets (*El Libro Español* April 1974, pp. 175–182): A high percentage of this was in educational and scholastic books. Only about 15% of these exports, however, were to other European countries. The United Kingdom's principal customers were the United States (around 25% of exports), Australia, Canada, the Republic of South Africa, and Nigeria. In 1971, the combined exports to these five countries would constitute 61% of British publishing exports. The most important companies—Oxford University, Longman, and Penguin—were responsible for more than half of the country's production. The British market also became the port of entry into Europe for American publishers, with companies such as Saunders, Harper, McGraw-Hill, and Wiley establishing headquarters in London.

The exportation models of the other great European publishing powers, France and Germany, would follow a similar pattern. In France, exports to European countries comprised 30.5% of the total. The principal customers were Belgium, Luxembourg, Canada, and Switzerland (together, they represented some 50% of French exports in the 1970s) as well as the French-speaking African countries. Germany exported principally to Switzerland and Austria (50% of the total in the 1970s, followed by the United States at 10%). The case of Italy is somewhat unusual: It exported 51% of its output to European countries and, to a lesser degree (around 20%), to the United States (*El Libro Español* April 1974, pp. 175–182). However, the figure for its exports to Europe would include a significant amount of business in French works printed in Italy. The Spanish case is also striking: Over 80% of Spanish exports went to Latin American countries.

As may be deduced from these data, European publishing exports were (and still are) strongly conditioned by the existence of former colonies and the extension of linguistic areas. The only model of publishing exportation to fall outside this pattern was that of the Netherlands. The country's geographical location and its commercial and intellectual tradition had built a dynamic publishing sector that sought a position in the international book market that was independent of linguistic conditioning. It found its niche in the publication of translations and foreign language works, especially scientific and technical books. At the beginning of the 1970s, Elsevier, the undisputed leader in the country's domestic market, was also the leading European publisher of books and journals in the fields of medicine, chemistry, and physics, producing 25% of all scientific and technical works published in the English-speaking world. At this time, most of the publishing output of the Netherlands (58.7% of exports) was being sold in Europe, as opposed to 26% from the United States (*El Libro Español* April 1974, pp. 175–182).

3.3 Roles of New Actors and Platforms in Managing a Cultural Multinational

Both European and American publishers were able, by different means, to meet the enormous international demand for books. How did the new growth strategies and business practices of the publishing industry affect publishers? One result of this process was an increase in the size of companies, bringing with it specialized management staff members, computerized accounting and management controls, systematically organized marketing services, research facilities, human resource departments, and, in general, a more professional and impersonal management. In 1970, an article entitled 'The Big Story in Books is Financial' observed that 'financially oriented executives are taking over where traditionalist genteel editors used to hold sway' (*Business Week* 16 May 1970). The changes affected both the role and education of publishers. Most professionals working in the publishing sector saw themselves primarily as publishers. They had usually learned by doing, eventually working for publishing houses that were regarded almost as universities, such as Macmillan, Faber, or McGraw-Hill. However, after the 1970s, a growing number of universities (such as Columbia and New York) began offering specific programs in publishing. As firms became larger and more complex, professional managers were hired to deal with the financial and commercial aspects of the publishing business. Their hands became at least as visible as those of genteel and formally educated publishers. Finally, professionalization also took hold of the European publishing business, and the practical education provided by companies such as Herder in Germany or the professional school of the Cercle de la Librairie in France began to be either replaced or complemented by the more formal education provided by the Oxford Polytechnic or the expanding number of business schools and public universities.

Thanks to the increase in both publishing output and the appearance of new formats and distribution channels, many publishers were transformed from small companies into large, diversified, and widely internationalized business groups. How can the regional character of a cultural industry be made compatible with the gradual globalization of the publishing industry? It was in this context, that of large international companies needing global strategies adapted to national cultural markets, that three key elements in the dynamic of today's literary publishers were consolidated: literary agents, international book fairs, and the use of mergers or acquisitions in their strategies of internationalization.

What was the role of literary agents within the publishing sector? The function of such agencies was, and is, to mediate between the author and publisher with the aim of achieving the highest revenue for the former while taking into account other parameters as well, such as the ability of the publisher to promote the author's work or to distribute it as widely as possible. After signing a contract, the agent was also charged with managing information regarding sales and royalties. In payment for their services, literary agents received a percentage of the income earned from sales. Such agencies had first appeared in the late 19th century in already developed publishing markets such as the United Kingdom and Germany. The first of which we have notice is A. P. Watt, created in the United Kingdom in 1875. This agency would handle the affairs of, among others, Rudyard Kipling and William Butler Yeats. From a business point of view, the figure of the literary agent was in effect that of a subcontractor. Before the 1950s, few literary publishers were subcontracting the reception and selection of authors' works through agents. Their small size and orientation toward a market that was more or less known to them made such an activity unnecessary. However, the new realities of the sector in the mid-20th century encouraged increasingly large and diversified publishers to use agents to build their catalogs. Thus, in the period following World War II, the number of literary agents operating around the world increased substantially.

Together with the literary agent, another striking phenomenon emerged in the 1960s: the international book fair. The most influential of these by far was that of Frankfurt. Its first edition (in 1949) would bring together 205 German exhibitors (Weidhaas 2007). In 1957, the number of participants had grown to 1,385 publishers from 22 countries (*El Libro Español* April 1958, 197). Publishers came (and still come) to Frankfurt to buy and sell publishing rights, making it a center of direct economic transactions as well as a space in which to exchange relevant information about the sector, both formally and informally.

At the fair, publishers would exhibit their 'dummies'—sample volumes with 32 or 64 pages of text and the rest blank—and attempt to negotiate joint publishing projects. These co-publications began as isolated connections between publishers in the segments of art and other illustrated books, which were very costly to produce and only profitable through the formula of simultaneous publication in several countries with the same illustrations. Little by little, this system was extended to include other types of books as well (Lacy 1967, p. 13). Indeed, printing a book in various languages, at a centralized plant for which each partner paid a fixed price for the plant and printing costs, became a standard practice beginning in the 1960s. Although other fairs would be created later in Bologna (established in 1963 and focused mainly on children's books), Cairo (1969), and London (1971), the Frankfurt fair remains to this day the great international meeting place of the publishing industry. In the context of growing internationalization that characterized the 1960s and 1970s, such fairs provided a nucleus of networks that facilitated international transactions and simplified the operations of multinational publishing houses.

3.4 Mergers and Acquisitions: A Way to Achieve International Competitiveness

The last significant change in the publishing sector in the 1960s was the beginning of business concentration. The publishing sector had reached its maturity, and profits per product unit had become lower and lower, obliging companies to increase their sales volumes. Therefore, mergers and acquisitions seemed to be not only another method but also the only system capable of enabling survival and expansion in the post-World War II business fabric.

In the United States, the statistics illustrate well the transformation of the American publishing market. In the period of 1958–1970, the structure of most of the leading publishing houses would shift from private ownership to public participation and/or form a part of a publishing or industrial group. In the United States, 18% of all mergers and acquisitions in this period were now being carried out by companies whose principal activity was media related, whether written, radio based, or electronic. In the period of 1960–1969, there were 183 mergers or acquisitions in the US publishing industry, 40% of which took place in the final two years (Greco 1995, pp. 230–231). These figures include some of the most important American publishing companies, such as Bantam Doubleday, Dell, Farrar Strauss & Giroux, McGraw-Hill, Random House, and Thomson.

Despite greater market atomization, in the Europe of the 1960s, the phenomenon of concentration would occur at the national level. In 1968, the signs were already being observed in Germany: 19 publishers were doing business of DM 5 to 50 million (among them Bertelsmann, Springer, and Fischer), while 56 others had turnovers of DM 50,000 to 500,000. In the mid-1960s, the turnover of 19 French companies represented 54.2% of the sector total in that country, while that of 192 small publishing houses was barely 7.3% (*El Libro Español* April 1974, pp. 175–182). In the United Kingdom, a dozen publishers were doing business of £2–10 million, while for a hundred other companies, this ranged from £50,000 to £2 million. In the Spanish-speaking area, the concentration process began somewhat later and would be greatly influenced by the crises in Latin America from 1982 onwards. In 1982, 23% of the sector exported 50% of Spain's total publishing output; in 1985, 4% of the sector exported 60% (Fernández-Moya 2012).

Along with these tools, agents, and fairs, publishers would come to use mergers and acquisitions as strategies of internationalization as they expanded. The most important European publishers, already well capitalized thanks to their presence in their own national markets and their volume of exports, chose to take the step toward foreign direct investment. Mergers and acquisitions in the 1970s, therefore, present a character unlike those of the previous decade. They were fewer in number but were qualitatively different, being much larger in size and involving the participation of international companies, principally European. The experience of an international expansion in close (cultural and geographical) European countries worked as a learning process to overcome a much higher barrier when they entered the American market.

The age of information was transforming the business of communication into a global business. This increasingly integrated market was chiefly English speaking, which made US publishers an attractive prey for the conglomerates of other countries seeking to establish an international presence. This was an attraction accentuated by the political and financial stability (i.e., low political and economic risk) of the United States and its vast internal market. The recession of the American economy in that decade, marked by the end of the Vietnam War and the oil crises, particularly that of 1973, would facilitate purchases at good prices and favorable exchange rates. In addition, the legal protection derived from the freedom of the press guaranteed by the US Constitution allowed foreign companies to own publishing companies, even if the ownership of radio and television companies was restricted to American citizens (Greco 1995, p. 233). In the 1980s, this pattern would continue. In the opinion of Albert Greco, an expert on the American publishing sector, the most significant transactions of the decade were the acquisition of Dell and Doubleday by Bertelsmann, that of Harper & Row by Australian media magnate Rupert Murdoch, and that of New American Library by the UK company Pearson. This period would also witness the entry of the Netherland's Elsevier and Canada's Thomson Corporation into the American market. These operations laid the foundations for the international concentration that would characterize the sector in the following period.

4 Case Studies

The three case studies of Bertelsmann, Salvat, and Pearson included in this section illustrate the different strategies developed by large European book companies in order to cope with mass production, the emergence of new publishing products, and the design of their international strategy. Note that all three companies, founded in the 19th century, became leaders in the middle decades of the 20th century. Over time, Bertelsmann and Pearson would consolidate their leadership. However, Salvat would be acquired by the Hachette-Lagardère group in 1988.

4.1 Bertelsmann

Starting as a small, religious publishing house, Bertelsmann has transformed itself into the fifth largest international publishing firm. Its identity is reflected by the extraordinary diversity of its portfolio. According to the business historian Harmut Berghoff, seven key factors have influenced the success of the German company: economies of scope, economies of scale, decentralization, a paternalistic corporate culture, growth from its own resources, market orientation, and freedom of action for managers (Berghoff 2010, pp. 8–11).

Founded in 1835 by the printer Carl Bertelsmann, this company focused for a very long time on the narrow religious (Protestant Christian) market. The turning point in Bertelsmann's trajectory came in the 1950s, during the so-called German 'economic miracle.' A string of innovations supported the rapid process of vertical integration. In 1950, the company launched its first book club, Bertelsmann Lesering. Its members were obliged to buy a certain number of titles every three months, allowing the company to anticipate demand and adapt its production capacity. Encouraged by the club's huge success, in 1956, Bertelsmann created Schallplatering, a music club. This was soon followed by Bertelsmann's own record label, Ariola, and the manufacturing firm, Sonopress. In the 1960s, the company entered the media sector, first through its own television production division and then through acquisitions (Ufa-Fernsehproduktion, Ufa-Werbefilm, Ufa-International, and Constantin Film). Between 1969 and 1973, Bertelsmann took control of the Hamburg publisher Gruner + Jahr (Fernández-Moya and Lubinski 2012).

To manage its growing complexity, Bertelsmann adopted a multidivisional structure comprising eight relatively autonomous units (Berghoff 2010, p. 29). The firm went public in 1971, exemplifying the transformation of a middle-sized family firm (*mittelständish*) into a modern, management-led media corporation and accelerating the firm's internationalization. Bertelsmann's first foreign subsidiary was established in Spain in 1962. It did so by introducing the Spanish-speaking area's first book club, Círculo de Lectores. To overcome language and cultural barriers, Bertelsmann opted for mixed teams. To achieve economies of scale and maximize profits, the Spanish affiliate was fully integrated into the central organization, a strategy that proved extremely successful. Spain's experience encouraged the company to create more subsidiaries in Austria (1966), the Netherlands (1967), Belgium (1967), Mexico (1969), Colombia (1969), France (1970), Portugal (1971), Argentina (1971), Venezuela (1971), Brazil (1972) and the United Kingdom (1977; Berghoff 2010, p. 32).

The company's internationalization strategy reached a turning point of its own in the 1970s. Until then, Bertelsmann had achieved an organic growth with modest outside investment (Berghoff 2013, p. 181). From this moment on, the firm also resorted to mergers and acquisitions as a means of going international. Bertelsmann was by no means the only European publisher to do this. As the industry became more concentrated, large companies such as France's Hachette, the UK's Pearson, or Italy's Mondadori would choose the acquisition of local firms as the fastest and easiest way to enter foreign markets (Van Lente and De Goey 2008).

Strongly positioned in the European market, the aim of Bertelsmann from the 1980s onwards was to be consolidated into the American market. The first step toward this was the acquisition of 51% of the American publishing house Bantam in 1977. It would purchase the rest of the company in 1981. In 1985–1986, it acquired Doubleday Dell. By 1989, the three merged companies were the seventh most important publishing company in the United States by market share (5.19%; Greco 1995, p. 2). The next step in this direction was the acquisition of Random House, which Bertelsmann bought and merged with Bantam Doubleday Dell. The operation was the largest single investment in the company's history, and it made Bertelsmann the publisher with the highest volume of trade in the English-speaking world at that time. Random House then included Alfred A. Knopf, Beginner Books, and Pantheon Books, which it had acquired in the 1960s, and it was one of the five leading publishers in the United States. Bertelsmann paid respect to the reputation of its new acquisition by designating its entire literature division under the umbrella of Random House. From this time on, Random House became the center of Bertelsmann's literary publications division. The firm now has a direct presence in Argentina, Australia, Austria, Canada, Chile, Colombia, Germany, India, Ireland, Japan, Korea, Mexico, New Zealand, South Africa, Spain, the United Kingdom, Uruguay, the United States, and Venezuela. A crucial move in this process was the acquisition of Sudamericana, an Argentinean company with a strong position in Latin American markets. After each acquisition, Bertelsmann maintained the original brands and symbols of the acquired companies and, in many cases, of the national culture with an intellectual allure that cannot be underestimated.

4.2 Pearson

The story of the largest publisher of the world illuminates the crucial role played by the media and the education market in the English-speaking market as well as the typical path of internationalization via mergers and acquisitions by non-publishing, diversified conglomerates.

Pearson was an outsider that entered the publishing industry to become a highly diversified industrial conglomerate. Originally, Pearson was a construction and engineering company founded by Samuel Pearson in 1844. It grew spectacularly via unrelated diversification in the first decades of the 20th century. In 1921, Pearson entered the media sector through the acquisition of the local newspaper group UK Provincial. Its diversification into the publishing business line continued with the purchase of Longman—already one of the most important textbook publishers in the United Kingdom—in 1968.

Pearson's growth accelerated after 1969 when the company went public. Under family control, Pearson became a holding company with five main business lines: banking and financial services, investment trust, newspapers and publishing, oil, and industrial participation. The British holding took a giant step in the race to become a major player in the European book market through the acquisition of Penguin—the paperback pioneer and a landmark in the English-speaking world—in 1970. Through Penguin's operation, publishing became Pearson's main source of profit in 1974: it showed a profit of 42% compared with 17% of the banking and finance business. Penguin also contributed to the internationalization of the holding. That same year, 56% of the total profit was generated in the United Kingdom and 44% overseas. Meanwhile, the publishing subsidiary Penguin Longman obtained barely a third of its sales revenue in the United Kingdom and had a growing presence in the Arab countries, Asia, Australia, Europe, the Americas, and Africa. In 1975, the acquisition of Viking Press would help reinforce Penguin's position in the United States.

Pearson's annual reports help understand how a consistent strategy of mergers and acquisitions since the 1980s allowed the British group to become a giant in the educational market Relevant operations involved Maskew Miller (1983), Addison-Wesley (1985), HarperCollins Educational Publishing (1996), NCS (2000), Kirihara (2001), Americana GS (2003), and Wall Street English (2009).

4.3 Salvat

The Spanish company Salvat constitutes a further example of fast organic growth in the European publishing market, a clear contrast with previous examples. Moreover, the case illustrates how language plays a vital role in creating a competitive advantage in the process of internationalization of a publishing firm.

The publishing house Salvat was founded in Barcelona in 1868 by Manuel Salvat. It specialized in medical publications, large-format books, dictionaries, and encyclopedias. By the end of the 19th century, the company underwent a successful process of internationalization focused on Latin America (Fernández-Moya 2009). Salvat's accumulated capabilities flourished in the 1960s, when the company rose to the very top of the Spanish publishing sector and led the ranking of exporting publishers until well into the 1980s. Salvat's leadership position was built upon two pillars: an entrepreneurial environment of modernization developed by the new generations of the proprietary family and its multinational status.

The entrepreneurial environment of modernization resulted in changes in the publishing industry's traditional business lines. To meet the fast growing demand, Salvat embraced mass production through two products: the formats of fascicles and pocket books. Regarding the distribution system, Salvat created its own distribution company called Marco Ibérica Distribución de Ediciones Sociedad Anónima (Midesa) in 1964, which was modeled on a similar company operating in Italy. Through Midesa, fascicles reached new sales channels: newsstands and department stores.

Regarding its condition as a multinational company, Salvat's earlier internationalization (accumulated knowledge and previously-formed contacts) and common language were its two profitable sources of competitive advantage. Furthermore, the fascicle format turned into a very profitable business that supported Salvat's growth in the international markets, first in Latin America and then in Europe. In association with Italian publisher De Agostini, Salvat entered the non-Spanish speaking areas: the Swiss, French, German, Belgian, and British markets. However, the center of Salvat's international market was Latin America. In fact, the main assets of its strategy of internationalization were its reputed brand and strong position in the largest Spanish-speaking markets. This Barcelona-based publisher managed to build an extensive business network, with offices in Buenos Aires, Mexico City, Caracas, Rio de Janeiro, and Bogotá, that allowed exports of up to 60% of its total output. In 1974, the company undertook an important step in the internationalization sequence: the installation of a production subsidiary, a printing plant in Mexico.

Based on its new growth strategies, in 1972, Salvat became Spain's largest publisher as well as one of the most profitable Spanish companies. The number of employees grew from 50 in the mid-1950s to over 4,000 (at home and abroad) in 1972 (Fundación Germán Sánchez Ruipérez 2006). Salvat's professionalization took place in at least three ways: the postgraduate education provided to the three Salvat brothers (members of the fourth generation); regular consulting by faculty from the Instituto de Estudios Superiores de la Empresa International (IESE); and IESE-trained managers for the company's domestic and overseas' offices. Professionalization was also a key element for the consolidation of international expansion, and it enabled sustainability of the increased organizational complexity of the multinational company.

Despite Salvat's leading position in the Spanish-language publishing sector, its sales records were still far below those of the main European publishers. In 1970, while Salvat's sales barely reached ESP 1 billion, Hachette and Bertelsmann reported sales of approximately ESP 32 billion and ESP 14 billion (FF 3 billion and DM 712 million), respectively. Thus, Salvat was a medium-sized company according to European standards. The company had successfully implemented an organic growth strategy (vertical integration, internationalization, and related diversification), yet the results were not as dramatic as those of the largest European publishers. The gap grew in the 1980s as concentration and competition levels increased, weakening Salvat's position in both the Spanish and international markets. As the firm was unable to compete with the giant publishing firms that entered the Spanish market, the proprietary family decided to sell the company to French publisher Hachette in 1986.

Conclusions and Directions for Future Research

In this chapter, we attempted to answer an intriguing question: How has the European publishing industry managed to globalize while maintaining headquarters in its home countries, operating within highly fragmented markets, and facing formidable cultural barriers?

The central argument of this chapter is that European publishers have succeeded in maintaining and developing their own competitive abilities in the international market through flexible strategies of internationalization. The mirror (and the competition) provided by the United States since the postwar period and the long-term impact of the 1970s crisis have conditioned such strategies. A variety of innovations have played important roles in this European dynamism. These have been both commercial (book clubs, fascicles, literary prizes, door-to-door sales, bookstands, etc.) and institutional (book fairs and literary agents) and have persistently defended the sector's collective interests at the local, national, and international levels. It is precisely here that questions arise regarding the least-known aspects of the sector—such as the role of regulation in general and price controls in particular—and these questions are currently most in need of research.

What is decisive, however, are the strategies of internationalization—inseparable from growth strategies—employed by these companies. As paradoxical as it may seem, in the long term, the fragmentation of the Old World markets has served as a catalyst for the creation of large multinational companies. During the so-called Golden Age, European publishers grew organically within their domestic markets by expanding their production capacities, adopting new commercial techniques, supporting vertical integration, and, in many cases, increasing exports to both European and colonial markets. The fact is that despite the inexorable advance of the English language, the linguistic diversity and cultural influence of certain European countries on their neighbors or former colonies came to have a positive impact on their success abroad. However, since the 1980s, mergers, acquisitions, and joint ventures have become more relevant than organic growth to the internationalization strategies of European firms. Mergers and acquisitions became the fastest way for publishers to grow, achieve economies of scale, and compete in the global market. As publishing is a cultural industry, publishers must overcome huge cultural barriers to go international, and this strategy enables them to compete in a national market as a national brand. Most groups have chosen to maintain the identity (and markets) of their acquired companies in order to create strong positions in their home markets by maintaining the strong positions the acquired companies have built.

The present essay is a first examination of an important but little-known subject: the keys to the competitive abilities of Europe's cultural industries, specifically that of the publishing sector. Here, we have focused on an analysis of the domestic sector and on gathering quantitative data that will enable an overview of the European sector as a whole. This has obliged us to leave some questions unanswered. We have already mentioned the need to further explore the role of regulation and fixed price policies. In general, we feel that it would be useful to look more closely at the differences between the various national publishing industries in Europe and at their institutional frameworks and business fabrics, as well as reconstruct specific cases that would provide insight into the microeconomic details of these transformations. Along these lines, subjects still needing study include crucial issues such as the ownership structures of European publishing groups and their degree of professionalization. A greater understanding of the factors behind the growth of the American publishing sector would also help to clarify some of these unresolved questions, all of which reflect the inherent limitations of this research and must be consigned to a future agenda.

Notes

1 Heading the ranking of the international publishing sector is Pearson (UK), Reed Elsevier (UK/NL/US), ThomsonReuters (US), Wolters Kluwer (NL), Random House (Germany), Hachette Livre (France), Holtzbrinck (Germany), Grupo Planeta (Spain), Cengage (US), and McGraw-Hill Education (US; *Publishers Weekly* 27 June 2014).
2 The number of titles is an excellent indicator of both production capacity and the cultural diversity of the industry. Moreover, this indicator is more reliable than the total production of one country. Another indicator, the average number of copies per title, refers to the industrial capacity of the printing sector. In 1964, UNESCO established a recommendation regarding the international standardization of statistics related to book production. It defined a book as 'a non-periodical printed publication of at least 49 pages, exclusive of the cover pages' (*Courier* September 1965, p. 15).

3 Data available at Angus Maddison project website, www.ggdc.net/maddison/
maddison-project/data.htm, accessed October 29th 2016.
4 Note that, while incorrect, the following three terms are usually thought of as
being synonymous: mass book, pocket book, and paperback.

References

Altbach, P.G. 1997, 'Book publishing', in Y. Courrier and A. Large (eds.), *World Information Report 1997/98*, UNESCO Publishing, Paris, pp. 318–327.

Barker, R.E. 1956, *Books for All, a Study of International Book Trade*, UNESCO, Paris.

Barker, R.E. and Escarpit, R. 1973, *The Book Hunger*, UNESCO, Paris.

Berghoff, H. 2010, 'From small publisher to global media and services company: Outline of the history of Bertelsmann, 1985 to 2010', in H. Berghoff (ed.), *175 Years of Bertelsmann: The Legacy for Our Future*, Bertelsmann, Munich, pp. 8–83.

Berghoff, H. 2013, 'Becoming global, staying local: The internationalization of Bertelsmann, 1962–2010', in C. Lubinski, J. Fear and P. Fernández Pérez (eds.), *Entrepreneurship, Governance, and Pathways to Internationalization*, Routledge, New York, pp. 169–190.

Business History Review 2015, 'Special issue on global business', *Business History Review*, vol. 89, no. 3.

Escarpit, R. 1965, *The Book Revolution*, UNESCO, Paris.

Federation of European Publishers 2013, *European book publishing statistics 2013*, Available from: <www.fep-fee.eu/-About-FEP-> [15 July 2014].

Federation of European Publishers 2014, *The whole world is here: Books in the digital age*, Available from: <www.fep-fee.eu/-About-FEP-> [15 July 2014].

Fernández-Moya, M. 2009, 'A family-owned publishing multinational: The Salvat company (1869–1988)', *Business History*, vol. 52, no. 3, pp. 453–470.

Fernández-Moya, M. 2012, 'Creating knowledge networks: Spanish multinational publishers in Mexico', *Business History Review*, vol. 86, no. 1, pp. 69–98.

Fernández-Moya, M. and Lubinski, C. 2012, 'Business groups in the publishing industry: A cross-cultural analysis of internationalization', Paper presented at the *XVIth World Economic History Congress*, 9–13 July, Stellenbosch University, South Africa.

Fundación Germán Sánchez Ruipérez 2006, *Conversaciones con editores en primera persona (Personal interviews with publishers)*, Papeles de la Fundación Germán Sánchez Ruipérez, Madrid.

Greco, A.N. 1995, 'Mergers and acquisitions in the U.S. book industry, 1960–89', in P.G. Altbach and E. Hoshino (eds.), *International Book Publishing: An Encyclopedia*, Fitzroy Dearborn Publishers, London and Chicago, pp. 229–241.

Hall, D.D. (ed) 2014, *A History of the Book in America*, University of North Carolina Press, North Carolina.

Lacy, D. 1967, 'Major trends in American book publishing', in K.L. Henderson (ed.), *Trends in American Publishing*, University of Illinois, Graduate School of Library Science, Champaign, IL, pp. 1–15.

Lara, J.M. 2002, 'Sector editorial: el caso de planeta (Publishing sector: the case of Planeta)', *Revista ICE*, vol. 799, p. 221.

Lipscomb, C.E. 2001, 'Mergers in the publishing industry', *Bulletin of the Medical Library Association*, vol. 89, no. 3, pp. 307–308.

Miller, L.J. 2006, *Reluctant Capitalists: Bookselling and the Culture of Consumption*, University of Chicago Press, Chicago.

Rak, J. 2013, *Boom! Manufacturing Memoir for the Popular Market*, Wilfrid Laurier University Press, Ontario.

Stevenson, I. 2010, *Book Makers: British Publishing in the Twentieth Century*, British Library, London.

Tebbel, J. 1987, *Between Covers: The Rise and Transformation of Book Publishing in America*, Oxford University Press, New York.

Throsby, D.C. 2001, *Economics and Culture*, Cambridge University Press, Cambridge.

Van Lente, D. and De Goey, F. 2008, 'Trajectories of internationalization: Knowledge and national business styles in the making of two Dutch publishing multinationals, 1950–1990', *Enterprise & Society*, vol. 9, no. 1, pp. 165–202.

Weidhaas, P. 2007, *A History of the Frankfurt Book Fair*, Dundurn, Toronto.

7 Small, Hidden and Competitive
The Japanese Chemical Industry Since 1980

So Hirano

Introduction

The chemical industry presents unique features that contribute to the discussion on the nature of industries and competitiveness. Indeed, unlike most of the cases tackled in this book, the chemical industry is not defined by a specific product (automobile, books, drugs, paper, screw, tobacco, or watches) or service (retail, shipping, or water construction) but by a process. This industry manufactures products by using chemical processes on raw materials. Another characteristic is the diversity of raw materials and finished products.

The petrochemical industry, which occupies a central position in chemical products, manufactures many products with molecular structures that contain carbon. Petrochemical products are mainly classified into basic chemicals and specialty chemicals. Basic chemical products include synthetic resins (polyethylene, polypropylene, etc.), synthetic fibers (nylon, polyester, etc.), and a variety of other products. Their characteristics are a low added value, and their mass production and competitiveness are based on price. Therefore, the competitive advantage for such goods lies in regions where it is possible to procure raw materials at low prices and where there are large-scale and highly efficient production facilities, namely the Middle East and shale gas production regions in the United States. Latecomers, such as South Korea, Taiwan, and China, are characterized by the existence of large-scale manufacturing facilities.

Moreover, specialty chemical products refer to a wide group of chemical goods that are produced in smaller quantities than basic chemical products but have high added value. These include functional chemicals, agricultural chemicals, active pharmaceutical ingredients, and a broad range of other products. Such specialty chemical products tend to be priced according to their value at the time of use and not cost (Grüne et al. 2014). Corporations in Western Europe and the United States, which have long accumulated technologies for the chemical industry, have retained a strong competitive edge in these high-value-added products. However, in recent years, Japan has also improved its competitiveness in functional chemical products, as will be examined in this chapter.

Literature on the chemical industry usually emphasizes the global domination of firms from Germany and the United States, as well as British, French, and Swiss firms in some cases. Japan is always referred to as a latecomer and a backward country that relies on foreign technology, as well as a country where firms in the chemical industry are unable to establish a globally competitive position, unlike firms in other sectors of the manufacturing industry. For example, in his work on the global chemical industry, Chandler (2005) considered Japan as only a target for US investments and did not pay any attention to Japanese companies. Other scholars, such as Aftalion (2001); Arora, Landau, and Rosenberg (1999); and Bower (1986) examined the high growth of the chemical industry in Japan after World War II, which even overtook Germany in 1980. However, they explain the reason for this development as mainly support from the state and its domestic orientation, because of which Japanese chemical companies cannot be considered as competitive on global markets. The most recent contributions to the literature (e.g., Grüne et al. 2014) focus on macro-level international comparisons in order to emphasize the major national trends in the chemical industry, but they failed to properly understand the changes that have taken place in Japan since the 1990s.

Nevertheless, although Japanese companies do not have a competitive advantage in the chemical industry as a whole, looking at some particular specialty chemicals gives a different perspective. The field of functional chemical products (in particular, electronic materials) is dominated by Japanese companies since the formation of this new industry in the early 1990s. The Japanese Ministry of Economy, Trade and Industry (METI) defines the functional chemicals industry as 'the branch of the chemical industry that delivers added value to customer products by utilizing proprietary technologies to propose solutions that add special functionality to materials' (Research Group on Enhancing Competitiveness in the Functional Chemical Industry 2013). Functional chemicals include a broad range of products, and electronic materials account for the largest proportion (Kawamoto 2003). Electronic materials are used in semiconductors (silicon wafers, photoresists, etc.), liquid crystal displays (resists, polarizing plates, protective films for polarizing plates, spacers, etc.), and other electronic products.

The producers of electronic materials have both high market shares and high profitability in the global market for such products. Moreover, as this industry is relatively new, it provides a good opportunity to discuss the issues of the construction and boundaries of industries, as addressed recently by Sokes and Banken (2015). One major characteristic of the development of these materials is the importance of cooperation with customers (the electronics companies) because the component (electronic material) and the end product (electronic device) must be developed simultaneously. The co-development of prototypes of new materials and new devices makes it possible to perfect the electronic products manufactured for the public.

Consequently, this chapter will address the following research questions: How were Japanese companies able to achieve competitiveness in electronic materials, while the chemical industry was historically weak in this country? How was it possible to keep this advantage in global markets? The chapter is divided into three sections. Section 1 presents the overall development of the chemical industry in Japan. Next, section 2 shows the emergence of a new sub-industry, namely the electronic material industry, in which Japanese firms had a dominant position. Finally, section 3 analyses the way in which Japanese producers of electronic materials were able to extend their competitiveness to the global market.

1 The Chemical Industry in Post-War Japan

The history of the development of the Japanese chemical industry after World War II is characterized by, on one hand, a fast catch up of production volume with advanced countries and, on the other hand, slow improvement of quality and added value. The petrochemical industry, which is at the heart of the chemical industry, was launched in Japan in 1958 via technology transfers from the United States and other Western countries. Since neither crude oil nor natural gas was produced domestically, imported petroleum-based feedstock was selected as the raw material. Consequently, Japan had no competitive edge in terms of technology or raw materials. However, the production output of Japanese petrochemical products surged to answer the rise in demand during the period of rapid economic growth from the mid-1950s to the early 1970s (Hirano 2016). A comparison of the output of ethylene, which is a basic material in the petrochemical industry, shows that by 1968, Japan had overtaken West Germany and was ranked second to the United States.

However, in terms of international competitiveness, Japanese chemical products were weak performers until the 1980s. Itami (1991) and Itami Laboratory conclude that the reason for the weak competitiveness was the trade deficit in chemical products. An overview of the trade balance for chemical products in 1988 reveals a $900 million deficit for Japan, whereas the United States had a surplus of $12.4 billion and West Germany a surplus of $19.9 billion. At the time, Japan experienced economic growth and significant surpluses in terms of the overall trade balance, but chemical products recorded a deficit. In the same year, the chemical industry also recorded a deficit in the technology trade balance. In short, the steel industry, electronic industry, automobile industry, and many other manufacturing industries were growing the export industry and recording substantial trade surpluses, whereas the chemical industry lagged far behind in terms of international competitiveness.

The ranking of the world's 30 largest companies in the overall chemical industry in 2013 shows this weak competitiveness of Japanese firms (see Table 7.1). Only five Japanese companies had ranked, and none were in the

Table 7.1 The World's 30 Leading Chemical Companies

Ranking	Company	Country	Chemical sales				Chemical operating profits		
			2013 ($ million)	Change from 2012 (%)	Chemical sales as of total sales		2013 ($ million)	Change from 2012 (%)	Operating profit margin
1	BASF	Germany	78,615	-4.60%	80		6,317	-6.20%	8.00%
2	Sinopec	China	60,829	5.00%	13		103	71.90%	0.20%
3	Dow Chemical	United States	57,080	0.50%	100		4,715	6.60%	8.30%
4	SABIC	Saudi Arabia	43,589	3.10%	86.5		12,795	1.70%	29.40%
5	Shell	Netherlands	42,279	-7.60%	9.4		N.A.	N.A.	N.A.
6	ExxonMobil	United States	39,048	0.80%	9.3		5,180	6.00%	13.30%
7	Formosa Plastics	Taiwan	37,671	5.90%	60.2		2,352	67.20%	6.20%
8	Lyondell Basell Industries	Netherlands	33,405	1.70%	75.8		5,087	17.50%	15.20%
9	DuPont	United States	31,044	2.70%	86.9		5,234	11.60%	16.90%
10	Ineos	Switzerland	26,861	-10.80%	100		2,137	-6.30%	8.00%
11	Mitsubishi Chemical	Japan	26,685	14.80%	74.4		507	121.10%	1.90%
12	Bayer	Germany	26,636	0.90%	49.9		4,409	1.00%	16.60%
13	LG Chem	South Korea	21,142	-0.50%	100		1,592	-8.80%	7.50%
14	AkzoNobel	Netherlands	19,376	-5.20%	100		1,193	-3.50%	6.20%
15	Air Liquide	France	19,153	-0.80%	94.7		3,569	1.10%	18.60%
16	Braskem	Brazil	18,994	15.40%	100		1,370	140.10%	7.20%
17	Mitsui Chemicals	Japan	18,916	11.50%	100		306	597.10%	1.60%
18	Linde	Germany	18,554	11.00%	83.9		5,108	13.00%	27.50%
19	Sumitomo Chemical	Japan	18,116	16.30%	78.8		688	136.90%	3.80%

20	Reliance Industries	India	17,778	10.40%	23.3	1,436	17.40%	8.10%
21	Evonik Industries	Germany	17,097	-3.70%	100	1,653	-22.50%	9.70%
22	Toray Industries	Japan	16,665	17.90%	88.5	1,152	22.50%	6.90%
23	Lotte Chemical	South Korea	15,017	3.40%	100	445	31.10%	3.00%
24	Yara	Norway	14,472	0.60%	100	1,963	-23.10%	13.60%
25	PPG Industries	United States	14,044	-0.90%	93	2,134	-3.00%	15.20%
26	Solvay	Belgium	13,768	-19.20%	100	1,179	-24.00%	8.60%
27	Chevron Phillips	United States	13,147	-1.20%	100	N.A.	N.A.	N.A.
28	DSM	Netherlands	12,773	5.30%	100	580	-11.90%	4.50%
29	Shin-Etsu Chemical	Japan	11,945	13.70%	100	1,781	10.70%	14.90%
30	Praxair	United States	11,925	6.20%	100	3,734	7.90%	31.30%

Source: American Chemistry Council (ACC) 2014, 'Guide to the business of chemistry 2014.'

top 10. Moreover, the three largest companies (Mitsubishi Chemicals, Mitsui Chemicals, and Sumitomo Chemicals) are general chemical companies and had very low profitability, with an operating profit of less than 2% for the first two companies and less than 4% for the third. Yet, there were also two smaller companies in terms of gross sales but with the largest profitability: Toray Industries, a producer of carbon fibers and various materials (operating profit of 6.9%) and especially Shin-Etsu Chemical, a manufacturer of functional chemicals (operating profit of 14.9%). The latter case shows that some Japanese chemical companies, positioned in niche markets, can be extremely profitable. This case will be analyzed in detail below.

Moreover, if one looks at today's trade balance of chemical products, there is a significant improvement since the late 1980s, which suggests that the Japanese chemical industry achieved international competitiveness. Although the trade balance was negative in post-war Japan, it became positive in 1988, and trade surplus continues to improve slightly since that year (Hirano 2016, p. 9). As indicated in Table 7.2, the trade balance for chemical products in fiscal year 2013 showed a strong surplus of approximately ¥1 trillion (approximately $9.36 billion at the exchange rate of the time). Looking at the trade balance by region reveals that trade with the United States and the European Union was running a small deficit, whereas trade with the Asian countries showed a substantial surplus. Moreover, the technology trade balance (excluding transactions between parent companies) ran a surplus of ¥25.1 billion in fiscal year 2012. In terms of industry, the amount of surplus for the chemical industry is ranked third behind the pharmaceutical manufacturing and the transportation equipment manufacturing industries. In addition, Japanese product quantities are still large in the world. The shipment value of Japanese chemical products is ranked third after China and the United States.

Electronic materials—a group of strong products unique to Japan—are the reason for the surplus in the trade balance. As indicated in Figure 7.1, Japanese corporations have built an oligopolistic position in materials for semiconductors, liquid crystals, and lithium ion batteries. The abovementioned Shin-Etsu Chemical holds the largest market share for silicon wafers, which is one of the materials for semiconductors. Until the 1990s, the majority of customers for these products were Japanese electronics companies,

Table 7.2 Exports and Imports of Chemical Goods in Million Yen (FY 2013)

	Exports	*Imports*	*Balance*
World	7,689,567	6,612,486	1,077,081
United States	744,695	1,180,081	–435,386
European Union	656,450	2,200,139	–1,543,689
Asia	5,788,964	2,361,113	3,427,851

Source: Trade Statistics of Japan 2013, Ministry of Finance of Japan (revised value).

and so the Japanese chemical companies were very competitive. They hold nearly 100% of the world market in liquid crystal displays (LCDs) and lithium ion batteries. However, as indicated in Figure 7.1, today, Japan is no longer competitive for end electronic products, such as semiconductors or LCDs, and only remains competitive for components. It seems that the chemical industry in Japan does not share the fate of the Japanese electronics industry.

Another reason why Japanese chemical products are enjoying a substantial surplus in the trade balance with Asia is the expertise of Japanese chemical companies in the field of electronic materials. At present, Samsung and other South Korean electronics companies are strongly competitive on LCDs and smartphones. Thus, the Korean trade balance has been running a

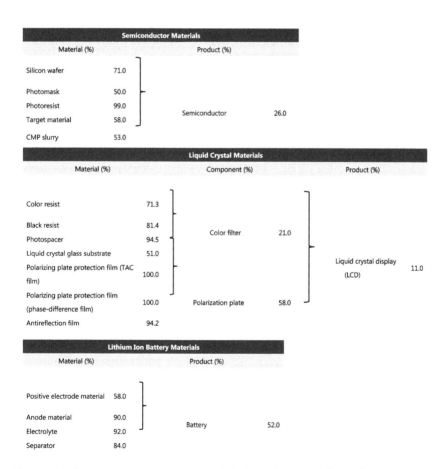

Figure 7.1 Japanese Companies' Share of the Electric Materials Market (2011)

Source: Compiled by Fukoku Capital Management, Inc. using data from the White Paper on Manufacturing Industries (Monodzukuri).

surplus since 1998. However, trade with Japan is in deficit, because Korean electronics corporations rely on Japanese imports for parts and electronic materials. Consequently, the growth of Korean electronics companies increases the sales of Japanese chemical firms. In the case of electronic products, Japan and South Korea are codependent.

2 The Creation of a New Industry

This section clarifies the way in which Japanese companies have emerged as the dominant players of a new industry—the industry of functional products for electronics. Despite their overall weakness compared with Western companies, some Japanese chemical companies were able to build competitive advantages in this new field.

The analysis conducted below is based on the work on 12 highly profitable chemical companies in Japan carried out by Kikkawa and Hirano (2011). The selection of the 12 firms was based on the following principles. First, a chemical company was defined as a company in which the combined net sales of chemical goods and synthetic fibers accounted for at least 30% of the consolidated gross sales. The population consisted of corporations with net sales in excess of ¥100 billion (approx. $928 million) in 2000. This resulted in a sample of 40 corporations. Then, the researchers calculated the operating margin (return on sales [ROS]) for these corporations from fiscal year 2000 to 2009. Corporations with an average ROS of at least 7.5% over this decade were considered as 'highly profitable corporations.' The average ROS for the entire Japanese manufacturing industry was 3.8% in the first half of the 2000s and 4.5% in the second half of the decade. Thus, the following twelve companies were selected using this method: Shin-Etsu Chemical Co., Ltd.; JSR Corporation; Nissan Chemical Industries, Ltd.; Nitto Denko Corporation; Kuraray Co., Ltd.; Nifco Inc.; ADEKA Corporation; Denka Co., Ltd.; Daicel Corporation; CHISSO Corporation; Tokuyama Corporation; and Hitachi Chemical Co., Ltd (this order follows ROS). Shin-Etsu Chemical is the only one to be ranked (28th) among the top 30 corporations in the world. The other highly profitable corporations are medium-sized corporations.

The process whereby these corporations were able to build a competitive advantage in the field of electronic materials is summarized in Figure 7.2 and discussed below.

2.1 Positioning in a Niche Market

Let us now consider in detail how Japanese chemical companies achieved competitive strength. First, when expanding their business, these corporations intentionally targeted niche markets, that is, operating platforms where the market scale is small and there is little competition (I).[1] For example, Nitto Denko has a policy of selecting operating platforms in

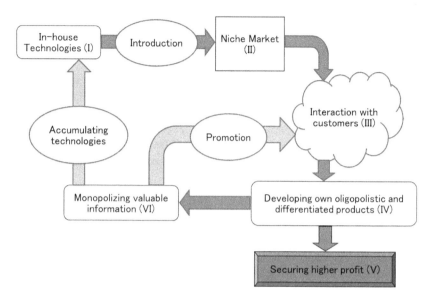

Figure 7.2 The Process of Achieving Competitiveness

growing international markets even if their scale is not so large as well as capturing the top share of those markets. At Kuraray, the criteria for entering a new market include taking the initiative as a first mover and securing a high share and not following other companies. Daicel Corporation has also focused on small-scale markets where the opportunities of success are good, specifically, where there are a maximum of three competitors at the time of market entry, each with a projected share of at least 30%. Such behavior was rare for Japanese corporations, which, unlike Western corporations, tended to be oriented toward increasing net sales rather than profitability. Many of the highly profitable chemical corporations in Japan developed the electronic materials field in the 1980s and 1990s when the markets were small.

Conversely, large chemical companies largely ignored the market for electronic materials where these medium-sized corporations made their moves. The major chemical companies in Western countries and in Japan focused rather on diversifying into the life sciences industry (pharmaceuticals, biotechnology, etc.), where profitability and market scale are relatively high (Shimamoto 2009). Even though they were located in the same region (Japan) as the abovementioned medium-sized chemical companies, the major Japanese companies overlooked the electronic materials business because of the small scale of the market. For example, photoresists, which are a chemical product used to manufacture semiconductors, only generated sales of several billion yen (several tens of millions of dollars).[2]

Consequently, Sumitomo Chemical Co., Ltd., which is one of the major chemical companies in Japan (ranked as the world's 19th largest chemical company in 2013; see Table 1), did not consider photoresists as an important businesses for the future. However, a market scale of several tens of millions of dollars was large enough to attract JSR, a small company with net sales of approximately $1.5 billion. Even if medium-sized chemical companies wanted to emulate the major corporations and enter the life sciences business, there was a financial entry barrier due to the huge investments necessary to enter this field. Consequently, large and medium-sized chemical corporations in Japan parted ways. Major chemical companies of Western Europe and the United States also showed no interest in electronic materials.

2.2 In-House Technology as a Major Resource

Second, another condition for a medium-sized chemical company to enter a new market is that it should be able to use its own technology (II) in this new market. The cases of both Nitto Denko and Kuraray show their ability to use in-house technical competence as a criterion for entering a new market. Let us look at the example of Kuraray in detail. Many flagship products at Kuraray are connected to a substance called POVAL made of polyvinyl alcohol (PVA). After World War II, Kuraray started producing a synthetic fiber called vinylon using POVAL as a raw material. It was the first company in the world to successfully develop products using POVAL and vinylon. In 1953, it enjoyed a significant success when it started to manufacture school uniforms made from vinylon. Unfortunately, at the start of the period of rapid economic growth, vinylon lost its competitive advantage to polyester, which was cheaper and of better quality than vinylon. However, Kuraray used POVAL, its in-house technology, to develop other products. Today, one of Kuraray's leading products is POVAL film, used as a material for the polarizing plates in LCDs. Currently, there is no substitute for POVAL film. Moreover, only two companies in the world have the technology for producing POVAL, and thus Kuraray has built an oligopolistic position. Kuraray supplies 80% of the market and The Nippon Synthetic Chemical Industry Co., Ltd. supplies the remaining 20%. Another flagship product at Kuraray is EVAL, which was developed out of research to improve POVAL. EVAL is a substance that is used to enhance the barrier properties of plastic containers, and it is indispensable for manufacturing gasoline tanks. Kuraray has captured 65% of the international market for EVAL.

2.3 Product Development: Close Interaction with
    the Electronics Industry

Third, the product development strategy of Japanese chemical companies is based on an intense cooperation with electronics manufacturers, who are their customers (III). Until the 1980s, Japanese electronics companies, such as Sony and Panasonic, had a strong international competitiveness. Thus, close interaction with these firms made it possible for Japanese chemical companies to benefit from experiences that were different from those of chemical companies in Western Europe and the United States. These companies were able to accumulate specific knowledge and technology as, in this period, electronics and chemical companies in Japan worked together to develop new, groundbreaking products. The development of LCDs is a case in point. Sharp, a pioneer in the commercialization of the LCD, was able to improve the image quality and durability of this product thanks to joint research with a chemical company, JSR. According to an executive of an electric appliances manufacturer, 'the LCD business would not have been viable without JSR products. JSR bears the lion's share of the credit for creating the current market for liquid crystal televisions'(Nikkei Business Publications 2006).

A similar relationship led to the co-development of the lithium ion battery by Sony (electronics) and Asahi Kasei (chemicals). Such joint research and development (R&D) activities explain why and how Japanese chemical companies were able to establish a monopoly on supplying electronic materials. Therefore, the strong competitiveness of Japanese electronics companies in the 1980s was also a consequence of the competitive advantage of domestic chemical companies. At the time, Japanese corporations had captured a high share of the market for both materials and finished products.

The interaction with electronic companies also led chemical companies to gain the following advantages. (1) Refined technologies. For example, in the case of JSR, the company refined its own technologies and accumulated advanced in-house technologies by complying with strict product quality demands from Toshiba and other customers. Hitachi Chemical, a subsidiary of Hitachi group, was able to improve its own technologies by answering the strict requirements of Hitachi, Ltd., the leading manufacturer of semiconductors at that time. (2) Development of new products. On occasion, information obtained from close customers led chemical companies to develop and launch new products. For example, Nitto Denko manufactures a protective seal for household sinks. This seal is a thin film affixed to stainless steel sinks to protect them from being scratched during transportation and installation. A customer decided to use this protective seal as a process material for semiconductors. Then, he approached Nitto Denko and complained about detachability problems when using the product as a process material for semiconductors. Nitto Denko redeveloped the product for its use as a semiconductor process material, and the new product sold very well. There are many cases of products emerging from interactions with customers who used existing products in ways that deviated from the original intent. The frequent exchange of information between chemical companies and their customers has been linked to new product development.

2.4 Management Performance: Forming Oligopolies to Achieve High Profitability

Forming oligopolies is the way in which Japanese chemical companies have successfully developed differentiated products (IV) and achieved high profitability (V). In the case of Kuraray, for example, the company increased its price negotiation ability within the supply chain by developing differentiated products. As a result, in 2006, when the prices for liquid crystal panels—the end product—dropped by 16% and the prices for polarizing plates and color filters—the components—dropped by 14–20%, Kuraray still managed a 15% increase in the price of POVAL film, the material used for polarizing plates. With several similar products, medium-sized chemical companies in Japan have increased their profitability. For example, the operating profit margin at JSR, sometimes nicknamed 'the department store for liquid crystal materials,' was 4.0% in the 1980s and a mere 2.9% in the 1990s, but it rose rapidly to 11.0% in the early 2000s. Similarly, the ROS at Nitto Denko was 4–6% in the 1990s but rose to approximately 10% in the 2000s.

The oligopolistic markets and the increase in the degree to which chemical components contribute to the functionality of electronic products are the reasons for their increased profits. In recent years, chemistry has continued to influence the whole industry, as chemical technologies and chemical products have become indispensable to a broad range of industrial production processes and to core components (Itami 2009). For example, the methods for improving the quality of semiconductors and other electronic devices have shifted from improving the processing technologies to improving the properties of chemical materials, so that it is no longer possible to ignore the importance of improving chemical materials. There are also cases in which it is not possible to manufacture the final product without sophisticated chemical materials. In the case of large-scale integrated circuits (LSI), the difficulty is that the LSI may not operate electrically unless new materials are introduced when switching to a new generation of products. Thus, Japanese chemical companies have been able to grow their margins by increasing the value of the chemical products used by the entire manufacturing industry.

On the other hand, profitability at major chemical corporations, including Mitsubishi, Sumitomo, Mitsui, and other former *zaibatsu* companies, is still relatively low. This results from a trade-off peculiar to large corporations. As indicated by the abovementioned examples, if corporations focus on profitability, they need to intentionally enter small markets. However, when a large corporation enters a small market, the market makes an extremely small contribution to its gross sales. Consequently, if a company pursues a growth strategy based on increasing or maintaining a large scale, it is difficult to enter such markets. There is a trade-off between profitability and growth. Selecting a new business is an extremely difficult issue for major corporations. Japan's large chemical companies have sacrificed profitability in the pursuit of growth.

3 The Shift Toward Global Competitiveness

The competitive advantage of Japanese chemical companies in electronic materials during the late 1980s and 1990s was deeply linked to cooperation with Japanese electronics companies and, consequently, to the global competitiveness of the latter. Then, we must discuss what happened to these chemical firms when Japanese electronics companies started to lose their competitiveness since 2000. How and why were they able to find and cooperate with new customers? This section addresses this question.

3.1 The Lasting Competitiveness of Japanese Component Makers

It is important to discuss the reasons why Japanese chemical companies have been able to maintain their competitive advantage even though corporations from emerging economies emerged and became established as new leaders of the electronics industry. Two points must be considered.

First, one must wonder how Japanese chemical companies were able to move quickly and systematically to new partners based outside Japan. Since the 1990s, they have gradually switched their collaboration from Japanese electronics corporations to European, North American, and East Asian companies. JSR, for example, has established business hubs for photoresists in Europe and North America and increased joint development by approaching Intel, IBM, and other leading semiconductor companies. In 1992, JSR also started to provide Korean and Taiwanese manufacturers with technical services. As a result, there has been a profound shift between the 1980s, when more than 90% of JSR products were intended for Japanese companies, and 2003, when 70% were intended for overseas corporations. When South Korea, Taiwan, and other emerging economies gained competitive clout in the electronics industry, JSR and many other Japanese chemical companies started to do business with companies from these countries, such as Samsung. Today, many Japanese chemical companies have factories in South Korea.

Consequently, Korean semiconductor and liquid crystal industries have been able to grow thanks to the presence of Japanese companies, which supply them high-performance materials. The antireflective coating for semiconductors (ARC) from Nissan Chemical Industries is a remarkable example. Japanese electronics companies did not adopt ARC because their processing techniques were accurate enough without using ARC. However, semiconductor makers in South Korea and Taiwan, where processing technologies were less developed, were keen to use the new technology and materials. Without using ARC and other components developed by Japanese chemical companies, Korean and Taiwanese firms would perhaps not have achieved their current competitive strength in sophisticated electronic products. It is also possible that the turn-around in semiconductor market shares between Japan and Korea is the outcome of the passivity of Japanese companies toward these new technologies.

3.2   Information as a Major Resource

Second, we must discuss why corporations in emerging economies have not been able to increase their competitiveness in materials production. During the 2000s, the share of East Asian nations in the global market for electronics end products overcame that of Japan. For example, Japanese corporations held 77% of the market for LCD televisions in 2002, but by 2005, the market share had reduced to 50%, and by 2010, it was less than 30% (Nishino 2012). Korean and Taiwanese corporations have won a large market share from Japan. However, Japanese chemical companies still maintain a high share of the market for materials for LCDs (see Figure 7.1). The situation is similar in the case of lithium ion batteries (decline in the market share of Japan) and materials for lithium ion batteries (maintenance of the high market share of Japan).

The non-emergence of chemical companies specialized in electronic materials in Korea and Taiwan results largely from the monopoly of Japanese chemical companies on information related to the co-development of materials (VI). This is one of the main resources in this industry, and it is strongly controlled by a few Japanese firms. For example, according to Mr. Muguruma, previous head of technical planning at Nitto Denko, 'it is extremely important to anticipate information about customer developments when researching and developing electronic materials because the product lifecycle is short' (Japan Management Association 2004). Corporations with the ability to anticipate such information are more efficient at R&D than corporations that cannot obtain such information. JSR was also able to focus the field of R&D because it had accumulated sophisticated technologies through its relationship with the best manufacturers in the world.

Japanese corporations have their own ways of accumulating information efficiently and effectively. JSR set up a centralized personnel system for the R&D department and the sales department to facilitate dialog with customers. They decided to rotate personnel between R&D and sales departments. This twofold experience in technology and marketing enables sales employees—'former researchers'—to have in-depth conversations about technology, understand customer needs, and identify future directions for technological progress related to the end product. Hitachi Chemical also had a similar insight. Hitachi Chemical recognized that the best method for understanding trends is to dispatch the best technicians to the best customers. Therefore, senior researchers at the Hitachi Chemical research laboratories also visit customers and take part in developing new products.

Japanese companies also invest heavily in evaluation facilities for prototypes to improve their ability to conduct dialog with customers. When developing semiconductor and other electronic materials, it is advisable to keep evaluating the physical properties of the prototype to determine if they meet customer demands for product quality. If the company has its own evaluation facilities, it is possible to improve prototypes and shorten the time spent on development. Such evaluation facilities are extremely expensive.

However, JSR, Nitto Denko, and other highly profitable companies have installed these facilities. They are used constructively for R&D.

Such close relationships with customers means that information converges on the existing corporations. It is easy to understand the situation if we consider it from the perspective of the customer, who needs a solution to some technical problem. Companies with the best technology, that is industry leaders, are of course the most likely to resolve the problem. Consequently, once a company has become an industry leader, an efficient and effective cycle is created wherein the industry leader accumulates a wide range of information, prompting it to develop new products. Mr. Muguruma at Nitto Denko, comments, 'When we take the top share of the market, we get a wide range of information ahead of anyone else. Customers consult us about many things from the concept stage of new product development. This is very gratifying' (Japan Management Association 2004). Conversely, unless a company is the industry leader or the runner-up, it will not build close relationships with its customers and thus will not be able to obtain the latest information. In short, in the area of functional chemical products, we have a situation in which 'oligopolies create oligopolies.'

In the end, corporations in South Korea and other emerging economies are facing an uphill struggle in the field of electronic materials. For example, LG, a major manufacturer of lithium ion batteries in South Korea, had a company in its group engaged in the manufacture of electronic materials for lithium ion batteries (LG Chem).[3] However, LG continues to procure about half of the key materials that influence performance from Japanese makers. In 2015, LG Chem decided to sell its plant for producing separators, an important material for lithium ion batteries, to Toray, a Japanese chemical corporation. The LG parent company decided that it would be more efficient to spin off the business and increase purchases from the Japanese maker than to keep the production of electronic materials in the group.

Even though governments in East Asian countries attempt to support the development of domestic industries of electronic and other materials, the results are not promising. In 2001, the Korean government adopted the 'Act on Special Measures for the Promotion of Specialized Enterprises, etc. for Components and Materials' to promote the transition to domestic production of advanced components and materials. Despite these efforts, trade balance remains negative. In 2001, the deficit with Japan was $10.5 billion, but by 2011, it had increased to $22.8 billion. Therefore, the South Korean government has extended special measures for another ten years, switched to a policy aimed at in-country training, and recently launched efforts to attract Japanese companies.

3.3 Financial Entry Barriers

Another answer to the second point is the fact that there is little room for new entrants because Japanese corporations made large investments when the market was expanding. For example, JSR extended its product's producing capacity when demand was rapidly growing (JSR Corporation 2008). As a result, JSR has limited the opportunities for other companies to enter the market. Other chemical companies in Japan also made financial investments when demand for electronic materials was increasing. They now hold a high market share.

All these companies chose niche markets to develop their business, and this position now contributes to preventing new entries. If the profit for electronic materials increases, outsiders may plan to enter such a market. Yet, first movers invested massively during the first phase of growth in order to limit the opportunities for new comers to enter the market. However, such strategies are only valid for niche markets. If the size of a market increases rapidly to become huge, the amount of investments also becomes enormous. In such a case, the medium-sized chemical companies would not be able to keep up with investments, and this would offer an entry opportunity to other corporations.

Another point related to investment is the importance of the medium size of Japanese corporations. In electronic materials and other industries where the product lifecycle is short, the supplier must react quickly to market change and refocus investments. Small-scale corporations have such flexibility. For example, Mr. Fujimoto, president of Nissan Chemical in 2004, made the following comment about the competitiveness of medium-sized companies in relation to capital investment: 'Speed is very important for electronic materials businesses. It is not enough to recognize (capital investment projects) when coming out of a management meeting, the senior management must take action on the same day. In terms of capacity for taking on risk, the medium-sized company is no match for the major companies. However, I believe it is the proper scale for an organization to move quickly' (Kagakukōgyōnippōsha 2004). The medium-sized chemical companies in Japan have been able to respond with rapid capital investment that has blocked new entrants because their scale was not large.

3.4 Features of the Process Industry

In addition to the points mentioned above, some typical features of the process industry provide another reason for why Japanese chemical companies have maintained their competitive advantage in global markets. Similar to other process industries, it is difficult to reverse-engineer chemical products. It is possible for corporations coming late to a market to understand the construction, specifications, components, and underlying technologies of most assembled products by means of reverse engineering. However, with chemical products, it is not easy to ascertain the composition of a substance. Even if the composition is identified, it is still not easy to ascertain the production method by simply testing the end product. There is a lot of know-how and tacit knowledge involved in manufacturing chemical products, including the pressure, temperature, time, and catalyst used at the time of production. This is also true of products manufactured by the steel industry (e.g., high-function steel plates).

Another feature of the process industries and particularly functional chemical products is the high cost of switching to a different component. In the case of flat-screen televisions, for example, electronics manufacturers build their facilities premised on the thermal shrinkage rates and other properties of the materials supplied by the materials manufacturers. If they use a material that is even a little different, they will face problems with the alignment of the red, green, and blue colors. The same is true for the photoresists used in semiconductors. When manufacturing semiconductors, the manufacturing equipment and materials must be approved for use in the semiconductor manufacturing process, that is, the process of record (POR). Products that have obtained for the POR are often used for a long time, or as long as a particular product generation is still manufactured. Consequently, once a customer has adopted a particular material, it will support the company's competitive edge over a long period of time.

These conditions are related to the process industry as a whole and not specifically to functional materials; thus, they cannot explain by themselves the reasons why Japanese chemical companies have maintained their competitiveness since the 1980s, despite the shift of electronics from Japan to East Asia after 2000. They are secondary reasons and general external conditions that have long been present in process industries, including the iron and steel industries.

Conclusion

This chapter has demonstrated that although Japanese companies are weak in the general chemical industry, they have achieved a high competitiveness in some specific parts of this industry, such as functional chemical products. Moreover, medium-sized—not large-scale—chemical companies have increased their competitiveness. Such a characteristic can be explained by four factors. First, these corporations have methodically avoided competition by intentionally selecting niche markets where major corporations, both from Japan and from Western countries, are not engaged. Although these markets are small, Japanese chemical companies found it easy to acquire an oligopolistic position. Second, these companies have made methodical use of their strong points, namely their in-house technologies. Third, having entered the markets, these corporations have collaborated intensively with their customers—the electronic companies—for product development. As a result, they have accumulated even more proprietary technologies and useful information. This has facilitated the manufacturing of unique and high-value-added products, which other companies cannot easily produce. The ability to control the niche market has also made the companies highly profitable.

Next, despite the electronics industry's move from Japan to other East Asian countries after 2000, it was difficult for chemical companies in these countries to catch up with Japanese chemical companies. In the electronic materials industry, 'information' from customers plays an extremely important role, and Japanese corporations have prevailed because they have a monopoly on skillfully procuring information. When the Japanese electronics manufacturers were losing their competitive edge, Japanese chemical companies quickly started to build business relations with electronics manufacturers in emerging economies, particularly in South Korea and Taiwan. As a result, they were able to maintain their sources of valuable information.

Another phenomenon is the fact that 'oligopolies create more oligopolies.' In order to improve the quality of their products, electronics companies would communicate their requests and issues regarding materials to the chemical companies. On these occasions, the electronics companies would seek responses from industry leaders because they are the most likely to resolve the problems. Consequently, once a company has become the leader in an industry, it gets exclusive access to valuable information. As a result, lower-ranked companies and potential new comers are disadvantaged in terms of product development because they cannot access information.

Lastly, I would like to outline the implications of the case discussed in this chapter. One of the major findings emphasizes that competition between developed and emerging countries in the manufacturing industry is not a mere question of high technical standards: Information appears to be a major source of competitiveness. It makes imitation based on pure technological factors difficult. The chemical industry shows that maintaining a monopoly on information related to technical improvements helps stabilize technical superiority, which in turn prevents emerging economies from catching up. Such incidental requirements are, of course, not limited to information but could also refer to technical development staff or rare resources that are indispensable to production. It is possible for a company to delay the transition from maturity to decline by fulfilling one of these incidental requirements in addition to technology. Seen from the perspective of the party trying to catch up, it is advantageous to first accumulate technologies in markets other than those where advanced countries have a controlling position if the focus is on profitability. If, for argument's sake, a company enters the same market as advanced countries and even acquires the same technologies, prices will drop to the same extent as the increase in supply until this results in a price war. Even if the market is small, it is better to aim to be the leader in a market where no advanced country has a presence. Working to expand such markets will facilitate companies' own competitive advantages.

Notes

1 The Roman numerals I to VI in the text correspond to the Roman numerals in Figure 7.2.
2 The description of photoresists is based on interviews with Asakura Tatsuo, President of JSR Corporation, in Matsushima and Nishino (2010). JSR Corporation (2008) was consulted for net sales. The 1988 net sales were calculated using the US dollar exchange rate at the time.

3 For the examples from Korea, refer to '*Hyundai•LG nado kankokuzei, nihon de gijutsusha saiyō, sentan sozai•buhin, jimaeshugi wo tenkan*' (*Nikkei shimbun* 17 June 2012, p. 7) and '*Toray, LG kagaku no kōjō baishū, ekokaa muke denchi zairyō seisan, shui no Asahi Kasei ou*' (*Nikkei shimbun* 16 September 2015, p. 11).

References

Aftalion, F. 2001, *A History of the International Chemical Industry*, Chemical Heritage Foundation, Philadelphia, PA.

Arora, A., Landau, R. and Rosenberg, N. 1999, 'Dynamics of comparative advantage in the chemical industry', in D.C. Mowery and R.R. Nelson (eds.), *Sources of Industrial Leadership*, Cambridge University Press, Cambridge, pp. 217–266.

Bower, J.L. 1986, *When Markets Quake*, Harvard Business School Press, Brighton, MA.

Chandler, A.D. 2005, *Shaping the Industrial Century: The Remarkable Story of the Evolution of the Modern Chemical and Pharmaceutical Industries*, Harvard University Press, Cambridge, MA.

Grüne, G., Lockemann, S., Kluy, V. and Meinhardt, S. 2014, *Business Process Management Within Chemical and Pharmaceutical Industries*, Springer-Verlag, Berlin.

Hirano, S. 2016, *Nihon no sekiyukagaku sangyo: bokko, kozo fukyo kara saiseicho he* [The History of Japanese Chemical Industry], Nagoya University Press, Nagoya.

Itami, H. 1991, *Naze sekai ni tachiokureta no ka: Nihon no kagaku sangyō* [Why Is Chemical Industry of Japan Delayed for Another Countries? Japanese Chemical industry]. NTT Shuppan, Tokyo.

Itami, H. 2009, 'Chemistry-oriented transformation of Japanese industry', *Chemistry & Chemical Industry*, vol. 62, no. 2, pp. 114–116.

Japan Management Association 2004, *Dokusousei jyūshi no purodakuto kakushin* [Attaching Importance of Originality in Product Innovation], JMA Management Center, Tokyo.

JSR Corporation 2008, *Kanō ni suru kagaku wo: JSR gojūnen no ayumi* [With Chemistry, We Can: The History of JSR on 50 Years], JSR, Tokyo.

Kagakukōgyōnippōsha 2004, 'Top interview', *Kagaku Keizai (Chemical economy)*, vol. 51, no. 8, pp. 2–8.

Kawamoto, M. 2003, 'Miraigata kagaku sangyō he kitai suru' (Expectation for chemical industry of new type), *Kagaku Keizai (Chemical Economy)*, vol. 50, no. 8, pp. 18–23.

Kikkawa, T. and Hirano, S. 2011, *Kagaku sangyō no jidai* [The Chemical Industry Will Spearhead the Way for Japan in the Near Future], Kagakukōgyōnippōsha, Tokyo.

Matsushima, S. and Nishino, K. (eds.) 2010, *Asakura Tatsuo Oral History*, Research Institute for Innovation Management, Hosei University, Tokyo.

Nikkei Business Publications 2006, 'Sentehisyō niche de nerau sekaiichi' (The first move wins without fail: Aiming to become the top in the world on the niche market), *Nikkei Business*, vol. 1337, pp. 52–54.

Nishino, K. 2012, *Nihon no erekutoronikusu sangyō: kiki ni chokumen suru sangyō kara yomitoreru mono* [Japanese electronics industry: Lesson from industry that faces a crisis], Strategy Report, Mitsui Global Strategic Studies Institute, Tokyo.

Research Group on Enhancing Competitiveness in the Functional Chemical Industry 2013. *Kinōsei kagakusangyō no kyōsōryokukyōka ni muketa kenkyūkai*

[Enhancing Competitiveness in the Functional Chemical Industry], Report, Ministry of Economy, Trade and Industry, Japan, pp. 1–17.

Shimamoto, M. 2009, 'Kagaku kigyō no sannyū•tettai bunseki' [The Analysis of the Entry and Withdrawal in Chemical Firms], in Hitotsubashi Daigaku Nihon Kigyō Kenkyū Sentā (eds.), *Nihon kigyō kenkyū no furontia*, Yūhikaku, Tokyo, pp. 41–69.

Sokes, R. and Banken, R. 2015, 'Constructing an "industry": The case of industrial gases, 1886–2006', *Business History*, vol. 57, no. 5, pp. 688–704.

Part III
Shift in Global Value Chains

8   Sourcing Competition across Industries

Japanese Department Stores and Global Fast Fashion

Rika Fujioka

Introduction

Traditionally, retailing has been regarded as a localized commercial sector composed of small-scale operations (Akehurst and Alexander 1995). Even global retailers such as Walmart and Carrefour need to target local demand and sometimes cooperate with local retailers to launch new stores in overseas markets. The local nature of the market requires retailers to be aware of local consumer culture, and retailers, therefore, cannot ignore the local market (Dawson and Mukoyama 2006). The world's largest retailer, Walmart, has 5,163 domestic stores, including Sam's Club in the United States, compared with 5,816 overseas stores in 2015, making about 47% of its stores domestic; net sales in these stores amounted to $346 billion out of the total $482 billion of company sales in 2015, making international sales just 28.2% of the total (Walmart 2015). The fourth largest retailer, Carrefour, has 5,650 stores in France out of a total of 12,296 stores, making 45.9% of them domestic; these generated €36.3 billion in net sales in 2015, which was 47% of the total net sales of €76.9 billion (Carrefour 2015). Most retailers—even global retailers—rely on domestic sales.

By contrast, manufacturers can more easily internationalize their business and take advantage of lower labor costs by transferring their factories to developing countries (Sternquist 2007). The largest automobile company, Toyota, has production bases in 28 countries, and it sold its cars in 170 countries in 2015. In 2015, it sold over 2.2 million cars in Japan, which was only 24% of its total global sales—quite a low percentage compared with that of global retailers (Toyota 2016). When manufacturers can provide desirable products and meet the demand of consumers worldwide, it is easier for them to realize a standardized business model for a global market than for retailers to attempt to internationalize their business.

There are several examples of failure with regard to retailers' attempts at internationalization, including that of Marks and Spencer (M&S; Burt et al. 2002), Japanese department stores (Fujioka 2013), and French hypermarkets (Dupuis and Prime 1996). Around 70% of all overseas Japanese department stores and supermarkets were closed down by their parent companies

(Kawabata 2011). Burt, Dawson and Sparks (2003) investigated the four types of failure in internationalization. The first is market failure, wherein retailers enter an overseas market with overly optimistic expectations, and sales do not meet the predictions. The second is competitive failure, wherein unforeseen regulations can impose restrictions on large retailers. Competition sometimes arises from factors outside the market, including political issues such as boycotts, new regulations on retailers, and economic issues such as depression. The third is operational failure, wherein retailers are simply not able to operate effectively outside their own culture or country. The fourth is business failure. Retailers should make decisions about their international business, not because of the international situation but because of the domestic market situation. If retailers begin to struggle in their domestic market, then they need to focus more on strengthening their position in the home country before continuing to pursue the global market.

Nevertheless, many retailers have expanded their market internationally for further development since the late 1980s. There are two common reasons for this: first, the push factor that retailers experience following the saturation of their domestic market, which drives them to reach beyond their home country, and second, the pull factor that draws retailers toward new potential markets (Alexander 1990; Burt 1991). Many studies on the internationalization of the retail industry have focused on this expansion of international outlets and their operations, how retailers adapt to the local market while building a standard business model for a global market, and the extent to which ideas are transferable from manufacturers to retailers (Alexander and Myers 2000).

In addition, while retailers' expansion of international sourcing under globalization is inevitable, there are few studies that shed any light on how retailers' global sourcing impacts their competitive advantage (Dawson and Mukoyama 2006). Much more analysis has been conducted on the expansion of overseas stores than on the success and failure of international sourcing. As large retailers have become increasingly powerful since the 1990s, their direct sourcing from manufacturers has also increased in order to reduce sourcing costs. Notably, after China entered the World Trade Organization (WTO) in 2004, global retailers invested in building a purchasing office and logistics center for direct sourcing from China. For example, Walmart built a logistics center for footwear in Quanzhou City, China, in 2005, and Aeon established a sourcing center in Shenzhen, China, in 2004. In addition, it was not only general merchandise stores such as supermarkets and department stores that began operating and sourcing internationally but also fast fashion retailers such as ZARA and H&M; moreover, these retailers of private label apparel were more successful at controlling their value chain and launching their stores worldwide than general merchandise stores.

Retailers expanded their stores internationally and increased the volume of direct sourcing as a result of their increased buying power in countries with lower labor costs. Fast fashion retailers, in particular, have contributed to the growing global competitiveness with their own brands in terms of sourcing, and, for example, Japanese department stores are now struggling to maintain their own value chains and competitive advantages in the face of this current trend of global sourcing. Few studies have so far investigated the impact of this sourcing competition among manufacturers on global retailers or the relationship of inter-industrial competitiveness between retailers and clothing companies. This chapter, therefore, focuses on the links between the fashion industry—including textile and clothing companies—and the retail industry and tackles the following questions from a historical perspective: How have Japanese department stores built competitive advantage with clothing companies since the 1960s, how have they responded to the global competition between manufacturers, and how have they found the shifting competitive business environment in terms of sourcing?

1 Globalization in the Fashion Industry

1.1 The Development of Chinese factories

In the 1980s, Japan, Italy, and France held leading positions in the fashion industry for textile production, while Hong Kong, Italy, and the United States were global leaders in clothing, as shown in Figures 8.1 and 8.2. However, in the 1990s, these leading positions shifted to China, and then to Turkey since 2000. China has increased its exports of both textiles and clothing since the 1990s. In 1980, Japan exported $5.1 billion of textiles throughout the world (almost twice that of China's exports of $2.5 billion), making it a global leader in the industry at the time. While Japanese exports have remained stable in the years that followed, China increased its textile exports to $7.2 billion in 1990, $41 billion in 2005, and $111.6 billion in 2014, which is about 10 times that of other leading countries such as Italy, South Korea, Turkey, and the United States in 2014. China similarly increased its exports of clothing from $1.6 billion in 1980 to $36 billion in 2000, and to $186.6 billion in 2014. Turkey also increased its exports from $0.1 billion in 1980 to $8.4 billion in 2014, and France increased its exports from $2.3 billion in 1980 to $11.6 billion in 2014. However, the huge scale of the development in China distinguishes it from other countries, and it has forced the entire textile and clothing production system to change radically.

There are two main reasons for the rapid expansion of the Chinese textile and clothing industry. First, Deng Xiaoping visited southern China, including Shanghai and Shenzhen, in 1992 and indicated that China should open up its economy to the rest of the world. Then, China introduced a policy of socialist market economy and promoted direct foreign investments, and the Chinese textile and clothing companies began establishing joint ventures with Japanese, American, and European companies. As many previous

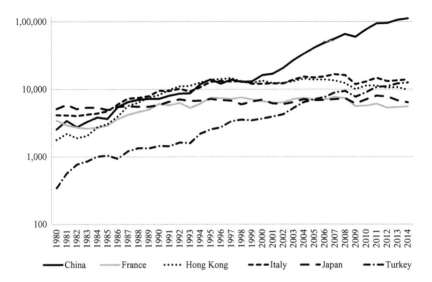

Figure 8.1 Exports of Textile, 1980–2014 (millions of US dollars)
Source: OECD.

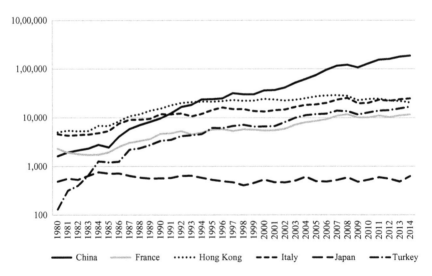

Figure 8.2 Export of Clothing, 1980–2014 (millions of US dollars)
Source: OECD.

studies have indicated, it was crucial for the textile industry to use cheap labor in order to make a profit (Dicken 1998; Lane and Probert 2009). For foreign companies, China represented an excellent means of sourcing low-cost labor and generating an attractive return. For Chinese factories, these foreign partners provided advanced skills for producing textiles and clothing. Chinese companies were, therefore, able to offer competitive prices compared with other countries, and the Chinese economy developed along with the growth of these textile and clothing joint ventures.

Second, Chinese factories became large vertically integrated. According to data from Mergent Online, Chinese clothing factories producing men's coats and business suits are much bigger than Italian factories. About 69% of Italian factories producing men's coats and suits are small companies with 10 or fewer employees. By comparison, about 63% of Chinese factories are larger companies with 51–100 employees. In addition to being larger companies, these factories are integrated vertically, so they include the whole production line from spinning and dying to sewing and packaging; in this way, they achieve economies of scale.

As a result of its size and development, China can offer competitive prices for manufactured products in a globalized market. This new competition with Chinese factories has changed the traditional structure of the division of labor in the fashion industry (Richardson 1996). Japanese factories, in particular, started to look for suitable partners to establish joint ventures in China, initially to work on the sewing process, and later to work on the spinning, dyeing, and finishing processes; this was achieved with vertically integrated partners. Japanese manufacturers also began sending their employees to China to build an international division of labor. This has since contributed to the gradual hollowing out of the fashion industry in Japan (Itami and his Laboratory 2001). Moreover, traditional suppliers who imported material from Taiwan, Hong Kong, and South Korea lost their share of the US market from the 1990s, and they subsequently shifted to low-cost production countries such as China (Sen 2008). In this way, the fashion industry has relocated to countries with a low-cost workforce, as businesses have reorganized themselves with an international division of labor made possible through globalization.

1.2 The Growth of Fast Fashion Retailers

Traditional retailers sell products they purchase from manufacturers or wholesalers, and their wide and original range of merchandise is crucial for attracting customers. However, GAP, Esprit, and The Limited were the first full-scale fashion retailers who began selling their own private labels in the late 1970s. They reduced the proportion of branded products they stocked, such as Levi Strauss, to avoid a price competition with other retailers who sold the same products and then introduced their own brands; these were designed and produced by sharing data within the value chain on customer fashion trends, type and amount of stock sold, and current operational capacity of each manufacturing factory (Azuma 2010; Li 2009). Since the 1980s, fashion retailers, for example, Laura Ashley and Next, increased the number of their outlets, launched overseas stores with their own concepts, and developed internationally. The buying power of these fashion retailers grew tremendously, and they became very powerful actors. As a result, manufacturers needed to respond to this new demand from retailers as quickly as possible (Dicken 1998).

Subsequently, fashion retailers who could control and grow their manufacturing of private labels developed into fast fashion retailers. Fast fashion retailers introduced a new business model to create fast-cycle fashion: They do not directly invest in design but are instead inspired by the most attractive and promising trends spotted at fashion shows. Fast fashion has the following characteristics. First, fast fashion has a rapidly increasing number of stores worldwide—preferably directly owned and operated outlets—so they can reach more and more customers around the globe. Second, fast fashion needs to connect customer demand with the upstream operations of design, procurement, production, and distribution through the development of information infrastructure. Third, fast fashion requires short development cycles, rapid prototyping, small batches, and variety, so that customers are offered the latest designs in limited quantities that ensure a sort of exclusivity. Fourth, fast fashion needs a very fast and highly responsive supply chain to be able to deliver with enough frequency (Tokatli 2008).

The big change was sparked by the growth of fast fashion retailers since the 1990s.[1] These currently include many different retailers such as ZARA, which has its own factories in Spain and Portugal, and H&M, which outsources the production process but controls its suppliers (Saito 2014). In order to control the entire supply chain, all of their products are private labels. The Japanese fast fashion retailer UNIQLO also shifted from branded products to its own labels in the 1980s and built its production base in China, later adding production bases in other developing Asian countries such as Bangladesh (Azuma 2011).

There are two aspects to this innovation: a new type of retail outlet and a new type of sourcing, both of which are closely interlinked. Fast-cycle merchandise is based on a model of mass distribution in which a large quantity of products are divided into small batches of display products at stores all over the world. At the point of sale, a variety of products are displayed with their prices, the latest fashion items are sold at short intervals with quick delivery, and dead stock is reduced by sharing customer data with suppliers through improvement in communication technology (Bhardwaj and Fairhurst 2010). As retailers sell large quantities of each particular design of clothing all over the world, they have a very fast turnover and do not replenish stocks once they are sold out in stores; in this way, customers feel confident that the designs they buy are not likely to be mirrored by others.

At the manufacturing level, fast fashion retailers build a value chain to produce a wide variety of products in large quantities using large manufacturers, mainly in China. ZARA, for example, takes two months to prepare the materials and make the first products for each season, and it can then continue to add high-selling products to its points of sale for three weeks. This means that in the mid-season, there are still plenty of high-selling products in stores to meet consumer demand (Saito 2014). H&M has introduced lines of clothing between basic clothing and high fashion; it starts by preparing the basic products for the next season a whole year in advance, and it outsources production of large quantities of each product to factories in countries with low labor costs to create economies of scale. For high-fashion products, H&M can respond in just two weeks at the earliest from designing the product to delivering it to the store, thus benefiting from economy of speed (Toba 2011). Fast fashion retailers, therefore, take the initiative to control their product quality and schedule and reduce all dead stock within the chain.

This collaboration between fast fashion retailers and large suppliers has other competitive advantages in addition to offering lower sales prices. Fast fashion retailers expect that bigger suppliers are more innovative than smaller suppliers (Azuma 2011; Fujioka 2016). These retailers, which have strong negotiating power due to the volume of their purchases, have taken the initiative to source their merchandise from innovative textile companies and clothing factories. Fast fashion retailers make good partners for these textile companies and clothing factories because their sales are steadily increasing, and these suppliers can work more efficiently with a single fast fashion partner. These retailers do present their suppliers with a challenging task, as it is difficult to respond quickly to their requirements; however, if the suppliers can successfully respond to the challenges, then they also have a chance to increase their sales and benefit from a source of innovation. This arrangement works to build a strong competitive advantage over other value chains.

For example, the partnerships between M&S and its pilot factories for 'Plan A' and between UNIQLO and Toray for 'Heattech' underwear are good examples of mutually beneficial partnerships between global retailers and large suppliers. M&S launched its 'Plan A' project to consider the environmental condition of our planet and limit emissions of carbon dioxide and other greenhouse gases. For this project, M&S reviewed all its suppliers and henceforth dealt with only those suppliers who could meet their new high environmental standards. In this way, M&S developed environmentally friendly products and led a sustainable form of development with its suppliers (Cuthbertson 2011; Grayson 2011).

UNIQLO also challenged tradition by creating new functions for clothing rather than just fashion. Its collaboration with manufacturers of advanced textile technology to create new textiles and materials means that UNIQLO can lead the creation of its own fashion (Choi 2011a, 2011b). One example is the Heattech fabric, a unique heat-retaining material created in collaboration with Toray, a leading Japanese textile company; another example is stretch jeans, which were developed with Kaihara, a leading Japanese denim company. UNIQLO's launch of innovative products with its manu-facturers results in both partners enjoying increased sales. Indeed, the cumu-lative sales of Heattech recorded the sale of almost 300 million pieces in 2011, following its initial launch in 2003 and its subsequent introduction of new fabric qualities such as stretch, antistatic, and antibacterial (UNIQLO 2012). UNIQLO also successfully achieved a low level of production failure with these new products with Toray (Azuma 2013). Innovations such as these often originate via mass production from global retailers such as fast fashion stores rather than from small, high-quality companies (Chandy and Tellis 2000; Itami and his Laboratory 2001). This is another source of com-petitive advantage for fast fashion retailers and suppliers.

2 Unique Development of Japanese Department Stores

2.1 *Increasing Sales in Department Stores alongside the Growing Fashion Industry*

Department stores were big players for fashion retailers in Japan. They espe-cially dominated the high-end market, and new fashion trends have come directly from department stores. Large clothing companies originally worked for department stores before fast fashion retailers emerged in the 1990s. Japanese department stores developed along a very different path from fast fashion retailers. They began increasing their sales along with the grow-ing clothing companies in the 1960s, when ready-to-wear clothing became popular in Japan. Ready-to-wear clothing formed the largest portion of sales in department stores, overtaking those of silk draperies for kimonos. Sales then increased dramatically in the 1970s and grew to over 60% of the total sales in department stores (Japan Department Stores Association 1980).

With the increased sales, new clothing wholesalers developed; these included established textile companies that transferred to ready-to-wear lines as well as newcomers. These companies began to hire in-house designers and oversee the entire production process from raw textiles to the finished product. The Japanese fashion industry was divided into sev-eral processes including spinning, dyeing, weaving, sewing, and finishing, and most of these factories were small or medium-sized companies. Tra-ditionally the textile wholesalers who controlled the production process within the major production area had control over the whole value chain from spinning to selling; however, new clothing wholesalers took over this control due to their understanding of consumer demand for ready-to-wear clothing at the point of sale. These new clothing wholesalers—located in the center of principal markets such as Tokyo and Osaka—were bigger than the clothing manufacturers and managed supply and demand in the fashion market.

In the 1970s, clothing wholesalers and department stores successfully built a win-win relationship. With a consignment and concession sales structure, department stores could sell a variety of products on a sale or return basis and renew their product portfolio without the risk of having to increase their stock; meanwhile, wholesalers could control the point of sale for their own merchandise, and they received direct feedback from their customers through the sales staff they employed in the stores. This relationship worked out very well and was the driving force for the development of the fashion market in Japan in the 1970s and 1980s (Takaoka 1997).

Once department stores' clothing sales increased and it became a common product for mass customers, the classification of sales areas changed. At the time, the sales areas were divided according to product category, with separate sections for skirts, shirts, trousers, and so on, which were produced by several different manufacturers. While department stores wanted to increase their clothing sales, each wholesaler also wanted to boost its own sales. For this reason, clothing wholesalers adopted a marketing strategy that presented their own concepts of different types of clothing. For example, a particular shirt and pair of trousers were coordinated with a new concept of 'urban casual' within a single sales area. Department stores, therefore, reorganized their sales areas from product categories to brand concepts. Clothing wholesalers adopted a particular image to present their products and were keen to foster customers who were loyal to their brand.

Every clothing company, therefore, built many product brands and expanded its sales areas with them in the 1970s (Oyamada 1984). With this variety of product brands, customers recognized and became loyal to different brand names, so department stores easily expanded their merchandise. By introducing many different brands within a single store, it would take much longer to reach a saturation point for each brand. This was the multi-brand strategy of clothing wholesalers in department stores. As a result, the variety of product lines contributed to the increase in their total sales, even though the sales of each brand are subdivided into many product brands. The combined sales of the clothing departments of all department stores amounted to ¥754 billion in 1970, increasing to ¥2.4 trillion in 1980 (Japan Department Stores Association 1970; 1980). The top clothing wholesaler in Japan, World Co. Ltd. (World), had sales of around ¥232 billion in 2003, yet the sales of its top brand accounted for only ¥26.6 billion (World 2003). World was established in 1959 and rapidly introduced many brands with the increasing sales areas of department stores since the 1980s; for example, it launched an average of nine new brands per year in the late 1980s and an average of 13 new brands in the early 2000s, although only a few of these brands remained on the market each year, as consumers were always looking for new types of products (World 2009). This multi-brand strategy was the driving force for the development of both department stores and clothing companies, and it shaped the Japanese fashion industry until the 1980s.

2.2 *The Changing Value Chains of the Japanese Fashion Industry*

The global shift in the fashion industry had a great impact on Japanese department stores. In 1991, about 80% of Japanese clothing products were made in Japan, and during this time, department stores and clothing companies competed within a domestic market. However, by 1997, this figure had decreased to 60% as clothing production in China boomed under globalization (Ministry of International Trade and Industry 1999); clothing companies, therefore, had to begin competing with large global companies. Manufacturers looking for the most efficient way to make their products realized that China was extremely well placed to offer a low-cost labor force that could handle the large-scale production of clothing for a mass market. Wholesalers retained their domestic design division but started to collaborate with Chinese sewing factories and wholesalers. Retailers who targeted the lower mass market, such as supermarkets and discount stores, could gain the advantage of using Chinese manufacturers with their appealing low prices; however, department stores needed to differentiate themselves from these stores, and thus they shifted to catering to much more high-end customers with exclusive Japanese products.

In order to respond to this globalization of the fashion industry and to avoid the hollowing out of this industry in Japan, the Japanese government implemented the industrial policies called for by the fashion industry (Matsushima and Committee on the History of Japan's Trade and Industry Policy 2012). As Chinese factories became larger and larger and focused on mass production with vertical integration, the Japanese government suggested that Japanese factories should focus on manufacturing a wide variety of products in small quantities with a fast product cycle. Japanese fashion industries, including retailers and manufacturers, did not want to get involved in a price competition with Chinese companies. Therefore, leading clothing wholesalers, such as World and Onward Kashiyama, introduced a flexible production system with an information and communications technology (ICT) network within their supply chain, so that everyone from retailers to manufacturers could share data and work effectively together to create a quick ordering system.

Clothing companies generally start working on each new fashion season a year in advance in Japan. Designers and merchandisers at the wholesalers need to plan ahead for the next season and decide which designs to use, what kind of materials they will need, where they will produce the clothing, and in which factories they will work. They need to anticipate the demand for the next season, set a production schedule, and then make and stock their products. Manufacturers want to reduce dead stock but also have enough products in their stores to avoid running out of stock. However, it is very difficult to anticipate consumer demand a year in advance, and there will inevitably be some dead stock with a make-to-stock manufacturing system.

To deal with this problem, clothing wholesalers attempted to postpone their production decisions and reduce this dead stock. World, for example, built an effective flexible production system in 1993 (Kato 1998). Manufacturers began producing 70% of the anticipated demand for the season and left the remainder as half-finished products such as textiles and undyed jumpers. After tracking the sales of these products and listening to customer responses, clothing wholesalers analyzed sales data and feedback from their own sales staff and adjusted the production plan to fit the actual demand within a single season. For example, World gathered sales data from all its stores on Mondays. On Tuesdays, the marketing, merchandising, production, and sales staff all came together to analyze these data and adjusted their production and merchandising plans for the next two weeks. Then on Fridays, the products they ordered two weeks ago would be displayed in the stores. In this way, Japanese clothing wholesalers reduced their dead stock and built a quick response production system with manufacturers. Nonetheless, they used this approach with their existing suppliers rather than reorganizing their supply chains and did not respond properly to the global shift in the fashion industry as fast fashion retailers did (Fujioka 2016).

3 The Growth of Fast Fashion Retailers and Department Stores' Response

3.1 Department Stores' Response to the Growth of Fast Fashion Retailers

Inditex, which operates ZARA, has developed effectively since the 1990s: its sales were €1.6 billion in 1998, €2.6 billion in 2000, and €16.7 billion in 2013 (Inditex 1998; 2000; 2013). The combined sales of the clothing department of all department stores in Japan totaled about €16 billion in 2013, which was the figure for Inditex's total sales in 2013 (Japan Department Stores Association 2013). This means that Inditex sources the same volume of products as all Japanese department stores combined. This involves indirect competition for suppliers who collaborate with other companies to purchase merchandise in larger quantities. While fast fashion retailers have built a win-win relationship with Chinese firms, which use a low-cost labor force at their vertically integrated, large factories, Japanese department stores are too small to compete with them.

For example, ZARA has only five sub-brands—ZARA WOMEN, ZARA BASIC, ZARA TRF, ZARA MEN, and ZARA KIDS; UNIQLO also reduced its total branded products from 400 stock keeping units (SKU) to 200 SKU and increased its ordering units when it decided to shift to its own labels in 2000 (Saito 2014). In contrast, the leading department store, Mitsukoshi, had 220 brands only for women's clothes within an anchor store in 2016 (Mitsukoshi 2016); the leading clothing company, World, had 120 sub-brands in 2009 (World 2009), and so they were less competitive with their suppliers. This is the main reason for the gap in transaction volumes between department stores and fast fashion retailers.

To understand the solution to this problem of high-volume sourcing, let us consider the following example. A Swiss department store, Manor, has responded to the new strategy of global sourcing by collaborating with other European department stores. Manor is the largest department store in Switzerland. Its market share of department store sales in Switzerland is around 60% and that of all retail sales in Switzerland is almost 5%. This means that Manor has quite a large share of the Swiss retail market. Manor's defining feature is its high sales of private label products, which are about 40% of its total sales. From the beginning of its business in 1902, it launched many private labels into its market—from clothing to household products and foods. Manor understands its domestic market and customers' lifestyles better than anyone does, and it uses this knowledge to design its own style of products (Fujioka 2014).

In 2003, ZARA opened its first store in Switzerland and then went on to increase the number of its stores. Because ZARA's products are in the same price bracket as those of Manor, this fast fashion store gradually began competing with Manor. Before that, H&M began launching its stores in 1978 and it affected the retail market in Switzerland, however, in terms of sourcing, ZARA had a huge impact on Manor. It has strong private-label product lines, while most other department stores have expensive branded products. Because of this, Manor first needs to compete with fast fashion retailers at the point of sale; second, it needs to compete to provide the best-value products and to collaborate with good-quality upstream companies. Manor competes with ZARA's supply chain, in which it plays a strong role through its design and manufacturing process.

Despite its leading position in the Swiss retail market, Manor is too small to compete with the large lot production system of Chinese clothing factories. As its low prices are crucial for a competitive advantage over fast fashion, about 80% of its clothing was imported from China in 2005 (*HandelsZeitung* 30 March 2005). However, the sales of Manor, the largest Swiss department store, amounted to just €2.3 billion in 2005, while the global sales of Inditex reached €6.7 billion in the same year. Manor has less buying power to negotiate with Chinese clothing manufacturers, compared with fast fashion retailers. Attempts at internationalization have not been successful for Manor. It tried to launch overseas stores in China, opening a pilot store in April 2004 in Shanghai and expanding to 15 stores in shopping centers across China (Manor Review 2004; *Neue Zürcher Zeitung* 7 Jan 2004). However, this did not work out well, and so Manor turned its strategic direction and focus toward China as a sourcing base (*HandelsZeitung* 15–21 April 2009; *Textil Wirtschaft* 2008).

Manor decided to increase its buying power by collaborating with other European department stores that had their own individual markets in order to purchase products in large quantities from low-cost Chinese manufacturers, who only deal with large lot production (Fujioka 2014). At first, Manor partnered up with Vroom & Dreesmann (V&D) in the Netherlands in 2008 and introduced its own brand, 'Yes or No,' which appeared in 62 V&D stores (Manor Review 2013). Manor then moved into partnership with Galaries Lafayette in France and Breuninger in Germany, and Manor now cooperatively buys large quantities of its private label products, while other European department stores can also purchase Manor's private labels on original equipment manufacturer (OEM) deals. As a result of this collaboration, Manor is able to benefit from the low-cost manufacturing prices offered by Chinese suppliers, and so remains competitive with the fast fashion industry, which does the same. Increasing the transaction volume in partnership with other department stores has, therefore, been the European department stores' response to the globalization of the fashion industry.

This collaboration has been successful for two main reasons. First, Manor and other European department stores are members of the International Association of Department Stores (IADS), so their managers frequently network with each other; they all know that they are not competing for the same target market. Second, Manor has strong private label product lines compared with other department stores, and it has an outstanding supply chain including a design team at its head office in Switzerland and a buying office in China (Manor Review 1997, 2004, 2007, 2011, 2013). Its buying office has connections with 480 suppliers who are mostly based in China, and it frequently communicates with the design team in Europe and factories in Asia. Its buying office in China then finds a suitable factory to make a trial model of the design, which is reviewed by Manor. Once the product is approved, the factory then scales it up to mass production. In this way, Manor is deeply involved in the production process and its own supply chain, similar to fast fashion retailers.

Consequently, European department stores have increased their production lots to benefit from low-cost sourcing. Before the year 2000, the clothing manufacturers for European department stores were based in European countries such as Italy and France. However, the market for clothing manufacturing in Europe has shrunk as a result of the competition with Chinese factories. European department stores then buy their clothing stock from Chinese suppliers. If they want to keep their prices competitive, they are left with no other option but to collaborate with each other. This was the solution of European department stores to address the new global sourcing competition in the fashion industry.

3.2 The Changing Competitive Advantage in Fashion Industry

Most Japanese department stores are bigger than Manor and other European department stores, and they target higher-income customers by selling much more expensive products. In addition, Japanese department stores do not consider themselves to be competing with fast fashion retailers. Therefore, it may be difficult for Japanese department stores to introduce the same strategy of collaborating with other department stores in terms of sourcing. However, Manor's case shows the extent of the competitive advantage of fast fashion retailers over department stores, which are severely affected by the sourcing methods of fast fashion retailers in addition to the competition from their stores at the points of sale.

Fast fashion retailers have a very different strategy from Japanese department stores: While fast fashion retailers focus on the latest fashion and produce their own private labels for an ever-increasing global market, most Japanese department stores focus on high-quality branded products for a domestic market. They also have different customers: consumers of fast fashion retailers in Japan are younger consumers in the mass market, while those of Japanese department stores are more conservative shoppers, mostly over the age of 40. Additionally, department stores usually select manufacturers who work very carefully with small lot productions through their wholesalers. Their ordering quantity is about 1,000 pieces for each item. In contrast, manufacturers of fast fashion retailers are large suppliers who have large and vertically integrated factories and produce several million pieces for each item. The strategy of fast fashion retailers is therefore in marked contrast with that of department stores.

Therefore, since the 1990s, the fashion industry has seen not only relocation of the main production region of the textile industry from Europe and Japan to China but also the restructuring of the value chain due to the introduction of large, vertically integrated Chinese clothing factories. This transformation to a global market and an integrated factory structure fits well with fast fashion retailers. Large Chinese suppliers can produce clothing in large quantities and with short development cycles, and they are the driving force of the development of fast fashion retailers. These retailers have become the perfect partners for Chinese suppliers, as together they are able to make value products efficiently. Some traditional companies think that fashion design is a creative and artistic process, and so it does not fit well with specific production demands for certain quantities and appealing functions. However, many manufacturers have now become involved in a sourcing competition with fast fashion retailers, except for a few haute couture manufacturers.

The difference between the merchandise of Swiss and Japanese department stores also affected their strategies. The Swiss and Japanese retail markets were particularly isolated from other global markets and were dominated by domestic retailers. The Swiss retail market developed uniquely with private labels of retailers such as Migros and Coop, as they were very familiar with the tastes and requirements of their domestic customers and could launch original and traditional products that fit with the Swiss lifestyle (Cohen 2005). Similarly, Manor developed its own private labels, although most department stores in the world mostly sell branded products. Since Manor mainly deals with private labels and is always looking for suitable suppliers, it faces intensive direct competition with fast fashion retailers in terms of sourcing.

Japanese department stores and wholesalers led the Japanese fashion market since the 1960s, as mentioned above. The structure of the Japanese fashion industry is very well suited for these department stores and wholesalers. With this relationship, the sales of department stores were ¥407 billion in 1960, increasing to ¥1.8 trillion in 1970, ¥5.7 trillion in 1980, and ¥9.3 trillion in 1990 (Japan Department Stores Association 1960; 1970; 1980; 1990). This distribution structure was the driving force for the development of the fashion retail market until the early 1990s, and it was a sustained competitive advantage of department stores in the domestic fashion market. Therefore, these Japanese department stores did not need to respond immediately in this new climate of globalization, because they mainly sold branded products that were sourced by wholesalers.

However, the competition between wholesalers for Japanese department stores and fast fashion retailers under globalization is becoming more intensified since the 2000s and this affects the competitiveness of department stores (Fujioka 2016). Japanese clothing wholesalers are struggling to maintain their long-term contracts with Chinese manufacturers because these Chinese companies now prefer to do large-scale, efficient business with fast fashion retailers rather than small-scale, more demanding work for Japanese wholesalers. Other Chinese manufacturers who have worked with Japanese department stores for a long time are now deciding to close their businesses and transfer to new industries, as it has become too difficult to maintain their low-cost labor force and competitive advantage in the face of competition from other developing Asian countries such as Vietnam and Bangladesh. As a result, Japanese department stores have now lost their competitive advantage.

Conclusion

This chapter investigates how fast fashion retailers impact department stores and how department stores have transformed their value chains in the face of globalization. It is clear that competition does not occur within a single industry but within linked industries. The development of Japanese department stores alongside their clothing wholesalers illustrates how these two industries have traditionally been separated in Japan in terms of sourcing. Following the establishment of fast fashion retailers, fashion companies compete with retailers, and retailers compete within their value chains including manufacturers and wholesalers. It is therefore important to identify the linked structure of the fashion and retail industries as the foundation of international competitiveness for department stores. While fast fashion retailers have built a strong partnership with Chinese suppliers and have developed globally, department stores are being strongly affected by the new globalized fashion industry and have needed to respond to these restructured value chains.

Many department stores worldwide are happy to remain in their domestic markets. However, even if department stores choose not to become global companies themselves, they still have global competition when it comes to purchasing their merchandise. As this competition has impacted not only their retail outlets but also their sourcing, the fashion industry has changed along with the new global value chains. Fast fashion retailers triggered this shift to global competition, and this new global fashion industry has affected department stores. Wholesalers in Japan took control of their merchandise between the 1970s and 1980s, and they were responsible for purchasing products for department stores during this time. This should have led to competition among wholesalers. These wholesalers depended heavily on department stores, and this was the competitive advantage of Japanese department stores within the value chain. However, since the late 1990s, one source of competitive advantage for fast fashion retailers has been having a production volume large enough to collaborate with highly skilled and low-cost Chinese manufacturers.

Buying power based on ordering quantity has been the foundation of the competitive advantage of fast fashion retailers. However, the source of this advantage is the innovative production system of fast fashion retailers with large manufacturers, not the buying power alone. Large manufacturers in China have now created innovations such as an environmentally friendly production system and a new type of fabric, and this provides a competitive advantage to their value chains. In turn, manufacturers that have not been able to collaborate with global retailers have lost their competitiveness and exited the market completely, shifting their focus to other businesses such as restaurants and the service industry. For retailers, it has become crucial to have a competitive advantage with the manufacturers of their products. It is therefore essential for retailers to get involved in building their own effective value chain in addition to working on their strategies at the points of sale.

Note

1 There are also negative aspects of the new business model of fast fashion retailers, such as the harsh working conditions of fast fashion factories in developing countries (Ito 2016; Klein 2000) and our new consumption habit of buying a huge amount of cheap clothing every season and then throwing it away after wearing it only a few times (Cline 2012).

References

Akehurst, G. and Alexander, N. 1995, 'The internationalisation process in retailing', *Service Industries Journal*, vol. 15, no. 4, pp. 1–15.
Alexander, N. 1990, 'Retailers and international markets: Motives for expansion', *International Marketing Review*, vol. 7, no. 4, pp. 75–85.
Alexander, N. and Myers, H. 2000, 'The retail internationalisation process', *International Marketing Review*, vol. 17, no. 4/5, pp. 334–353.
Azuma, N. 2010, 'Suichoku togogata iryouhin senmonten chain kourisho wo meguru ninshiki to jitsuzai—H&M no jirei wo chushin ni' [Issues on vertically

integrated specialist clothing retail—The case of H&M], *Aoyama Keiei Ronshu*, vol. 45, no. 3, pp. 197–215.

Azuma, N. 2011, 'Iryouhin senmonten gyotai no shijo senryaku to gyomu shisutemu ni kansuru kenkyu—UNIQLO (fast retailing) ni jirei wo chushin ni' [Issues on the strategy of specialist clothing retail and operation system—the case of UNIQLO (fast retailing)], *Aoyama Keiei Ronshu*, vol. 46, no. 1, pp. 121–158.

Azuma, N. 2013, 'The rise of virtually integrated specialist clothing retail multiples and the evolution process of retail format—from the experiences of UNIQLO: Fast retailing', *Proceedings of the 30th Sino-Japanese Modern Engineering and Technology Symposium*, pp. 1–13.

Bhardwaj, V. and Fairhurst, A. 2010, 'Fast fashion: Response to changes in the fashion industry', *The International Review of Retail, Distribution and Consumer Research*, vol. 20, no. 1, pp. 165–173.

Burt, S. 1991, 'Trends in the internationalization of grocery retailing: The European experience', *The International Review of Retail, Distribution and Consumer Research*, vol. 1, no. 4, pp. 487–515.

Burt, S., Dawson, J. and Sparks, L. 2003, 'Failure in international retailing: Research propositions', *The International Review of Retail, Distribution, and Consumer Research*, vol. 13, no. 4, pp. 355–373.

Burt, S., Mellahi, K., Jackson, P. and Sparks, L. 2002, 'Retail internationalization and retail failure: Issues from the case of Marks and Spencer', *The International Review of Retail, Distribution, and Consumer Research*, vol. 12, no. 2, pp. 191–219.

Carrefour 2015, *2015 Annual Report*. Available from: <www.ecobook.eu/ecobook/Carrefour/2015/view/RA-EN.html> [6 August 2016].

Chandy, R.K. and Tellis, G. 2000, 'The incumbent's curse? Incumbency, size, and radical product innovation', *Journal of Marketing*, vol. 64, pp. 1–17.

Choi, E. 2011a, 'Paradigm innovation through the strategic collaboration between TORAY & UNIQLO: Evolution of a new fast fashion business model', Working paper, 11–01, Institute of Innovation Research, Hitotsubashi University.

Choi, E. 2011b, 'The rise of UNIQLO: Leading paradigm change in fashion business and distribution in Japan', *Entreprises et Histoire*, vol. 64, pp. 85–101.

Cline, E. 2012, *Overdressed: The Shockingly High Cost of Cheap Fashion*, Penguin Group, New York.

Cohen, M. L. 2005, 'Migros: Migros- Genossenschafts- Bund' in T. Grant and M. H. Ferrara *International Directory of Company Histories*, vol. 68, St. James Press, Gale Virtual Reference Library. pp. 252–255. Available from: <http://go.galegroup.com.eur.idm.oclc.org/ps/i.do?p=GVRL&sw=w&u=erasmus&v=2.1&it=r&id=GALE%7CCCX3429500005&asid=0b0e6ec20585f3aeb0899bea71a2e1d0.> [20 Dec 2016]

Cuthbertson, R. 2011, 'Aiming to be the world's most major retailer through innovation: Interview with Mike Barry, Head of Sustainable Business, Marks & Spencer', *Retail Digest*, vol. 2010 (Summer/Autumn/Winter), pp. 64–71.

Dawson, J. and Mukoyama, M. 2006, 'The increase in international activity by retailers', in J. Dowson, R. Larke and M. Mukoyama (eds.), *Strategic Issues in International Retailing*, Routledge, Abingdon, pp. 1–29.

Dicken, P. 1998, *Global Shift: Transforming the World Economy* (3rd ed.), Paul Chapman Publishing, London.

Dupuis, M. and Prime, N. 1996, 'Business distances and global retailing: A model for analysis of key success/failure factors', *The International Journal of Retail & Distribution Management*, vol. 24, no. 11, pp. 30–38.

Fujioka, R. 2013, 'The pressures of globalization in retail: The path of Japanese department stores, 1930s–1980s', in M. Umemura and R. Fujioka (eds.), *Comparative Responses to Globalization: Experiences of British and Japanese Enterprises*, Palgrave Macmillan, London, pp. 181–203.

Fujioka, R. 2014, 'Oushu hyakkaten niyoru iryohin PB no tenkai' [The development of private labels in the European department stores], in T. Yahagi (ed.), *Dual Brands Strategies: NB and/or PB*, Yuhikaku, Tokyo, pp. 336–356.

Fujioka, R. 2016, 'Fast fashion no taito to hyakkaten no kiro: Apparel' [The development of fast fashion retailer and at the crossroad in retail competitiveness: Apparel industry], in T. Kikkawa, T. Kurosawa and S. Nishimura (eds.) *Global Business History*, Nagoya University Press, Nagoya, pp. 90–110.

Grayson, D. 2011, 'Embedding corporate responsibility and sustainability: Marks & Spencer', *Journal of Management Development*, vol. 30, no. 10, pp. 1017–1026.

Inditex 1998; 2000; 2013, *Annual Reports*. Available from: <www.inditex.com/investors/investors_relations/annual_report> [29 May 2014].

Itami, H. and his Laboratory 2001, *Nihon no seni sangyou: naze korehodo yowaku natte shimattaka* [Why did Japanese Textile Industry Decreased Their Competitiveness], NTT Shuppan, Tokyo.

Ito, K. 2016, *Fast fashion wa naze yasui?* [Why Are Fast Fashion Products Cheap?], Komonzu, Tokyo.

Japan Department Stores Association 1960; 1970; 1980; 1990; 2013, *Nihon Hhyakkaten Kyokai Tokei Nenpo* [Report on Annual Data of Japan Department Stores Association], Japan Department Stores Association, Tokyo.

Kato, T. 1998, 'Apareru sangyo niokeru seihan tougou no rinen to genjitsu' [Idea and reality of vertical integration in the apparel industry], *Kikan Keizai Kenkyu*, vol. 21, no. 3, pp. 97–117.

Kawabata, M. 2011, *Ajia shijo o hiraku: Kouri kokusaika no 100 nen to shijo groubaruka* [Opening Asian Markets: A Century of Internationalisation in Retail and the Globalisation of Markets], Shinhyoronsha, Tokyo.

Klein, N. 2000, *No logo: Taking aim at the brand bullies*, Flamingo, London.

Lane, C. and Probert, J. 2009, *National Capitalisms, Global Production Networks: Fashioning the Value Chain in the UK, USA, and Germany*, Oxford University Press, New York.

Li, S. 2009, 'Amerika ni okeru SPA moderu no seisei to hatten' [The development of SPA model in US], *Waseda Shogaku*, vol. 420/421, pp. 127–169.

Manor Review, 1997, 'Organisationstalent in Shanghai', September, p. 8.

Manor Review, 2004, 'Yes or No; jetzt auch in China', June, pp. 6–9.

Manor Review, 2007, 'donnons du style á la vie', December, pp. 4–15.

Manor Review, 2011, 'Sourcing', June, pp. 14–15.

Manor Review, 2013, 'Sourcing & Partnerships', April, pp. 24–25.

Matsushima, S. and the Committee on the History of Japan's Trade and Industry Policy 2012, *The History of Japan's Trade and Industry Policy, 1980–2000: Consumer Goods Industries*, vol. 8, Research Institute of Economy, Trade, and Industry, Tokyo. (in Japanese)

Ministry of International Trade and Industry 1999, *Senni vision* [Vision of Textiles], Tsuusan sangyo chosakai shuppanbu, Tokyo.

Mitsukoshi 2016, *Brands per each floor*. Available from: <www.mistore.jp/floor brand/list?pageNo=5&countPerPage=20&storeCode=50&brandSrcCtgId= 0002000> [21 December 2016].

Oyamada, M. 1984, *Nihon no fashion sangyo* [Japanese Fashion Industry], Diamond sha, Tokyo.

Richardson, J. 1996, 'Vertical integration and rapid response in fashion apparel', *Organization Science*, vol. 7, no. 4, pp. 400–412.

Saito, T. 2014, *UNIQLO vs ZARA*, Nihon Keizai Shimbun Shuppansha, Tokyo. (in Japanese)

Sen, A. 2008, 'The US fashion industry: A supply chain review', *International Journal of Production Economics*, vol. 114, pp. 571–593.

Sternquist, B. 2007, *International Retailing* (2nd ed.), Fairchild, New York.

Takaoka, M. 1997, 'Sengo fukkou ki no Nihon no hyakkaten to itaku shiire' [Department stores business in Japan between 1945 and 1956: Formation of the Japanese-style trade practices], *Japan Business History Review*, vol. 32, no. 1, pp. 1–35.

Textil Wirtschaft 2008, 'Manor: Die Macht in der Mitte', 47, pp. 24–27.

Toba, T. 2011, 'Fast fashion no jigyo system' [Operation system of fast fashion], *Sekai Keizai Hyoron*, vol. 658, pp. 89–98.

Tokatli, N. 2008, 'Global sourcing: Insights from the global clothing industry—the case of Zara, a fast fashion retailer', *Journal of Economic Geography*, vol. 8, pp. 21–38.

Toyota 2016, *2016 Annual Report*. Available from: <www.toyota.co.jp/jpn/investors/financial_results/2016/> [21 December 2016].

UNIQLO 2012, *Heattech and Ultra-Light Down Coat*. Available from: <www.fastretailing.com/jp/ir/library/pdf/presen120926_ht.pdf#search=%27%E3%83%A6%E3%83%8B%E3%82%AF%E3%83%AD+%E3%83%92%E3%83%BC%E3%88%88%E3%83%86%E3%83%83%E3%82%AF+%E6%9E%9A%E6%95%B0+%E7%B4%AF%E7%A9%8D%27> [8 December 2016].

Walmart 2015, *2015 Annual Report*. Available from: <http://s2.q4cdn.com/056532643/files/doc_financials/2015/annual/2015-annual-report.pdf> [6 August 2016].

World 2003, *2003 Annual Report*. Available from: <http://corp.world.co.jp/company/financial/accounts.html> [29 May 2014].

World 2009, *WORLD 50th Anniversary Book*, World, Kobe. (in Japanese)

9 "Swiss Made" but Global
From Technology to Fashion in the Watch Industry, 1950–2010

Pierre-Yves Donzé

Introduction

Literature in business history offers two main interpretations for tackling the issue of sources of competitiveness. On the one hand, there is big business, whose resources and organizational facilities make it a key actor in the world economy, as has been emphasized by Chandler (1994) and his followers. On the other hand, there is the perspective of industrial districts and clusters, which attaches greater importance to resources anchored in a region and to territorial economies (Sabel and Zeitlin 1984). However, there are also works which tend to transcend this opposition, one of the first being Porter (1990), which underscored that the competitiveness of multinational enterprises (MNEs) is also related to their localization in specific clusters and nations. Moreover, since the mid-1990s, several scholars working on industrial districts have researched the role of leading firms and MNEs within districts, and their role on overall regional dynamics (Markusen 1996; Colli 2002; Catalan & Ramon-Munoz 2013). In addition, other scholars stress the importance of geographically localized resources for MNEs (Dunning and Lundan 2008, pp. 594–597). The objective of this chapter is to contribute to this discussion on the importance of localized resources for the competitiveness of firms, as well as on the concept of national industry, using the case of the watch industry during the years 1945–2010 and focusing on the four main players (Switzerland, Japan, USA and Hong Kong), which represented around 65% of the world market in the 1950s (in volume, see Table 9.2) and a growing share until today. This chapter will discuss why and how an industry strongly rooted in national territories during the 1950s was gradually reorganized on a global scale during the following decades.

According to most scholars, the watch industry is a typical case where competition has been and still is based on nations and regions rather than enterprise. Literature has emphasized in particular Switzerland's domination of world markets since the late 18th century. Despite the emergence of competitors, in the United States in the 1860s to 1870s and in Japan between the 1960s through the 1980s, Switzerland was able to overcome crises and to re-establish itself as the world leader. The common explanation for this success stresses the necessity for a small nation to export—and then be competitive—and the organization of the Swiss watch industry as a cluster—or industrial district—concentrated in the Western part of the country (Landes 2000; Donzé 2011a). The attention given by scholars to nations rather than enterprises led some of them to explain the evolution of the global watch industry since the 18h century as a succession of dominant nations (Glasmeier 2000). In this narrative, a strong focus has been placed on the struggle between the Swiss watch industry and its Japanese—or even "Asian"—rivals. The association of Hong Kong and Japanese watch-makers as firms specialized in the production of cheap quartz watches, in comparison with the Swiss, is a common view shared by the majority of Western scholars. Indeed, many of them make no distinction when referring to "Asian manufacturers" (Stephens and Dennis 2000, 496). For example, Tajeddini and Trueman (2008) maintain that the Swiss watch industry "had been almost completely driven out of the low and mid-range sector of the market by low-cost, highly accurate quartz watches made in Hong Kong and Japan." Yet even if competition in this industry was mainly based on nations back in the 1950s, this chapter argues that major changes occurred in the following decades and resulted in a sweeping change towards competition between global firms. Accordingly, this chapter analyses the nature and the process of these changes and questions the current meaning of nations, regions and localization in the industry.

The choice of sources to tackle competitiveness in the watch industry is not neutral and greatly influences the output of the analysis. Two main kinds of data are available to scholars: foreign trade and production statistics for the various countries involved in this industry and the ranking of the world's leading watch companies.

First, the use of statistics sheds clear light on competition between the main watchmaking nations of the world between 1950 and 2010 (see Figure 9.1). This source makes it possible to identify three phases of development. First, the years 1950–1975 featured great stability, with the United States being the leading producing country but nearly absent from the world market (its exports amounted to a paltry 1.8% of production between 1950 and 1973) and thus not very competitive. Switzerland and Japan experienced steady growth and began to compete head on in the late 1960s. As for Hong Kong, its presence on the world market was still insignificant.

Second, the years 1975–1985 were a decade of deep upheaval, against the backdrop of the emergence of electronic watches. Whereas Switzerland was in stagnation, the American watch and clock industry entered a period of gradual decline which was to continue until 2010. This period marked the triumph of East Asia, with Japan establishing itself as the Number 1 producing and exporting nation, and of Hong Kong, which made a noteworthy entry into this market.

Third, the years 1985–2010 were devoted to the restructuring of international competitiveness, as reflected by the successful comeback of

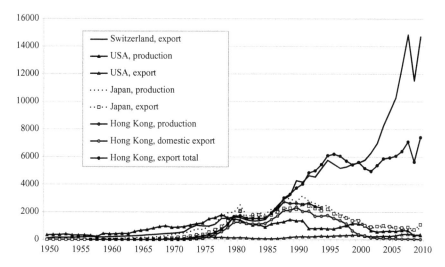

Figure 9.1 Production and Export of Watches and Clocks, in Millions of USD, 1950–2010

Source: *Statistique annuelle du commerce extérieur de la Suisse*, Berne: Administration fédérale des douanes (1960–2010); *Annual Survey of Manufactures*, Washington: U.S. Bureau of Census (1950–2010); *U.S. Exports*, Washington: U.S. Bureau of Census (1950–2010); *Kikai tokei nenpo*, Tokyo: MITI/METI (1950–2010); *Nihon gaikoku bokei nenpyo*, Tokyo: Ministry of Finance (1950–2010); *Hong Kong Trade Statistics Export & Re-Export*, Hong Kong: Census Department (1950–2010); *Hong Kong's Manufacturing Industries*, Hong Kong: Hong Kong Trade Development Council (1994–1996).

Note: Production for Switzerland is unknown.

Switzerland, which repositioned its watch industry towards luxury, and the remarkable growth of Hong Kong, no longer as a basis for production (which collapsed in 1990) but for the re-export of watch products to neighboring China, where Hong Kong's entrepreneurs located their plants. As for the US, it continued to slide, as did Japan, which started to go under.

Export and production statistics thus make it possible to highlight overall trends for the world watch industry and to differentiate between the development paths of different nations. Yet these data give an inaccurate overview, which only partially reflects the way in which competitiveness in this industry has actually evolved. This is because they were compiled by national authorities focusing on nation-based issues, as a result of which they offer a national vision of competitiveness. Using other sources gives a fundamentally different view.

The global ranking of the largest watch enterprises is another way to approach competitiveness in the industry. Owing to a lack of data for numerous enterprises not listed—especially in Switzerland—it is not possible to arrive at exact figures. In any case, some investment banks have compiled such rankings based on their own estimates. This chapter uses the ranking of watch companies (based on value, not volumes) established by the bank Vontobel, the most widely used by watch industry analysts. Table 9.1 shows the world's 20 largest watch companies, giving the production sites for their products. Two main features can be highlighted. First, this ranking shows that a very large share of manufacturing is in the hands of a very few firms. The top 20 companies have a combined 78.4% share of world markets, while the three largest have nearly half (45.8%).

Table 9.1 World's 20 Largest Watch Companies, 2012

Company	Country	Production centres	Watch sales (CHF millions)	Market share (%)
Swatch Group	Switzerland	Switzerland, France, Germany, Hong Kong, Thailand, China	6,955	18.3
Richemont	Switzerland	Switzerland	5,960	15.7
Rolex	Switzerland	Switzerland	4,500	11.8
Fossil	USA	Hong Kong, Switzerland	1,970	5.2
LVMH/Bulgari	France	Switzerland, Hong Kong	1,785	4.7
Citizen	Japan	Japan, Hong Kong, Thailand, China, Switzerland	1,490	3.9
Seiko	Japan	Japan, Hong Kong, Thailand, China, Singapore	1,295	3.4
Patek Philippe	Switzerland	Switzerland	1,150	3.0
Casio	Japan	Japan, Hong Kong, Thailand, China	800	2.1
Audemars Piguet	Switzerland	Switzerland	640	1.7
Chopard	Switzerland	Switzerland	600	1.6
Movado Group	USA	Switzerland, China, Hong Kong	465	1.2
Breitling	Switzerland	Switzerland	350	0.9
Franck Muller	Switzerland	Switzerland	300	0.8
China Haidan	Hong Kong	China, Hong Kong, Switzerland	280	0.7
Morellato & Sector	Italy	Switzerland, Hong Kong	250	0.7
Kering	France	Switzerland	250	0.7
Folli Follie	Greece	Hong Kong	250	0.7
Festina	Spain	Switzerland, Japan, Spain	250	0.7
Ulysse Nardin	Switzerland	Switzerland	220	0.6

Source: *Watch Industry*, Zurich: Vontobel Equity Research, 2013 and author's estimates for production centres.

Second, there is wide geographical diversity of firms. Most are headquartered in Switzerland (9), Japan (3) or the United States (2), but some are also based in countries where the watch industry is not particularly flourishing, like France (2), Italy (1), Spain (1) and Greece (1). What is more, only one firm is based in Hong Kong, whereas this city has become one of the leading watch exporters. Accordingly, a significant distinction may be made between producing and exporting nations, on the one hand (Figure 9.1), and the nationality of the world's largest watch companies, on the other hand (Table 9.1). This can be explained by the fact that most of the watch companies do not produce their own parts in-house, but rather source their supplies from other companies. Among the top 20, those companies which produce their own watches are in a minority: Swatch Group, a few Swiss companies specialized in luxury goods (Rolex, Patek Philippe, Audemars Piguet, as well as some of the companies held by the Richemont, LVMH and Kering groups, but only for some specific products) and the three Japanese watchmakers. All of the other companies in the top 20 distribute—and sometimes assemble—watches bought from Swiss, Japanese and Hong Kong watchmakers. Competitiveness no longer relies on the mastery of production technology, but rather on the ability to make effective use of global supply chains, as can also be seen today in other consumer goods industries like textile and fashion (Lane and Probert 2009; Campagnolo and Camuffo 2011). This difference between production sites and the main players explains the presence within the top 20 of watch companies established in countries with a watchmaking industry which is apparently not competitive in terms of export data (Fossil, Morellato & Sector, Folli Follie, and Festina).

The fundamental distinction between production sites and the nationality of the most competitive companies, which can be seen in the global watch industry at the beginning of the 21st century, is the outcome of a particular historical development. Indeed, this industry was largely organized on a national basis at the end of World War II. In the following sections, this article offers an analysis of the dynamics of this industry between the 1950s and 2010, with a view to identifying those factors which led to a radical change in the basis for competition.

1 The Global Watch Industry in the 1950s

At the end of World War II, the global watch industry was, broadly speaking, structured along national lines. The volume of Swiss production for the 1950s—an estimation based on export statistics, considering the small size of Swiss domestic market—amounted to nearly half of the total, while the top five nations taken together represented more than 80% (see Table 9.2). However, the figures published in Table 9.2 are for production volume and thus do not accurately reflect the competitiveness of each nation, due to the large variety of products, with some countries like the US specializing in

Table 9.2 World Production of Watches and Watch Movements, Millions of Units and %, 1950–1959

	Millions of units	%
Switzerland	348.4	48.2
USA	92.4	12.8
USSR	84.1	11.6
France	39.6	5.5
Japan	24.7	3.4
Other	134.1	18.5
World	723.3	100

Source: Estimation of the Federation of the Swiss Watch Industry published by Landes David S., *Revolution in Time: Clocks and the Making of the Modern World*, Cambridge: Harvard University Press, 2000 (second edition), p. 423.

the production of inexpensive, low-quality mechanical watches (called "pin-lever watches" or "Roskopf watches"); others like Japan opting for quality watches; and European countries, Switzerland included, producing both kinds of watches. Nevertheless, the key point highlighted by this table is the high concentration of production in a small number of countries, where this business was considered to be a "national industry" at the time. The national roots of watchmaking are essentially due to institutional factors.

At first, as far as Switzerland was concerned, the national character of the watch industry was a direct consequence of the cartel set up in the 1920s and recognized by the federal government in 1934 (Koller 2003; Donzé 2011a). Within this system, all enterprises involved in watchmaking in Switzerland were obliged to source their supplies of parts exclusively from other Swiss enterprises at price conditions defined by the cartel. The import of parts was strictly forbidden, except for a few French and German enterprises which had long-standing business relations with Swiss watchmakers. In addition, exports of parts and machine tools were strictly controlled, preventing Swiss watch companies from relocating their production abroad. Finally, the establishment and purchase of watch companies were subject to official authorization. This system, set up in order to maintain an industrial structure composed of small and medium-sized enterprises (SMEs) and to keep employment in Switzerland, explains the national character of the Swiss watch industry in the 1950s. While Swiss watchmakers did not invest abroad, except for sales subsidiaries, unlike most of the Swiss entrepreneurs of other sectors which organized globally early on (Müller 2012), inward foreign direct investment (FDI) was extremely rare. The very few watch companies with foreign capital were subsidiaries of American watch companies, established in Switzerland to secure their supplies of parts and movements and founded before cartelization, such as Gruen Watch (1903), Bulova Watch (1911) and Benrus Watch

(1927) (Richon 1998). However, these enterprises represented only a tiny share of the Swiss watch industry, which numbered 1863 companies in 1950 (Convention patronale 2008, p. 13).

In the United States, the national character of the watch industry was the twofold consequence of an "oligopolistic structure" (Glasmeier 2000) and of economic protectionism. The American watch industry in the 1950s was essentially limited to three companies: Bulova, Hamilton and Timex. These firms benefited from growing custom protectionism from the interwar years onwards, which became more pronounced in the 1950s. After World War II, the strategic importance of the watch industry on military grounds led to State backing. For example, Hamilton was very active in the production of war material during the Korean War (Glasmeier 2000, 184). As for Bulova, it appointed former General Omar Bradley as Chairman of its Board of Directors in 1958 (IDCH 2001). As a result of this proximity to State and of protectionism, American watch companies were not very interested in foreign outlets: exports amounted to a paltry 1.3% of domestic production in 1960.[1] The only exception to this national character of the American watch industry was the company United States Time Co. (Timex) (IDCH 1999), which was founded in 1941 to produce war material and which focused on the mass production of low-quality mechanical watches after the war. At the end of the 1950s, it adopted an active strategy of outward FDI and began to transfer production facilities abroad, stepping up the pace over the following decade.

The case of Japan was similar to that of America, even if the products were different. The Japanese watch industry was highly concentrated: the two groups Hattori & Co. (brand Seiko) and Citizen Watch production accounted respectively for 51.4% and 31.8% of national watch production in 1960 (volume).[2] Moreover, these two companies had all their production facilities on Japanese territory, and there were no watch companies with foreign capital in Japan. In addition, Japanese watch companies benefited from custom protectionism during this period, with imports being subject to quotas until 1961. As a result, the domestic market was the main outlet for this industry, which exported only 2% of its production in 1960.[3] However, the main differences with the United States were the absence of production of war material and the existence of cooperation and joint research between private companies, State agencies and universities (Donzé 2011b). This was instrumental in strengthening the feeling of a national industry developing to compete with other nations.

Accordingly, this quick overview has made it possible to highlight the existence of watch industries in several countries. Their national character was the consequence of a virtual absence of FDI and of protectionism, which safeguarded the domestic market for domestic companies. The State was a major player in maintaining such a structure, either on military grounds (USA), or to support employment (Switzerland) and industrial development (Japan).

2 The First Wave of FDI and Its Effects (1960s)

The organization of a deeply nation-based industry was challenged in the 1960s by institutional and technological factors, which broke down national borders and led to the first phase in the international division of labour.

One institutional factor which had an impact on industrial organization was the gradual phasing out of State protectionism. In Switzerland, the watch cartel, organized by the State since 1934, was steadily dismantled between 1961 and 1965, under pressure from the largest watch companies. They wanted to develop and rationalize their means of production in order to cut production costs and boost their ability to compete with American and Japanese companies, whose large-scale organizational structures enabled them to market cheaper products (Donzé 2011a). Moreover, the United States and European nations gradually abandoned their protectionist customs policies during this decade (Dirlevanger, Guex and Pordenone 2004). Consequently, the enterprises of the world's leading watch nations began to face growing competition while gaining new opportunities for expansion.

As for technological factors, they mainly consisted of the implementation of mass production systems for watchmaking. They were developed in the late 1950s and spread in the 1960s, through various process innovations, such as automation of movement production. However, final assembly remained difficult to automate. These new production technologies enabled companies to plan rationalization, realize economies of scale and ramp up production, all of which were essential push factors driving foreign expansion.

These changes in the institutional and technological environment led to the first wave of FDI which affected all of the watchmaking nations. Four cases may be singled out. First, a reference must be made to the emergence of the first real MNE in the watch business, with Timex, whose production amounted to 8 million pieces in 1960 and 22 million in 1969.[4] In 1971, it employed a total of 7,000 persons and its main production centres abroad were based in Hong Kong and Taiwan for Asia, as well as in Scotland (Dundee), England (Feltham), France (Besançon), Germany (Pforzheim) and Portugal (Chaneca da Caparica) for Europe (Blanc 1988, p. 45). These plants mainly produced watches for domestic markets, except those in Hong Kong and Taiwan, which supplied all Asian markets.

Second, the major Swiss watch companies moved to relocate production abroad. This was particularly the case of the company Ebauches SA, created in 1926 to control the production of movement blanks (i.e. movements without regulating parts), which attempted to extend its activities in Europe by successively purchasing two movement blank firms: Durowe in Germany (1965) and SEFEA in France (1967) (Ebauches 1973). In addition, Chronos Holding, founded in 1966 by the ASUAG trust (which controlled Ebauches SA in particular), the Federation of the Swiss Watch Industry and seven banks took a 19.9% stake in the capital of Gruen Industries in the United States (1967) (Richon 1998). Yet the foreign expansion of Swiss companies was still limited, as rationalization was first implemented domestically through M&A.

Third, Hong Kong emerged as a major venue for the production of parts and the assembly of watches for Swiss, American and Japanese companies (Donzé 2012). While the technology of automated mass production was possible for watch movements, activities relating to the production of external parts (cases, straps and dials) and final assembly were relocated to cheap labour regions, mainly in Hong Kong. As a result, the Federation of the Swiss Watch Industry intervened to improve the quality of parts made in Hong Kong. For example, in 1966 it signed a technical assistance agreement with the Federation of Hong Kong Industries.[5] Subsequently, the major Swiss watch groups invested directly in the British colony. Hong Kong became a key supplier for the Swiss watch industry. While Swiss imports of cases jumped from 1.6 million pieces in 1961 to 8 million in 1970, Hong Kong's share was growing fast: 21.9% in 1961 and 60.8% by 1970. As for the Japanese watch companies, even if they did not invest directly in Hong Kong at the time, they also relied on it as a major parts supplier. The value of Japanese imports of watch parts from Hong Kong soared, rising from 141,000 yen in 1960 to 1.3 billion by 1980.[6]

As for the assembly of watches, it led in particular to the opening of a subsidiary of the American company Timex Corporation, which founded Timex Hong Kong Ltd. in 1967.[7] Next, the Japanese group Hattori & Co. set up a production subsidiary, Precision Engineering (1968).[8] Yet Swiss watchmakers were not absent. For low-range models (*pin-lever watch*), for example, there was the company opened by one of the biggest watch companies in Switzerland, Baumgartner Frères Granges, BFG Far East (1970) (Blanc 1988, p. 148).

Thus, an industry based on outsourcing developed in Hong Kong during the 1960s. The number of enterprises active in watchmaking in the city jumped from 61 in 1960 to 229 in 1970.[9] Most were SMEs specialized in subcontracting and dependent on foreign big business.

Fourth, inward FDI in Switzerland developed, but almost exclusively from American firms. Bulova bought up two manufacturers, Recta (1963) and Universal (1966), while Hamilton purchased Büren Watch (1966) and Benrus took a minority interest in Ulysse Nardin (1965) (Richon 1998). For these companies, the objective was to enlarge their production facilities of high-quality mechanical watches for the American market, through the purchase of small, specialized manufacturers in Switzerland. Consequently, such FDI followed a logic consistent with the strategy developed at the beginning of the 20th century.

Accordingly, the first wave of FDI which could be observed worldwide in the watch industry during the 1960s led to an initial phase of international division of labour. Competitiveness on world markets was closely related to production costs, a factor which led companies to relocate parts of their production. This new industrial organizational structure was characterized by a strong hierarchy, with decision-making centres in the US and Switzerland and production subsidiaries embedded in a relationship of dependency, aimed at either horizontal extension of production, as in Europe, or vertical division of labour, as in Hong Kong. The organization of the largest firms tended to transcend national boundaries, but their management and ownership were still very much locally anchored.

3 The Impact of Electronics (1970–1985)

The most important changes occurred in the years 1970–1985, a period during which the local roots of the watch industry declined in favour of new actors. However, this sea change was not consistent with the first phase of internationalization seen in the 1960s; rather, it marked a major break.

These years are usually known as the period of the "quartz revolution" (Landes 2000, p. 364), a phenomenon which has been a focus of scholars' attention. Technology was the change which had the greatest impact, in the form of the advent of quartz watches. This product innovation had various effects on industrial organization around the world. One major consequence was that it put an end to the first wave of internationalization which had begun in the 1960s and had relied essentially on the expansion of low-range watch producers. The development of quartz watches made it possible to market cheaper, more precise products than pin-lever watches, which completely lost their advantage. Two of the world's leading watchmakers, who had been key drivers of the international division of labour, left the watch business. The Swiss firm Baumgartner Frères Granges (BFG) went into recession in 1975 and closed down in 1982.[10] As for Timex, it closed nearly all its foreign plants in the second half of the 1970s and converted to subcontracting production outside watchmaking (IDCH 1999).

The other American firms which played an essential role in internationalization also experienced difficulties due to quartz watches. Bulova and Hamilton found themselves facing unsolvable problems as a result of disastrous technical choices—the diapason watch for Bulova and the electrical watch for Hamilton. The watch division of the Hamilton group was purchased in 1974 by the Société suisse pour l'industrie horlogère (SSIH, a group founded in 1930, including in particular the watch companies Omega and Tissot), who wanted to acquire Hamilton's retail network in the United States (Sauer 1992). As for Bulova, it was taken over in 1976 by Stelux (see below) and sold a few years later to Loewe (1979). Its production centres in America (1978) and Switzerland (1982) were shut down (Richon 1998).

In Switzerland, this period of major changes is usually called the "watch crisis." Indeed, the volume of exports went from 24.2 million pieces in 1950 to 40.9 million in 1960 and peaked at 84.4 million in 1974, before dropping to an annual average of 31.3 million in 1982–1984.[11] As for the number of workers, it decreased from some 90,000 employees in 1970 to less than 47,000 in 1980 (Convention patronale 2008, p. 13). During this decade of recession, the Swiss watch industry experienced extensive restructuring, the most well-known instance being the merger in 1983 of the SSIH and the trust which controlled the production of movements and parts, ASUAG, giving birth to a new company, the Société suisse de microélectronique et d'horlogerie (SMH, Swatch Group since 1998), on the advice of the consultant Nicolas G. Hayek. Industrial rationalization also led to the closure of many enterprises, with the number of firms in the watch business declining sharply from 1,618 in 1970 to 634 in 1985 (Convention patronale 2008, p. 13). Nevertheless, foreign companies did not take advantage of this crisis to pour inward FDI into Switzerland: American firms left Switzerland and were not replaced by newcomers.

The Swiss watch companies primarily pursued the international division of labour to secure the supply of external parts. The largest groups strengthened their commitment to Asia, like SSIH which in 1971 purchased in Swiss Time Hong Kong, founded two years previously by a couple of Swiss entrepreneurs. In 1978, SSIH opened a second case-making plant, in Singapore, Precision Watchcase Ltd., in a joint venture with Japanese industrialists (Blanc 1988). In addition, the Swiss federal government slashed customs duties for imports of Hong Kong and Singapore manufactured goods by 30%, thereby encouraging the relocation of parts manufacturing to these countries.[12] SMEs also followed this strategy, in particular, case makers, who opened production subsidiaries in Asia in the 1970s. This was, for example, the case of Henri Paratte & Cie, who opened Parathai in Bangkok (1972), and Ruedin SA, who took a stake in Swisstime Philippines Inc. (1978) (Kleisl 1999, pp. 176–177). Consequently, the share of Swiss watches equipped with foreign cases increased sharply during this period.

However, the relocation of production by Swiss companies was limited by the adoption of a federal decree on the use of the "Swiss Made" label, which obliged Swiss companies to maintain some production activities in Switzerland—primarily the production of at least half of all movement parts and the final assembly—to qualify for this label.[13] This was a very pragmatic measure, aimed at reaping the benefits of the advantages of both the international division of labour for low value-added activities and the prestige linked to the "Swiss Made" label. For enterprises located in Switzerland, this was the beginning of a new kind of location advantage.

East Asia was the main region to take advantage of changes resulting from the advent of electronics, but the situation differed considerably between Japan and Hong Kong, contrary to what is usually stressed in literature. During this period, Japan carved out a position as the Number 1 watchmaking nation, and the watch industry was still firmly rooted in the national territory. The Japanese watch industry did not include any firms with foreign capital, and the bulk of the production was realized domestically. Like their

Swiss rivals, Japanese watch companies relocated only some external parts production abroad, mostly in Hong Kong and Taiwan.

The Hong Kong watch industry experienced a boom within this new technological context. The assembly, then the production, of analog quartz watches began in 1975, followed by digital watches the following year. Market share gains came at lightning speed: by 1976, Hong Kong's domestic production of four million quartz watches had made it the second largest producer in the world (volume), behind Japan (7.3 million).[14] The shift to electronic watches was very fast: they already accounted for 68.3% of the total value of Hong Kong's watch exports in 1980, then 88.2% in 1985 and 94.8% by 1990.[15] Above all, electronic watches made it possible for Hong Kong to establish itself as a leading watch nation. The total value of its watch and clock exports was USD 285.8 million in 1975, USD 1.6 billion in 1980 and USD 3.8 billion in 1990.

The industrial structure of the watch business also underwent a dramatic change. Quartz watches indeed enabled Hong Kong's entrepreneurs to overcome their technological dependency on traditional watch nations. It enabled the emergence of numerous new small independent companies. The redeployment of workforce expresses this shift. Between 1974 and 1978, while the overall size of the workforce remained stable, the proportion of employees in companies with foreign capital dropped from 49% to 25%. The emergence of newcomers weakened the position of foreign firms and reinforced the national character of this industry. Assembling electronic movements with imported components in Hong Kong and exporting finished watches to the world market became the new business model of this industry.

For Hong Kong watch companies, the shift to electronics let them free themselves from their historical dependency on large foreign watch firms. They were still dependent on external partners for the supply of CMOS chips and digital displays. Yet these suppliers were not watch companies, but rather electronic components makers.[16] Beyond technological issues, electronic watches played a key role in the emergence of Hong Kong's watchmakers because they gave them direct access to markets, something they did not hitherto have. Marketing and distributions skills were acquired relatively quickly. In 1987, Hong Kong watch companies were represented for the first time at the Basel Fair, the largest watch distribution event in the world.[17]

4 A New Basis for Competitiveness: Global Supply Chains (Since 1985)

Organizational changes in the world watch industry in 1970–1985 led to the emergence of global rather than national production systems. Two main models predominated.

First came a new generation of vertically integrated MNEs with production facilities organized globally and closely controlled by headquarters.

Their numbers were very low, as they essentially consisted of Swatch Group (Switzerland) and the Japanese companies Seiko, Citizen and Casio. Founded in 1983 through the merger of the two largest Swiss watch groups (SSIH and ASUAG), Swatch Group engaged during the second half of the 1980s in intense rationalization of production to restore its cost-competitiveness with its Japanese rivals (Donzé 2014). This strategy was marked by the opening of production subsidiaries in Thailand (1986), Malaysia (1991) and China (1996). Consequently, the number of employees in Switzerland dropped from about 80% in 1983–1985 to 54% in 1998. Besides, the production of these Asian plants was intended to supply not only Swatch Group's assembly plants in Switzerland but also world markets for electronic watch movements. During 2000–2004, overall Swatch Group production of Swatch Group averaged 120 million pieces (watches and movements), that is, some 20–30 million "Swiss Made" pieces (the level of Swiss exports at that time) and 90–100 million non-Swiss pieces.[18] The latter were primarily quartz movements sold to assembly makers outside Switzerland, mainly based in Hong Kong and China, who designed watches for a large variety of customers (OEM makers).

The Japanese watch companies show a similar profile and became global MNEs in the 1980s (Donzé 2017). The case of Seiko is very representative of this transformation. This group adopted a strategy of relocating assembly and production in Asia, especially China, in order to cut costs. In 1988, the subsidiary of Seiko Instruments Inc. (SII) in Hong Kong, Precision Engineering Ltd. (founded in 1968) began outsourcing the assembly of electronic watches to a new company founded in Guangzhou, Seiko Instruments (Whampoa) Factory. A second company was opened in 1996 in Shenzhen (Sai Lai Factory), then all SII production on Chinese soil was restructured in the late 2000s and centralized at a new plant in Guangzhou (2012). In addition, SII headquarters in Japan also opened some directly controlled production subsidiaries, in Thailand (1988), China (Dailan SII, 1989), Malaysia (1990) and South Korea (2004).[19]

As a result of this reorganization of the watchmaking production system, a growing share of watches and movements were manufactured outside Japan. This proportion increased significantly over time, rising from 17.8% in 1995 to 24.2% in 2000 and 45.8% in 2010.[20] Thus, in 2009–2010, nearly one out of two Japanese watches was made outside Japan. A second major effect of this radical change was that production volumes remained stable. Whereas production in Japan tended to decrease since 1998, the overall output of Japanese watch companies stayed more or less the same, despite the 2009 drop due to the world financial crisis, amounting to some 700 million pieces.

Second, a new organizational model appeared in the 1980s: global supply chains. This model is characterized by the absence of vertical integration and the division of labour between numerous independent firms (parts makers, assembly makers, designers, brand companies and distributors). Hong Kong watch companies are at the centre of these chains. The city's location advantage comes from the accumulation of knowledge since the 1960s: watch design, through the outsourcing of production of external parts; easy access to quartz movements; and proximity to low-cost labour-intensive production facilities in China. Hence, Hong Kong entrepreneurs positioned themselves as indispensable intermediaries in the manufacturing of watches under license (Berger ans Lester 1997). Whereas headquarters, together with product design and marketing, stayed in Hong Kong, the production and assembly of watches were gradually transferred to the economic zone of Shenzhen and to Dongguan, both located in Guangdong province. However, these Chinese plants did not supply all the movements used by Hong Kong watch companies, which also purchased Swiss or Japanese movements, depending on their customers' wishes (Trueb 2005, p. 364). Consequently, the domestic production of watches entered a phase of decline. After peaking at HK$ 13.5 billion in 1990, it amounted to only 7.4 billion by 1993.[21]

Until the mid-1980s, the growth of Hong Kong watch exports relied on the domestic production and assembly of finished watches. The share of re-exports out of overall exports, which was very high when Hong Kong was essentially a commercial hub (89.9% in 1960), declined dramatically from its 1970 total of 50.8%, amounting to 18.9% by 1985. The relocation of production facilities to China ended in the late 1990s and resulted in a very high growth of re-exports from Hong Kong, which rose from 36.1% in 1990 to 75.5% by 1995 and have stood at more than 90% since 2000. On the whole, however, these were no longer essentially watches re-exported to the entire Far East by Swiss, Japanese and American firms, as used to be the case until the 1970s, but rather products manufactured in China. Watch imports from China grew by leaps and bounds: USD 49.9 million USD in 1980 and 7.43 billion in 2010).[22] While the value of these imports accounted for only 17.4% of re-exports in 1980, they amounted to 63.9% in 1990 and have represented more than 75% since 2000.

However, even though some Hong Kong watch entrepreneurs distribute watches bearing their own brands, the key driver of their success has been OEM manufacturing activities. They supply several of the world's top 20 watch companies, such as Fossil (USA), Moretallo & Sector (Italy) and Folli Follie (Greece). Beyond these few examples, there is the fashion industry in general (Benetton, Burberry, Puma, Tommy Hilfiger, etc.), which has made watches key components of its diversification strategy since the 1990s (Degoutte 20057) and usually sources its supplies from Hong Kong watch companies, sometimes through marketing and design companies based in Switzerland.

5 The Importance of Being Swiss

In the context of an industry which has globalized intensively since the late 1980s, one must wonder what place Switzerland occupies and why watch production is still strongly anchored in the country. Since 2000, Switzerland has established itself as the unchallenged Number 1 export nation, with the value of watch exports rising from USD 5.6 billion in 2000 to 14.7 billion in 2010, while Hong Kong has stagnated at an average of USD 6 billion during this decade (see Figure 9.1). What is more, in 2012 Switzerland was home to many of the companies in the top 20: nine have their headquarters in the country, while eight others have production facilities on Swiss soil.

Switzerland's key role in the global watch industry is the consequence of an institutional factor which turned into a marketing resource during the 1990s, the "Swiss Made" legislation. At the time of its implementation in 1971, this measure designed to compensate for liberalization was aimed at keeping part of the production of Swiss watch movements in Switzerland to ensure their quality. At the time, the industry was dominated by mechanical watches (99.6% of Swiss watches exported in 1970)[23] and it was felt that only production in Switzerland was likely to maintain an image for good quality—and thus a good reputation—in the minds of business and political elites.

Yet the Swiss watch industry experienced a shift towards luxury in the 1990s, against a backdrop of strong growth for the luxury goods market since this decade. Global sales of this industry skyrocketed from 77 billion euros in 1995 to 173 billion in 2010 (Bain and Company 2012). This context offered an opportunity for the repositioning of the Swiss watch industry, whose change since the 1990s was characterized by a decrease in the volume of watches exported and a steep rise in their value. After reaching a new peak of 50.9 million pieces in 1993, the volume of watch exports plummeted to 35.9 million pieces in 2000 and 31.9 million in 2010.[24] During this same period, however, the value of mechanical watches became the key driver for growth. Between 2000 and 2010, mechanical watches went from 9.7% to 19.7% of the volume of exports, but from 47.5% to 71.9% in terms of value.[25] These changes in the nature of products reflect the radical shift in their use. Swiss watches are no longer useful objects bought for their precision; rather, they have morphed into luxury fashion accessories which convey an image of tradition, excellence and authenticity (Sugimoto, Terasaki and Nagasawa 2012). Hence, the persistence of Switzerland as a producing nation does not come from specific and traditional knowledge *per se*, but rather from the possibility to use location in Switzerland as a way to build a luxury brand whose identity is based on crafts and historical dependency. Hence, the "Swiss Made" label appears to be the guarantee that a watch made in Switzerland is a product of a tradition, and then a luxury fashion accessory.

In this context, the meaning of the Swiss Made legislation changed. Indeed, it no longer aims to maintain product quality, which can be easily achieved elsewhere in the world, but rather to guarantee the truthfulness of an essential marketing resource. Thus, the objective of possessing luxury brands in their brand portfolios has led numerous foreign watch companies to invest in Switzerland since the late 1990s, like the French luxury group Moët Hennessy Louis Vuitton (LVMH), which took over TAG Heuer and Zénith (1999); Fossil (USA), which bought up Zodiac (2001); Festina (Spain), which purchased Candino (2002); and China Haidan (Hong Kong), which successively acquired Eterna (2011) and Corum (2012).[26]

Conclusion

This chapter has emphasized the profound organizational change which occurred in the watch industry between 1950 and 2010, characterized by a shift from nation-based competition to a globalized industry. Yet this change was not a linear and natural process; rather, it resulted from a radical change in two kinds of factors—technological and institutional. They made a national industry more globalized, even if location still matters.

Two types of technological factors led to a global industrial organization. First, process innovation, with the mass production of low-range mechanical watches in the 1960s, made possible a first phase of relocation very similar to the classical model of the mechanical industry in the late 19th century, as embodied by Singer Manufacturing Company (Davies 1976). The companies Timex (USA) and BFG (Switzerland) restructured internationally and became major players in this industry thanks to their organizational capabilities. Yet this first phase of internationalization ended in failure, because it was predicated upon a product without a future.

Second, there was the key impact of electronics and quartz watches, developed in the second half of the 1960s and mass produced from the late 1970s onwards. This product innovation enabled any entrepreneur to acquire watch movements with ease: they suddenly became accessible and extremely cheap. Since then, their production has gradually been concentrated in cheap labour areas, especially in South-East Asia, then in China since the 1990s, which has made Hong Kong entrepreneurs indispensable intermediaries and suppliers of watches for nearly the entire world market—except for the so-called "Swiss Made" watches.

As for institutional factors, these were essentially legal measures restricting FDI and relocation, like the Swiss watch cartel or customs protectionism in Japan and the United States. Yet these measures were largely abandoned in the 1960s, allowing firms to restructure internationally. Even the Swiss Made legislation was a very pragmatic measure which has enabled semi-globalization of the production of watches by Swiss companies since the 1970s.

Beyond these technological and institutional changes, the major shift in the nature of the product itself must be stressed. The advent of electronics and social change has given way to new uses for watches since the late 1980s: they have stopped being useful objects bought and carried for their precision and have become fashion accessories, either cheap (Hong Kong made) or luxurious (Swiss made). Within this paradigm shift, brand management has emerged as the key factor for success in world markets, and international competitiveness has relied since the 1990s on the ability to build and manage a brand portfolio. Nevertheless, despite this major change, territorial anchorage and regional roots remain important. The emergence of global supply chains does not mean that the world has become flat. On the contrary, Switzerland and Hong Kong appear as major nodes within these networks, even if design, production and marketing are increasingly dissociated, as can be seen in other industries like textile and fashion (Lane and Probert 2009).

Finally, one can argue that firms, not regions or nations, compete on world markets. The idea that watchmaking was a "national industry" throughout the world during the 1950s, linked to locally rooted knowledge, results from the fact that institutional factors prevented inward FDI and made it difficult for national companies to move abroad. Hence, Switzerland was by far the world's most competitive nation at the time, due to the competitiveness of its firms. As they were based in a small country, they had to export—and then to face local competition abroad (Katzenstein 1985). The deep changes experienced by this industry during the 1960s and the 1970s led Swiss, Japanese and Hong Kong companies to adopt new kinds of cross-border organization, with global production networks. Since the 1980s, localization still matters, but for different reasons: for its role of intermediary between cheap labour and ordering parties, in the case of Hong Kong, and as a place to access marketing resources for luxury brands, in the case of Switzerland.

Notes

1 Own calculation on the basis of U.S. Commodity Exports and Imports, Washington: U.S. Census Bureau, 1960 and *Annual Survey of Manufactures*, Washington: U.S. Bureau of Census, 1960.
2 Own calculation on the basis of *Kikai tokei nenpou*, Tokyo: MITI, 1960 and production statistics provided by Hattori & Co. and Citizen Watch.
3 Own calculation on the basis of *Kikai tokei nenpou*, Tokyo: MITI, 1960 and *Nihon gaikoku boeki nenpyo*, Tokyo: Ministry of Finance, 1960.
4 *Kokusai tokei tsushin*, 1970, p. 477 and estimates of the Federation of the Swiss Watch Industry published by Landes (2000), p. 423.
5 Swiss Federal Archives, E2200.10 Hong Kong, Agreement between the Swiss Federation of Watch Manufacturers and the Federation of Hong Kong Industries, 2 November 1966.
6 *Nihon gaikoku boeki tokei*, Tokyo: Ministry of Finance, 1960–1980.
7 *Tokei no honkon shijo chosa hokokusho*, Tokyo: Nihon kikai zushutsu kumiai, 1980, p. 4.
8 "Seiko gurupu no kaigai senryaku,"*Noryoku kaihatsu shirizu*, vol. 87, 1982, pp. 14–15.
9 *Hong Kong's Manufacturing Industries*, Hong Kong: Hong Kong Government Industry Department, 1996.
10 *L'Impartial*, 9 September 1982.
11 *Statistique du commerce de la Suisse avec l'étranger*, Berne : Administration fédérale des douanes, 1950–1984.
12 Archives of the Union des Fabricants Suisses de Boîtes, Bienne, annual report, 1972.

13 *Ordonnance du 23 décembre 1971 réglant l'utilisation du nom «Suisse» pour les montres*, Berne: Conseil fédéral, 1971.
14 *Tokei no honkon shijo chosa hokokusho*, Tokyo: Nihon kikai zushutsu kumiai, 1980, p. 5.
15 *Hong Kong's Manufacturing Industries*, Hong Kong: Hong Kong Government Industry Department, 1996.
16 *Tokei no honkon shijo chosa hokokusho*, Tokyo: Nihon kikai zushutsu kumiai, 1980, p. 28.
17 *L'Impartial*, 2 February 2000.
18 Swatch Group, *Annual Report*, 2000–2004.
19 www.sii.co.jp (last access: 22 November 2012).
20 *Nihon no tokei sangyo tokei*, Tokyo: Nihon tokei kyokai, 2010.
21 *Hong Kong's Manufacturing Industries*, Hong Kong: Hong Kong Government Industry Department, 1996.
22 *Hong Kong Trade Statistics Import*, Hong Kong: Census Department, 1980–2010.
23 *Statistique annuelle du commerce extérieur de la Suisse*, Berne : Administration fédérale des douanes, 1970.
24 The historical peak of the volume of exports was reached in 1974 with 79.8 million watches, but a large proportion were low-range mechanical watches (47%), a product which collapsed after 1975. Subsequently, the volume of exports fell to a low of 28.9 million pieces (1983).
25 *Statistique annuelle du commerce extérieur de la Suisse*, Berne : Administration fédérale des douanes, 2000–2010.
26 *Le Temps*, 11 October 2001, 18 January 2002, 6 March 2012 and 25 April 2013.

References

Bain & Company 2012, *2012 Luxury Goods Worldwide Market Study*, Bain & Company, Milan.
Berger, S. and Lester, R.K. (eds.) 1997, *Made by Hong Kong*, Oxford University Press, Oxford.
Blanc, J.F. 1988, *Suisse-Hong Kong, le défi horloger. Innovation technologique et division internationale du travail*, Éd. d'En bas, Lausanne.
Campagnolo, D. and Camuffo, A. 2011, 'Globalization and low-technology industries: The case of Italian eyewear', in P.L. Robertson and D. Jacobson (eds.), *Knowledge Transfer and Technology Diffusion*, Edward Elgar, Cheltenham/Northampton, pp. 138–161.
Catalan, J. and Ramon-Muñoz, R. 2013, 'Marshall in Iberia: Industrial districts and leading firms in the creation of competitive advantage in fashion products', *Enterprise & Society*, vol. 14, no. 2, pp. 327–359.
Chandler, A. 1994, *Scale and Scope: The Dynamics of Industrial Capitalism*, Harvard University Press, Cambridge, MA.
Colli, A. 2002, ' "Pocket multinationals": Some reflections on 'New' actors in Italian industrial capitalism,' in H. Bonin et al. (eds.), *Transnational Companies 19th–20th Centuries*, Plage, Paris, pp. 155–178.
Convention patronale 2008, *Recensement 2007*, CP, La Chaux-de-Fonds.
Davies, R. 1976, *Peacefully Working to Conquer the World: Singer Sewing Machines in Foreign Markets, 1854–1920*, Arno Press, New York.
Degoutte, C. 2007, 'Stratégie de marques dans la mode: convergence ou divergence des modèles de gestion nationaux dans l'industrie du luxe (1860–2003)?', *Entreprises et Histoire*, vol. 46, pp. 125–142.

Dirlevanger, D., Guex, S. and Pordenone, G.F. 2004, *La politique commerciale de la Suisse de la Seconde Guerre mondiale à l'entrée au GATT (1945–1966)*, Chronos, Zurich.

Donzé, P.Y. 2011a, *History of the Swiss Watch Industry From Jacques David to Nicolas Hayek*, Peter Lang, Berne.

Donzé, P.Y. 2011b, 'The hybrid production system and the birth of the Japanese specialized industry: Watch production at Hattori & Co. (1900–1960)', *Enterprise & Society*, vol. 12, no. 2, pp. 356–397.

Donzé, P.Y. 2012, 'The changing comparative advantages of the Hong Kong Watch Industry (1950–2010)', *Kyoto Economic Review*, vol. 170, pp. 28–47.

Donzé, P.Y. 2014, *A Business History of the Swatch Group*, Palgrave Macmillan, Basingstoke.

Donzé, P.Y. 2017, *Industrial Development, Technology Transfer, and Global Competition: A History of the Japanese Watch Industry Since 1850*, Routledge, New York.

Dunning, J.H. and Lundan, S.M. 2008, *Multinational Enterprises and the Global Economy*, Edward Elgar, Cheltenham/Northampton.

Ebauches, S.A. 1973, *Industrie horlogère européenne: une expérience suisse: Ebauches SA—Lip, 1967–1973*, Ebauches SA, Neuchâtel.

Glasmeier, A.K. 2000, *Manufacturing Time: Global Competition in the Watch Industry, 1795–2000*, The Guilford Press, New York.

IDCH 1999, 'Timex', in *International Directory of Company Histories*, 25, St. James Press, Detroit, MI, pp. 479–482.

IDCH 2001, 'Bulova Corporation', in *International Directory of Company Histories*, 41, St. James Press, Detroit, MI, pp. 70–72.

Katzenstein, P.J. 1985, *Small States in World Markets: Industrial Policy in Europe*, Cornell University Press, Ithaca, NY.

Kleisl, J.D. 1999, *Le patronat de la boîte de montre dans la vallée de Délémont: l'exemple de E. Piquerez S.A. et de G. Ruedin S.A. à Bassecourt (1926–1982)*, Alphil, Delémont.

Koller, C. 2003, *"De la lime à la machine." L'industrialisation et l'Etat au pays de l'horlogerie. Contribution à l'histoire économique et sociale d'une région suisse*, Communication suisse et européenne, Courrendlin.

Landes, D.S. 2000, *Revolution in Time: Clocks and the Making of the Modern World* (2nd ed.), Harvard University Press, Cambridge, MA.

Lane, C. and Probert, J. 2009, *National Capitalisms, Global Production Networks: Fashioning the Value Chain in the UK, USA, and Germany*, Oxford University Press, Oxford.

Markusen, A. 1996, 'Sticky places in slippery space: A typology of industrial districts', *Economic Geography*, vol. 72, no. 3, pp. 293–313.

Müller, M. 2012, 'Internationale Verflechtung', in P. Halbeisen, M. Müller and B. Veyrassat (eds.), *Wirtschaftsgeschichute der Schweiz im 20. Jahrhundert*, Schwabe, Basel, pp. 339–465.

Porter, M. 1990, *The Competitive Advantage of Nations*, The Free Press, New York.

Richon, M. 1998, *Omega Saga*, Fondation Adrien Brandt en faveur du patrimoine Omega, Bienne.

Sabel, C. and Zeitlin, J. 1984, 'Historical alternatives to mass production: Politics, markets and technology in nineteenth-century industrialization', *Past & Present*, vol. 108, pp. 133–176.

Sauer, D. 1992, *Time for America. Hamilton Watch, 1892–1992*, Sutter House, Lititz.

Stephens, C. and Dennis, M. 2000, 'Engineering time: Inventing the electronic wristwatch', *The British Journal for the History of Science*, vol. 33, pp. 477–497.

Sugimoto, K., Terasaki, S. and Nagasawa, S. 2012, 'Emotional value communication strategy: Case of the Swiss Watch Industry', *International Symposium on Management Engineering*, pp. 147–152.

Tajeddini, K. and Trueman, M. 2008, 'The potential for innovativeness: A tale of the Swiss watch industry', *Journal of Marketing Management*, vol. 24, no. 1–2, pp. 169–184.

Trueb, L.F. 2005, *The World of Watches: History, Technology, Industry*, Ebner Publishing International, New York.

10 How to Sail a Sinking Ship

Adapting to the Declining Competitiveness of the European Shipping Industry

Stig Tenold and Jari Ojala

1 Shipping: A Special Case?

International seaborne transport is—by definition—an activity that crosses borders. Due to the nature of the service produced, the factors of production are much more mobile than in any other sector (perhaps with the exception of the airline industry). As ships and seamen work all over the world, their link to the 'home country' is often very limited and practically always weaker than similar links in any other goods or service production industry. Consequently, shipping is sometimes referred to as 'the world's first globalized industry' (Fink 2011). The shipping industry is, therefore, particularly relevant to the theme of this anthology—analyzing industries in a global environment, rather than studying firms in their local or national surroundings. The focus of this chapter is the declining competitiveness of European shipping in the face of global competition, as well as the political and business responses to this challenge.

The footloose nature of both the labor force and production capital implies that national and regional competitiveness can be challenged easily, as has indeed been the case in shipping over the last fifty years.[1] During the 15th century, Europe's position as the world's maritime center became clearly established, and this hegemonial role was maintained well into the 20th century. However, after World War II, and particularly after the shipping crises of the 1970s and 1980s, Europe's position was challenged by other maritime nations.

This chapter consists of two main parts. In the first part, the question of competition in world shipping in the post-war period is analyzed. After a short discussion of how competitiveness in this particular sector can be measured, we explain the leading role of European countries at the start of the period. Over the subsequent decades, European market shares became increasingly challenged, and the leadership shifted both from and within Europe. This development is discussed through an analysis of revenue generation and cost structures in shipping.

In the second part of the chapter, we show how institutional innovation—particularly the use of Flags of Convenience and the so-called 'open registers'—have been paramount in enabling shipping companies in European countries to maintain a relatively strong position. By adopting new regulations, which, in principle, enabled companies to slice up the value chain and outsource uncompetitive parts of the production process to low-cost countries, some European countries have managed to remain competitive. The shipping industry thus provides a case for studying general location choices of industries in global value chains, as discussed in the introduction of this volume.

2 Measuring Competitiveness in the Shipping Industry

What determines competitiveness in the shipping industry, and how can it be measured? Similar to most other industries, the answer for the shipping industry depends on the unit of analysis. The basis for the competitive strength of a shipping company differs from that of a nation, which again differs from the factors that make a region or continent competitive. At the same time, developments at the different levels of aggregation affect each other; it is difficult to have a competitive nation (on an aggregate basis) if the nation's companies are not competitive (on an individual basis). Similarly, Europe's competitiveness can be seen as the aggregate of various European countries' competitiveness. As we will show, 'European development' involves a variety of national starting points, trajectories, and responses. Most of our analysis is based on the 'typical' or 'aggregate' European experience relative to the rest of the world. The different developments are discussed in nationally-focused analyses; for example, the case of the Greek success is discussed in Harlaftis (1995), the British tragedy in Hope (1990), and the varied Nordic experiences in Tenold, Iversen and Lange (2012).

The competitiveness of the shipping industry based in a given country or region is a combination of the capabilities of its firms, the possibilities offered by the surrounding environment, and the demand of the markets in which they operate.[2] Moreover, the number and strength of the firms operating in the same geographical area and the vitality of related industries in the maritime cluster might have a decisive effect on competitiveness, as has been the case in some European countries (Sornn-Friese 2003; Wijnolst 2006).

Like in other chapters in this volume, the definition of industry competitiveness is problematic, and measuring competitiveness is challenging. In shipping, the drivers behind the competitiveness—in addition to factor costs—have been technological change and specialization, organizational innovation and development, and institutional changes. All of these changes occurred in globalizing markets with an undercurrent of growing demand for shipping services. Technological and institutional innovations led to declining freight rates that increased the market competition further. Moreover, during the post-war era, shipping companies also faced increased competition from other transport industries: Airplanes conquered the markets that had previously been dominated by passenger ships, whilst trains and trucks bypassed inland and coastal water transport in a number of countries (Boyce 2001). It is easy to forget that inland water transport may, in fact, also be international (Klemann and Schenk 2013). We, however, do not focus on this inter-industry competition but on the competition at the intra-industry level.

Due to the high mobility and easy transferability of the means of production (the ship), the size of a company's fleet should be a good measure of competitiveness. Shipping is characterized by strong cycles, resulting in relatively long periods of low revenues and ensuring that uncompetitive companies lose their capital. Thus, in the medium to long term, market forces will ensure that companies that are unable to compete will see their fleets dwindle, and the same will hold for nations and regions.[3] This will be the measure used—with some qualifications—in this chapter. However, before we discuss the development of shipping competitiveness and its basis, a few clarifications are in order.

When we use the term 'shipping,' we are concerned primarily with the provision of transport services from location A to B, and the term 'shipping companies' refers to corporations that organize and provide these services. At the end of the chapter, we will extend the analysis to include a brief discussion on 'the maritime industries' in a more general sense, saying a few words about the auxiliary service industries that make shipping possible. The bulk of the analysis, however, deals with shipping companies and their activities; in other parts of the maritime milieu, there are other competitive forces at play. Shipbuilding, for instance, does not have the same ability as shipping to combine capital and labor from different countries. Consequently, labor costs are extremely important, and this is partly an explanation of the greater decline of European shipbuilding than that of the European shipping industry.

Despite the massive loss of market shares for European shipbuilding, certain types of ships (high-tech, customized, and innovative) are still built in Europe. This is a result of the diversity of the industry and its market—such differentiation also pertains to the shipping industry. Just like in many other sectors, even though mass manufacturing has moved to low-labor-cost countries, high-cost producers and countries maintained competitiveness in luxury or high-quality niches, protected markets, and so on. This is the case for shipping as well. Indeed, among the various segments of the shipping market, there is substantial variety with regard to both the product that is produced and the ability to outsource parts of the production process.

The shipping industry is fairly diversified, encompassing small ships for transporting goods and passengers for coastal trade as well as tankers, bulk carriers, and container ships that trade between continents. Our focus is the international segment of the industry—ships performing transport services in international waters.[4] However, even this is a diverse activity, covering short and long trades served by a variety of specialized vessels for liquids, gases, commodities, and passengers.

This heterogeneity is relatively recent. At the beginning of the 20th century, the vast majority of the world's ships were versatile general cargo carriers that could carry all types of commodities or liners that carried passengers as well as cargo. Today, the situation is very different, as ships have become much more specialized.[5] Now, there is usually limited competition on the customer side—a cruise tourist would never consider booking holiday space on an oil tanker, and an oil cargo would never occupy a stateroom on a cruise ship. However, there are still important relations on the input side. Often, oil tankers and cruise ships compete for the same type of labor, capital, and berth space.

Another important consideration is the manner in which shipping services are produced. Shipping is a truly internationalized industry, in which the potential to source factors of production where they are cheapest is higher than in practically any other industry. Ships are usually financed in an international market, and today several nationalities may work onboard the same vessel, making the idea of a single 'home country' for the labor force absurd. At the same time, we see that there is a tendency of shipping companies (and supporting businesses) to be lumped together in certain cities and countries. This 'clustering' must, of course, be considered when we analyze shipping competitiveness.

As Figure 10.1 shows, the European share of the world fleet has dropped from more than 50 per cent to around 20 per cent during the past 50 years.

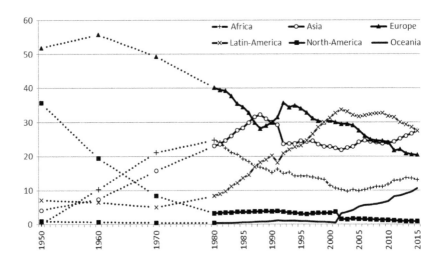

Figure 10.1 World Fleet by Flag, 1950–2015 (Per Cent Share of World Tonnage)

Source: Statistisk Sentralbyrå 1951, *Statistisk årbok 1951*, Oslo, p. 393; Lloyd's Register of Shipping, *Statistical tables* (various issues), Lloyd's Register of Shipping, London; and UNCTAD, *Maritime transport* (various issues), UNCTAD, Geneva. Based on dead weight tons (dwt) from 1970 onwards and grt (gross register tons) before that. Before 1980, the annual entries have been interpolated based on the development from the start to the end of the decade.

At the same time, Latin America and Oceania have increased their relative shares in world shipping. This analysis, based only on the flag of the ship, does not reveal the complexities in the development of shipping tonnage and competitiveness. The flag—namely, the country in which the ship is registered—does not necessarily reveal the location of actual ownership of the ship. Rather, it reveals the existence of a number of countries specialized in 'ship registry.' To wit, the leading country in Latin America is Panama with around 20 per cent of the fleet, more or less the same market share as Europe.[6] The rapidly growing share of Oceania is almost completely accounted for by more than ten per cent of the world fleet registered in the Marshall Islands, which comprise 29 atolls and five separate islands with slightly more than 50,000 inhabitants. The registry is administered by an American company, International Registries, Inc., based in Reston, Virginia.[7] Nevertheless, Figure 10.1 provides a broad empirical description of the evolution of the global shipping industry.

Figure 10.1 reveals that the concentration of the registry of the world fleet has greatly reduced in the post-war period. In 1950, more than 85 per cent of the world fleet was registered in the two leading centers: Europe and North America.[8] Today, the registration of the world fleet is much more evenly distributed. The share of each of the five regions comprises 10 to 30 per cent of the world fleet, with only North America falling outside this range.

3 The European Shipping Industry: A Competitiveness-Based Explanation of the Decline

At the start of the 20th century, Europe dominated world shipping; with the United Kingdom at the vanguard, the European countries held a hegemonic position in the industry. This position was closely linked to the leading role that Western Europe played in international trade and politics. The European shipping lines supplemented the telegraph cables—tentacles of the European colonial empires—facilitating control of a large share of the world's trade, capital, and people.

Around 1910, more than 80 per cent of the world fleet was registered in Western Europe (Lloyd's Register of Shipping 1972, pp. 66–67).[9] In hindsight, such a market share was clearly unsustainable. The two World Wars had a particularly detrimental influence on the fleets of European countries, and the breakdown of international relations in the interwar period also had a harmful effect. There were, however, differences within Europe in these periods. In particular, Greece, Norway, and Germany saw strong fleet growth and modernization in the interwar period, while the British fleet declined both in absolute and relative terms from the early 1920s to the late 1930s (Sturmey 2010). Still, even as late as 1950, more than half the world fleet was registered in Europe. If we accept the premise that fleet size reflects competitiveness, how can we explain the dominating position of the European ship owners?

In the first half of the 20th century, the European hegemony was partly a reflection of the fact that the region could still benefit from past glories. European shipping companies had spent decades—in some cases, more than a century—building an infrastructure that facilitated their business. Moreover, as shipping was—and is—a relatively capital-intensive sector, there were relatively few contenders. The European first-mover advantage was strengthened by the acquisition of superior skills and technology. Other countries (with the exception of North America and, to some extent, Australia and New Zealand) simply did not have the capital required to compete on a large scale in this industry. The other non-European exception was Japan, which, after the opening of the country in the second half of the 19th century, put much effort in establishing a navy and a merchant marine (Chida and Davies 2012). In his seminal book on British shipping, Sturmey (2010, chapter 1) emphasized four 'conditions of supremacy': colonies, industrialization, population growth, and establishment advantages. Europe's dominant position in international shipping was founded upon—and facilitated—the continent's dominant position in world trade and politics.

In the first decades after World War II, Europe was 'much more maritime' than today (Miller 2012). The central role of Europe in trade and manufacturing meant that the maritime dimension was very evident in most coastal European cities. The United Kingdom is a case in point: London, Liverpool, Glasgow, and Cardiff had bustling ports that stretched all the way into where people lived and provided employment to tens of thousands. In the northeast of England and on the Clyde, the biggest employer was the shipyards, which built a large proportion of the ships that traversed the world's oceans. These merchant vessels were manned primarily by Europeans and provided an attractive employment alternative. Trade and transport went hand in hand, and nowhere more so than in Europe.

Today, more than 90 per cent of the world's ships are built in Asia; the once bustling ports have moved out of the city centers, and giant and powerful cranes have replaced the muscles of the longshoremen. In the first postwar decades, there were some changes in the ownership of the world fleet, but the drastic transformation of the market shares did not take place until the shipping crises of the 1970s and 1980s. As the empirical data showed, this was when Europe's market share saw the most rapid decline.

When discussing the development of European shipping over the last decades, two features have to be explained. First, why did the European share decline? Second, what can explain the shifts in the relative strength of the shipping industries in various European countries; why did some countries (e.g., the United Kingdom and Sweden) lose terrain, while others (e.g., Greece and Denmark) prospered?[10]

In order to explain these shifts, it is useful to look more closely at the cost and revenue structure of shipping. Like in other industries, shipping companies are able to stand out among their peers if they can acquire higher revenues (sell at higher prices) or produce at lower costs. In his standard textbook on maritime economics, Martin Stopford (2009, p. 219) defines the 'key variables' in shipping as (1) the revenue received from chartering/operating the ship, (2) the cost of running the ship, and (3) the method of financing the business. Within these three areas, Europe initially had absolute advantages. However, due to technological, economic, and political developments, these locational advantages evaporated as shipping increasingly became subject to international prices.

Table 10.1 illustrates the basis for the competitiveness of a given shipping company or of a specific country's shipping industry. The crucial role played by European traders and customers gave a proximity to 'the market' that can explain why European ship owners dominated intercontinental trades. In other words, their market knowledge provided superior revenue-generating capabilities and consequently a hegemonic position. With regard to the costs of running ships and the method of financing the business, the advantages were based upon a specifically European skill set, more than 'costs' *per se.*

With the introduction of steam in the late 19th and early 20th centuries, the technological requirements increased, and a new set of skills—which existed almost solely in Europe—was necessary (Hynninen, Ojala and

Table 10.1 Revenues and Cost Structure in Shipping

	Factor	Inputs	Form	Notes
(1)	Revenues	'Market knowledge'	Mainly international	Proximity to customers Some national preference in particular segments
(2)	Operating costs	Crew, maintenance, insurance, provision	Increasingly international	Previous restrictions on foreign labor; increasing need for skills
	Voyage costs	Bunkers, port costs, tugs, pilots	Always international	Always linked to location, not nationality Fuel costs more important
	Administration	Shore-based functions, management, etc.	Mainly local	Part of the 'maritime cluster' Increased possibilities for outsourcing specific tasks
(3)	Capital costs	Equity and debt capital, access to technology	Increasingly international	Equity: increasingly international; Mortgages: 'always' international

Pehkonen 2013). Indeed, with the transformation from sail to steam, access to capital and skilled labor cemented Europe's advantages. At the same time, two distinct operational modes developed within Europe. Broadly speaking, the British, German, and French shipping companies dominated the liner trades, providing scheduled services through fast and modern ships, often linked to their respective colonial networks. In other countries, tramp shipping dominated. Ship owners in Norway, Sweden, Denmark, and Greece offered their services in a global market, their ships constantly plying the seas looking for goods to transport. Thus, the shipping industries of the leading European powers were closely linked to their own trade and empires. The smaller nations emerged as 'cross-traders,' fulfilling a transport need wherever one existed. In the longer run, this turned out to be a more sustainable business model.

The European economic development was (and is) closely related to the sea. During the 19th century, the United States shifted from a maritime, ocean-dependent economy to an inward-looking and land-expanding country. In Europe, however, and particularly in the North Sea/Baltic region and the Mediterranean, there were few efficient alternatives to maritime transport. Both within Europe and in Europe's relation to other parts of the world, shipping companies, ships, and seafarers provided the vital links.

Up until World War II, the European position in international shipping also reflected the continent's role as the center of international trade and production. For instance, Europe accounted for more than two-thirds of the world trade during 1876–1880 (Yates 1959 cited in Kenwood ans Lougheed 1999, p. 80), whilst Europe's share of the world fleet, at around 74 per cent, was around ten per cent larger than the share of world trade (Ojala and Tenold 2016). Table 10.2 details the factors that account for Europe's leading role before the shipping supply was 'globalized.' Before World War II, a combination of empires, tradition, path dependence, and limited economic

Table 10.2 European Advantages before the 'Globalization' of Shipping Supply

	Factor	Basis for the European advantage
(1)	Revenues	Control of international trade, infrastructure—customers, brokers, etc.
(2)	Labor	Maritime knowledge, skills, and tradition at relatively low cost
	Business environment	'Maritime clusters'—practically all the main auxiliary services (insurance, banking, classification societies) were based in Europe
(3)	Capital (financing)	Wealthiest part of the world, well-functioning financial system
	Capital (technology)	Center of world shipbuilding and naval architecture

capabilities elsewhere meant that challengers to the European crown were rare.

As long as Europe in general, and the United Kingdom in particular, was the nave of the network of international trade, the control of the world's shipping industry was simply an extension of this status. However, one dominant feature of the post-war world development is the spread of industrialization and relocation of manufacturing production, particularly to countries in East and Southeast Asia. A part of the basis for Europe's hegemony thus disappeared. Figure 10.2 illustrates the strong growth in the East and Southeast Asian share of the world gross domestic product (GDP) and the corresponding decline in the role of Western Europe.

The development would have been even more dramatic if we looked at manufacturing volumes rather than GDP. Japan, followed by two generations of 'tigers' and then China, has taken over as the 'workshop of the world,' implying that a larger share of the demand for shipping originates in this region. Manufacturing is based on the transformation of raw materials into finished goods, and import of raw materials is one of the most shipping-intensive economic activities. In the period of 1970–2000, the roles of Asia and Europe were reversed, as seen in Figure 10.3. Asia had overtaken Europe as the main importing region for raw materials by 1990.[11] Since then, the development has continued: in the new millennium, Asian imports have increased by more than 230 per cent, compared with five per cent in the case of Europe.

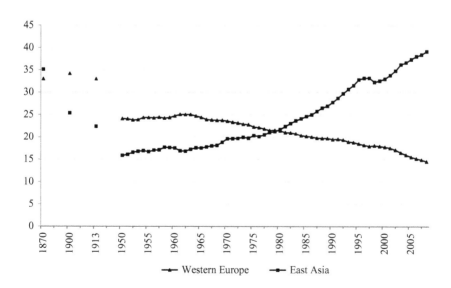

Figure 10.2 World Production—the Long-term Shift (Per Cent of World GDP)

Source: *The Maddison-Project* 2008, Available from: <www.ggdc.net/maddison/maddison-project/home.htm>. [Accessed: January 7, 2016].

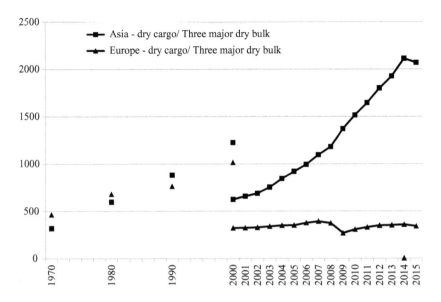

Figure 10.3 World Dry Cargo Seaborne Imports—the Recent Shift, Million Tonnes

Source: Based on two series that are only partly overlapping. Data for 1970, 1980, 1990, and 2000 refer to "Dry cargo goods unloaded" from "World seaborne trade according to geographical area" in UNCTAD, *Maritime Transport 2000*, Geneva. Asia refers to Japan, "Socialist countries of Asia" (China, Vietnam, and the Democratic Republic of Korea) and "Southern and Eastern Asia," while Europe refers to 22 countries in Western Europe as well as Turkey. The data for the period 2000–2015 are from Clarkson's Shipping Intelligence network, referring to seaborne imports of the three major dry bulk goods; iron ore, coal and grain. There is some variation in the countries included in the data set, but the series are consistent across time.

The demand development, based on growth and shifts of the world production, particularly manufacturing, is part of the story of Western Europe's reduced role in international shipping (and the concomitant rise of Asia). However, not only is the reduced competitiveness a result of demand side considerations and developments, but the European ability to supply shipping services at competitive rates has also been seriously challenged, as shown in Table 10.3.

Many functions—ownership, employment, port activities, and shipbroking—have followed in the wake of the shift of revenue-generating activities from Europe to Asia. New and newly successful 'maritime clusters' in Asia—Tokyo, Hong Kong, Shanghai, and, in particular, Singapore—have increased in importance.[12] However, many functions, institutions, and agents remain in Europe or are controlled by European companies.[13] Indeed, Europe maintains hegemony within ship financing, classification, and insurance, and around 40 per cent of the world fleet is still controlled by European interests.

Table 10.3 Market Structure after the 'Globalization' of Shipping Supply

	Factor	Basis for the 'post-globalization' transformation
(1)	Revenues	Reflect the increasing role of Asia in world trade—customers, charterers, brokers, etc. have moved in tandem with the shift in world manufacturing
(2)	Labor	Cost as the most important parameter—diffusion of skills and gradually increased potential for outsourcing
	Business environment	New 'maritime clusters'—mainly in Asia—reflecting changes Many auxiliary services still based in Europe
(3)	Capital (financing)	International investors and banks, increasingly 'faceless'
	Capital (technology)	Center of world shipbuilding moved to Asia

This is a stark contrast to the situation in shipbuilding (Todd 2011). There is still some production of luxury and technologically advanced ships in Europe. However, more than 90 per cent of the new ships delivered in 2014, measured in gross tons, were built in three Asian countries: China (36 per cent), South Korea (34 per cent), and Japan (21 per cent; UNCTAD 2015, p. 43).

The basis for the drastically different developments between the two industries is the manner in which the shipping industry—as opposed to shipbuilding—has been able to slice up the value chain and outsource the relatively low-skill, high-cost functions such as seafarers to countries with lower labor costs. This transfer was based on two institutional innovations: Flags of Convenience and 'open registers.'

4 Institutional Innovations and European Competitiveness

The regulation of shipping is partly private and partly public. Since the 18th century, there has been an element of 'self-regulation' of ship standards through classification societies. Private sector institutions have undertaken the certification of vessels and their seaworthiness, while the flag state—the country whose flag the ship flies—may also enforce certain requirements. The latter regulations include elements such as crew requirements (both the demand for certificates and number of crew), tax conditions, trading restrictions, and so on. Traditionally, Navigation Acts (e.g., the United Kingdom 1651–1849) or cabotage restrictions (the US Jones Act 1920 onwards) have been the most important types of trading restrictions.[14]

Government regulation of maritime labor was primarily a 20th century phenomenon. For instance, in 1913, as much as 'twenty-six percent of all seamen on Norwegian steamers were foreigners' (Fischer and Panting 1985, p. 190). Subsequently, restrictions on foreign labor were introduced and enforced more strictly in most European countries. As a result, the degree of correspondence between vessel flag, ownership, and crew increased. One way in which such restrictions could be overcome, however, was by re-flagging the ships; thus, there were US transfers to Panama in the interwar period and to Liberia after World War II.

Nonetheless, in the first post-war decades, the governments of most European countries restricted the ability to 'flag out' ships to Flag of Convenience countries. As Yrjö Kaukiainen (1994) points out in the article with the telling title 'From Low-Cost to High-Cost Shipping: Finnish Maritime Labour Costs after the Second World War,' around 1950, 'only some six percent of global merchant tonnage was on the "convenience" registers while in 1980 the proportion was over thirty percent.' The trend has continued subsequently. By 2015, the three leading flags—Panama, Liberia, and the Marshall Islands—accounted for almost 42 per cent of the world fleet, measured by deadweight tonnage (UNCTAD 2015, p. 42).

Up until the early 1970s, the strong demand for shipping capacity and the introduction of labor-saving ships utilizing economies of scale implied that the employment of seamen from high-wage countries was not too much of a handicap. However, the combination of the rapidly spreading use of Flags of Convenience and the depressed shipping market after the 1970s oil price increases changed all that. With more than a decade of freight rates that hardly covered variable cost, ship owners tried to save money wherever possible. The lobbying for more lenient labor requirements—and thus lower wage bills—rested on two main arguments. First, the owners wanted a 'level playing field' with Flag of Convenience countries and others that could use cheap labor. Second, the high mobility of the production capital—the ship—implied that the threat of closing down all activity by selling to foreigners was credible. In the case of, for instance, a factory, such a sale would usually have little effect on employment, taxes, and so on, as the location of the factory was fixed. In the case of shipping, however, any link to the home economy could disappear the moment the ship was sold (Sletmo 2001).

In the end, the 'globalized' element of shipping, which posed a major threat to the continued existence of the European shipping sector, enabled the countries to find a sustainable development path. European governments responded in two ways. First, the access to register ships abroad was improved in many countries. Ship owners would then be able to use foreign, low-cost labor in the international market, while the activity in domestic waters and in onshore offices was more or less unchanged. Governments accepted the reduction in the number of seamen, bartering it against continued employment in the shipping companies' offices. In the latter part of the 1980s, some countries introduced 'open registers,' also referred to as 'double registry,' where ships that traded *only* in foreign waters could combine the home country's flag with inexpensive foreign crews. The two most successful such institutions were the Norwegian International Ship Register and the Danish International Ship Register. In both instances, the new regulations provided an alternative to the sale of tonnage that, due to the level of European labor costs, had become uncompetitive.

Though flagging out was a common practice in many seafaring nations from the 1980s onwards, double registry was a more complicated question (Sletmo 1989; Sletmo and Holste 1993). This was something to be decided by governments, so the negotiating power of ship owners in political decision making may explain whether an open registry was introduced or not. In Norway and Denmark, for example, ship owners had an important position and considerable lobbying power (Iversen and Tenold 2014; Sornn-Friese and Iversen 2014), but in many countries, they did not. A case in point is another Nordic country, Finland, where almost 60 per cent of the tonnage was flagged out by 1990, but where there was no consensus on how to deal with the reduced competitiveness (Ojala and Kaukiainen 2012, pp. 129–155). Special committees discussed the issue, but the Finnish authorities chose direct subsidies to shipping companies, rather than an open registry. The recession of the early 1990s changed the situation, and, in 1991, a law on a parallel registry of foreign-going tonnage was enacted, although it was eagerly opposed by seamen's labor unions. By the year 2000, 63 per cent of the Finnish-flag tonnage was on this double registry (Soukola 2003; Wasström 2000). Still, the decline of the Finnish fleet shows that institutional innovation in itself is not enough to ensure competitiveness.

The attempt to overcome the high costs of domestically based labor led to several responses in different European countries. When the introduction of labor-saving technology proved to be fruitless, a combination of flagging out, open registries, and accommodating policies solved the reduced competitiveness following strong wage growth.[15] In some countries, European seamen were sacrificed in order to ensure the survival of shipping companies. In other countries, the attempt to maintain old and inflexible regulations resulted in a competitiveness shock that killed off all or most of the shipping companies.

Low labor costs alone are not enough, however. The 'globalization' of shipping supply also has a financial side. European countries have been successful in introducing regulation that ensured investment in shipping capacity. The basis for this is twofold: tax and finance. First, the shipping industry has gradually developed toward a regime in which tax has limited or no importance in choosing a location. Again, the impetus came from the Flags of Convenience and the ship owners' lobbying for fairness and a 'level playing field.' Today, most European countries, including those within the European Union, operate with a tonnage tax regime. Here, the conditions are almost 'tax free' and limited to a small fee per ton, like in most Flag of Convenience countries (Roe 2009).[16]

The movement toward this solution was gradual, but it is evident that the governments' reduced 'claim' on the surplus of the shipping companies is one element that has ensured the resilience of the industry. Still, this is a relatively recent phenomenon, not functioning fully until the new millennium. The tonnage tax solution became politically acceptable because European shipping companies contributed to public coffers through personal and employment tax contributions related to the office workers of shipping companies. In a worst-case scenario, both the ships and land-based organizations would have disappeared, leading to no taxable activity at all (Knudsen 1997).

The European maritime environment has also benefitted from an impressive ability to raise capital for shipping investments. In European countries, there have been—and are—some extremely efficient ways to raise capital. In Germany, for instance, the existence of limited partnerships (*Kommanditgesellschaft*) has ensured a steady inflow of money from 'doctors and dentists' looking for investments that are beneficial from a tax perspective. The major shipping banks are also European, and in their perimeter, a number of 'project developers' and 'project brokers' ensure that Europe has an efficient system to raise private capital for shipping investments.

Table 10.4 is a relatively recent comparison of the flagging and ownership of the world merchant marine. The left-hand-side shows the registration of the world fleet. With the exception of Greece, the countries in the Top 10 are either Flags of Convenience (the Top 3 plus Bahamas, Malta, and Cyprus) or rapidly growing shipping nations in Asia. These are followed by

Table 10.4 Shipping Top 15—by Registry and Control (dwt) 2015

	By registry (dwt)	%		By control (dwt)	%
1	Panama	20.1	1	Greece	16.1
2	Liberia	11.7	2	Japan	13.3
3	Marshall Islands	10.0	3	China	9.1
4	China, Hong Kong	8.6	4	Germany	7.0
5	Singapore	6.6	5	Singapore	4.8
6	Malta	4.7	6	South Korea	4.6
7	Greece	4.5	7	China, Hong Kong	4.3
8	Bahamas	4.3	8	United States	3.5
9	China	4.3	9	United Kingdom	2.8
10	Cyprus	1.9	10	Norway	2.7
11	Isle of Man	1.3	11	Taiwan	2.6
12	Japan	1.3	12	Bermuda	2.4
13	Norway	1.2	13	Denmark	2.1
14	Italy	1.0	14	Turkey	1.6
15	United Kingdom	1.0	15	Monaco	1.4

Source: Based on information from UNCTAD 2015, *Maritime transport 2015*, UNCTAD, Geneva, pp. 42, 36. Interestingly, some of the controlling 'nations'—for instance Bermuda and Monaco—reveal that the problem of nationality has now gone one step further.

another 'European' Flag of Convenience and some nations that have been most important in the post-war period but where the tonnage under their own flag has been reduced.

The right-hand-side, on the other hand, is based on actual ownership. The data show that many of the countries that have dominated shipping over the last century continue to do so. Moreover, the only real challenges have come from Asian countries. Still, it is interesting to see that a number of formerly important European shipping nations have fallen by the wayside. The decline of the United Kingdom is spectacular, but countries such as France and Sweden have also gone from having large merchant marines to becoming more or less invisible in today's shipping sector (Poulsen, Sjögren and Lennerfors 2012, pp. 100–128). These countries do still have a handful of shipping companies that manage to compete and are still present in the industry, but it would be wrong to claim that they have any kind of vital 'shipping environment.'

Table 10.5 provides an overview of the varied experiences in the leading European shipping nations anno 1970. With the exception of Sweden, all these countries saw their fleets increase in absolute terms. However, only Greece, with its spectacular development, as well as Germany and Denmark, managed to grow faster than the world fleet *per se*. All the other nations saw their share of the world fleet decline by more than half, with Sweden, France, and the United Kingdom as the worst examples.

The preceding analysis has focused primarily on ships and shipping companies, but how does the picture look if we extend it a bit to include other parts of the maritime cluster? There is no doubt that within shipbuilding, the

Table 10.5 Subsequent Development of the Largest European Shipping Nations in 1970

		Fleet 1970	Share 1970	Fleet 2015	Share 2015	Fleet	Share
1	United Kingdom	38.7	11.4	48.4	2.8	+25%	−75%
2	Norway	31.4	9.3	46.4	2.7	+48%	−71%
3	Greece	17.0	5.0	279.4	16.1	+1,543%	+222%
4	Germany	12.3	3.6	122.0	7.0	+892%	+94%
5	Italy	10.3	3.0	22.0	1.3	+114%	−57%
6	France	9.5	2.8	11.2	0.6	+18%	−79%
7	The Netherlands	7.4	2.2	17.0	1.0	+130%	−55%
8	Sweden	7.2	2.1	6.4	0.4	−11%	−81%
9	Denmark	5.1	1.5	36.2	2.1	+609%	+40%
10	Spain	4.5	1.3	N.A.	N.A		

Source: Fleet in million dwt, and share based on dwt; information on registry from Lloyd's Register of Shipping 1970, *Statistical tables 1970*, Lloyd's Register of Shipping, London, and on controlled fleet from UNCTAD 2015, *Maritime transport 2015*, UNCTAD, Geneva, p. 42. However, dwt is a very crude measure of shipping, and in some instances, a transformation toward more expensive and advanced tonnage may neutralize some, or even most, of the decline.

European countries have lost their previous dominant position. European shipbuilding today is confined to pockets of specialized and high-technology construction, whereas the high-volume trades have gone primarily to Asia, where South Korea, China, and Japan construct 90 per cent or more of the world shipping capacity.[17] With regard to the volume transported through various ports, Europe is also lagging far behind, with Asia again being the most dynamic continent.

Within other maritime activities, however, Europe is still *the* dominant arena internationally. Important economic activities such as ship finance, ship insurance, maritime law, and ship classification constitute an auxiliary framework within which shipping services are produced (Starkey and Murphy 2007). European companies still dominate these arenas, and such activities have followed the building and ownership of the vessels to Asia primarily via foreign direct investment of European firms.

Two factors, in particular, have enabled these auxiliary companies to remain competitive, even with high European costs. The first is proximity to and long-standing relationships with their customers: shipping companies and charterers. The second is an important organizational capability: command of specific, knowledge-intensive processes and procedures. Within areas such as contract law (both financial and maritime), naval architecture, marine underwriting, naval engineering, and so on, highly skilled European employees are not necessarily uncompetitive compared with their Asian counterparts. In fact, in the emerging maritime clusters in Asia, the high demand for such skills, combined with their limited supply, implies that the costs might be even higher than in 'sunset' European countries.

While the ownership of the world fleet has moved east and there has been an even stronger dislocation in shipbuilding, the European heritage has created some resilience with regard to the framework in which shipping business is conducted.

Conclusion

At the beginning of the 20th century, Europe's strong position in the world economy was mirrored in the maritime power of the continent. Britannia ruled the waves, and the most important contenders were other European nations. Few other countries had the skills or capital to compete with European shipping companies.

The spread of industrialization and a higher standard of living has reduced the European supremacy, in both world shipping and the world economy. As the other chapters in this volume show, the changing competitiveness has led to large changes in the manner and geographical locations of production. The global character of the shipping industry has created extremely strong competitive pressures. European adaptations to this—technological and, particularly, institutional innovations—have partly alleviated these pressures.

The basis for the European decline was partly the shift in the world economy and partly the manner in which the 'national' dimension of vessel ownership was challenged as the industry became increasingly borderless. Interestingly, this challenge initially came from European entrepreneurs such as Aristotle Onassis and Erling Dekke Næss, who built large fleets outside European jurisdiction and regulation. Onassis, born in present-day Turkey, controlled an international business empire with important links to Greece, Monaco, Panama, the United States, and Uruguay. Dekke Næss, born in Bergen, was one of the early adopters of Flags of Convenience (or Flags of Necessity, which was his preferred term) and also the architect behind the Norwegian International Shipping Register in the 1980s.

How do you sail a sinking ship? How do you try to compete as your advantages are gradually eroding? Some European companies and countries have managed to introduce technological and institutional innovations that have alleviated the competitiveness problems. Other European companies and countries have ignored the problems. As a result, their fleets have sunk, totally or to such an extent that the industry has more or less disappeared.

Notes

1 We primarily look at market share when discussing the competitiveness of various regions. However, we will take into account data and definition issues both with regard to the measurement unit (various tonnage measures versus value) and the reporting unit (flag versus ownership).
2 In the case of the latter element of demand, in principle, there should be no differences among companies in the *international* segment of the industry. Nevertheless, national policies may play a role, as we shall see.
3 Exceptions to this can be found where subsidies or market protection ensure survival. However, in such instances, one might rightly claim that the protection and subsidies create a competitiveness that transcends the market setting. For a discussion of market shares as a measure of competitiveness, see the detailed discussion in Norway (1983, pp. 31–39). In the short term, capacity utilization—whether ships are trading or not—is also a measure of competitiveness, though one for which valid and reliable data are increasingly hard to find.
4 As a rule of thumb, domestically based market segments—local ferry services, for instance—have not been subject to international competition to the same extent.
5 This has also facilitated an element of national specialization within shipping segments. Classification societies categorize the world's ships into 13 broad types, primarily based on specifications such as construction and cargo suitability. With a world fleet of more than 100,000 ships (larger than 100 gross register tons), differences in both design and size create heterogeneity. Going back to the beginning of the last century, the main differentiation was between sailing and steam vessels, though with some size differentiation then as well.
6 Shares are based on UNCTAD (2015); they are based on decadal data before 1980 and annual data subsequently.
7 Interestingly, the businessmen behind the Marshall Islands registry had previously managed the Liberian flag, but struck a deal with the island state after 'Liberia descended into bloody civil war' (*Tradewinds* [Oslo] 17 March 2016, p. 12).

8 The US data include the American reserve fleet, which, at the start of the period, comprised more than 2,500 ships and meant that the US share appeared to be three times higher than the share of the active fleet. However, the role of the reserve fleet declined across time as ships were sold, deactivated, or scrapped. By March 2016, around 100 vessels remained. United States Maritime Administration n.d., *National defense reserve fleet*. Available from: <www.marad.dot.gov/ships-and-shipping/strategic-sealift/office-of-ship-operations/national-defense-reserve-fleet-ndrf/>. [25 April 2016].

9 Due to aggregation of the data, the 1910 figure includes ships registered in the British dominions of Australia and Canada. The main shipping nations outside Western Europe were the United States (ten per cent of the world fleet), Japan (3.1 per cent), and Russia (0.8 per cent).

10 Ojala and Tenold (2016) discuss the empirical basis for and dynamics of these two processes.

11 The picture is the same for crude oil imports. In the European case, the seaborne imports fell from 608 to 480 million tons from 1970 to 2000, while the Asian countries listed above saw seaborne crude oil imports increase from 230 to 501 million tons over the same period.

12 Surprisingly, a recent cross-country analysis of competitiveness of the shipping industry by Lee et al. (2014) does not even mention Singapore, which, by many accounts, has been the most successful Asian (and indeed world) maritime cluster over the last decades. An interesting take on the various types of clusters can be found in Zhang and Lam (2013).

13 In fact, in some cases, European agents—brokers, banks, and subsidiaries of European shipping companies—play a leading role in the new maritime clusters in Asia.

14 On the British system, see for instance, Palmer (1990); on the Jones Act, see for instance, Whitehurst (1985); a recent analysis on the navigation acts from the Nordic perspective is conducted by Ojala and Räihä (2017).

15 It is important to point out that the high costs of domestic labor were not based purely on wages; rota systems with shorter working hours and improved social benefits (including paid journeys home) also added significantly to the costs compared with those from hiring seamen from developing countries.

16 For an introduction to the system before this, see Mayr and McGrath (2006).

17 This depends on the manner in which the shipbuilding output is measured. In dead weight tonnage, the share is more than 90 per cent, but if the sophistication of the tonnage is taken into account, for instance, by looking at the value of shipbuilding contracts, Europe becomes more visible.

References

Boyce, G. 2001, 'Transferring capabilities across sectoral frontiers: Shipowners entering the airline business, 1920–1970', *International Journal of Maritime History*, vol. 13, no. 1, pp. 1–38.

Chida, T. and Davies, P. 2012, *The Japanese Shipping and Shipbuilding Industries: A History of Their Modern Growth*, Bloomsbury, London.

Fink, L. 2011, *Sweatshops at sea—merchant seamen in the world's first globalized industry from 1812 to the present*, University of North Carolina Press, Chapel Hill, NC.

Fischer, L.R. and Panting, G.E. 1985, *Change and Adaptation in Maritime History: The North Atlantic Fleets in the Nineteenth Century*, Maritime History Group, St. John's, Newfoundland.

Harlaftis, G. 1995, *A History of Greek-Owned Shipping*, Routledge, London.

Hope, R. 1990, *A New History of British Shipping*, J. Murray, London.

Hynninen, S.M., Ojala, J. and Pehkonen, J. 2013, 'Technological change and wage premiums: Historical evidence from linked employer—employee data', *Labour Economics*, vol. 24, pp. 1–11.

Iversen, M.J. and Tenold, S. 2014, 'The two regimes of postwar shipping: Denmark and Norway as case studies, 1960–2010', *International Journal of Maritime History*, vol. 26, no. 4, pp. 720–733.

Kaukiainen, Y. 1994, 'From low-cost to high-cost shipping: Finnish maritime labour costs after the Second World War', in P. Holm, M.L. Hinkkanen and J. Thór (eds.), *Northern Seas Yearbook 1994*, Fiskeri- og søfartsmuseet, Esbjerg, pp. 33–43.

Kenwood, A.G. and Lougheed, A.L. 1999, *The Growth of the International Economy 1820–2000*, Routledge, London.

Klemann, H.A.M. and Schenk, J. 2013, 'Competition in the Rhine delta: Waterways, railways and ports, 1870–1913', *The Economic History Review*, vol. 66, no. 3, pp. 826–847.

Knudsen, K. 1997, 'The economics of zero taxation in the shipping industry', *Maritime Policy & Management*, vol. 24, no. 1, pp. 45–54.

Lee, C.B., Wan, J., Shi, W. and Li, K. 2014, 'A cross-country study of competitiveness of the shipping industry', *Transport Policy*, vol. 35, pp. 366–376.

Lloyd's Register of Shipping 1972, 'Table 17: merchant fleets, 1908–1972', in *Statistical Tables 1972*, Lloyd's Register of Shipping, London.

Mayr, T.P. and McGrath, R.H. 2006, 'Tramp shipping: The role of taxation in international resource allocation', *Maritime Policy & Management*, vol. 24, no. 3, pp. 261–283.

Miller, M. 2012, *Europe and the Maritime World: A Twentieth Century History*, Cambridge University Press, Cambridge.

Norway 1983, 'Skipsfartens konkurranseevne' [The competitiveness of shipping], Government white paper, Universitetsforlaget, Oslo.

Ojala, J. and Kaukiainen, Y. 2012, 'Finnish shipping', in S. Tenold, M.J. Iversen and E. Lange (eds.), *Global Shipping in Small Nations: Nordic Experiences After 1960*, Palgrave MacMillan, Basingstoke, pp. 129–155.

Ojala, J. and Räihä, A. 2017, 'Navigation acts and the integration of North Baltic shipping in the early nineteenth century', *International Journal of Maritime History*, vol. 29, no. 1, pp. 1–18.

Ojala, J. and Tenold, S. 2016, 'Maritime power and merchant shipping: The shipping/trade-factor from the 1870s until today', *NHH Department of Economics Discussion Paper 2016/12*, Bergen: NHH – Norwegian School of Economics.

Palmer, S. 1990, *Politics, Shipping and the Repeal of the Navigation Laws*, Manchester University Press, Manchester and New York.

Poulsen, R.T., Sjögren, H. and Lennerfors, T. 2012, 'The two declines of Swedish shipping', in S. Tenold, M.J. Iversen and E. Lange (eds.) *Global Shipping in Small Nations: Nordic Experiences After 1960*, Palgrave MacMillan, Basingstoke, pp. 100–128.

Roe, M. 2009, 'Maritime governance and policy-making failure in the European Union', *International Journal of Shipping and Transport Logistics*, vol. 1, no. 1, pp. 1–19.

Sletmo, G.K. 1989, 'Shipping's fourth wave: Ship management and Vernon's trade cycles', *Maritime Policy & Management*, vol. 16, no. 4, pp. 293–303.

234 Stig Tenold and Jari Ojala

Sletmo, G.K. 2001, 'The end of national shipping policy? A historical perspective on shipping policy in a global economy', *International Journal of Maritime Economics*, vol. 3, no. 4, pp. 330–350.

Sletmo, G.K. and Holste, S. 1993, 'Shipping and the competitive advantage of nations: The role of international ship registers', *Maritime Policy & Management*, vol. 20, no. 3, pp. 243–255.

Sorrn-Friese, H. 2003, *Navigating Blue Denmark: The Structural Dynamics and Evolution of the Danish Maritime Cluster*, Danish Maritime Authority, Copenhagen.

Sorrn-Friese, H. and Iversen, M.J. 2014, 'The establishment of the Danish International Ship Register (DIS) and its connections to the maritime cluster', *International Journal of Maritime History*, vol. 26, no. 1, pp. 82–103.

Soukola, T. 2003, *Järjestö jäänmurtajana. Suomen merimiesunioni työmarkkinaosapuolena ja suomalaisten laivatyöntekijöiden turvallisuuden vankentajana 1944–1980* [History of the Finnish Seamen's Labor Union 1944–1980], Otava, Helsinki.

Starkey, D.J. and Murphy, H. 2007, *Beyond Shipping and Shipbuilding: Britain's Ancillary Maritime Interests in the Twentieth Century*, University of Hull, Hull.

Stopford, M. 2009, *Maritime Economics*, Routledge, London.

Sturmey, S.G. 2010, *British Shipping and World Competition*, International Maritime Economic History Association, St. John's, Newfoundland.

Tenold, S., Iversen, M.J. and Lange, E. (eds.) 2012, *Global Shipping in Small Nations: Nordic Experiences After 1960*, Palgrave MacMillan, Basingstoke.

Todd, D. 2011, 'Going east: Was the shift in volume shipbuilding capacity from Britain and continental Europe to the Far East and elsewhere during the latter half of the twentieth century inevitable?' *The Mariner's Mirror*, vol. 97, no. 1, pp. 259–271.

UNCTAD 2015, *Maritime Transport 2015*, UNCTAD, Geneva.

Wasström, K. 2000, *Finlands och EU:s sjöfartspolitik* [Shipping Policies in Finland and in EU]. University of Turku, Turku.

Whitehurst, C.H. 1985, *American Domestic Shipping in American Ships: Jones Act Costs, Benefits, and Options*, American Enterprise Institute for Public Policy Research, Washington, DC.

Wijnolst, N. (ed.) 2006, *Dynamic European Maritime Clusters*, IOS Press, Amsterdam.

Yates, P.L. 1959, *Forty Years of Foreign Trade*, MacMillan & Co, London.

Zhang, W. and Lam, J.S.L. 2013, 'Maritime cluster evolution based on symbiosis theory and Lotka—Volterra model', *Maritime Policy & Management*, vol. 40, no. 2, pp. 161–176.

11 Three Markets and Three Types of Competitiveness

Pulp and Paper Industry

Takafumi Kurosawa and Tomoko Hashino

Introduction

Paper is a universal and familiar product for any industrial society. Although digitization eroded its dominance as an information carrier, one can hardly live without paper's use in printing, packaging and wrapping material, sanitary products, and a variety of industrial materials. Paper has over 2,000 years of history and has been consumed in virtually all regions of the world. On the supply side, almost all major industrial nations have a paper industry. These features make it an ideal object of long-term historical analysis of the industry-specific patterns of competitiveness.

Each region had its own specific supplier-consumer relationship. Despite considerable global integration in the flow of raw material (wood, wood-chip, and waste paper) and semi-finished products (pulp), the world market had been divided into the continental size of regional markets.

However, treating these regions as geographical units of analysis does not suffice for the analysis of competitiveness, especially when we look at the entire value chain, which includes not only paper production, but also raw material supply, pulp production and processing/consumption of paper. This is because each region has two types of sub-regions and actors, namely 1) nations, regions, and firms with competitiveness in the upstream of the production process and material flow (forestry and pulp production) and 2) the aforementioned actors with competitiveness in their downstream (paper making and processing/consumption of paper). The former can be categorized as 'resource-push,' and the latter as 'consumption-pull.' In addition, the third category ('hybrid integration') can be introduced, to explain another pattern of competitiveness wherein both the features of 'resource push' and 'consumption pull' are combined. This chapter investigates the history of pulp and paper industry in Europe, North America, and East Asia (mainly Japan) by applying these three categories. For this purpose, we analyze not only the paper industry, but also the pulp industry and other related sectors.[1]

This chapter addresses the following questions: What are the features of the paper industry, and what are the main determinants of its location and competitiveness? Which part of the world has competitiveness in this industry and why? How did it shift over time, and what were the main drivers of the change? What type of geographical unit or typology of region can be applied to identify both structural elements and historical changes in the industry?

The first section of this chapter analyzes the status-quo of the global paper industry. Section 2 outlines the characteristics of the pulp and paper industry and analyzes the 'industry specific time and space.' Section 3 provides basic features of the historical development of the three major markets in the 20th century (North America, Europe, and Japan). Section 4 introduces two analytical concepts (consumption pull and resource push). Section 5 discusses the third category (hybrid integration) focusing on Japan. Section 6 summarizes structural changes in the global competitive landscape in the 21st century.

1 Pulp and Paper Industry in Today's World

1.1 The Presence of Rich Economies and Forest-Rich Regions

Before analyzing historical developments, the global market landscape should be presented. Table 11.1 shows the top 20 paper producing countries in 2013.

The table shows a strong presence of large economies and the considerable share of forest-rich countries in the northern hemisphere. China (world share: 26%) and the United States (18.3%) have a dominant position, followed by Japan (6.5%) and Germany (5.6%). Except for the inverse position of China and the United States, the first to fourth ranks correspond to gross domestic product (GDP) of the respective countries. Some industrialized and prosperous economies with relatively large populations, such as Korea, Italy, and France, as well as forest-rich nations with a strong tradition of the pulp and paper industry, such as Canada, Sweden, and Finland, form the second group. In contrast, the United Kingdom, the world's fourth paper producer during the 1960s (4.8% in 1964), dropped to the 19th position, with only 1.1%.

What is the size of consumption of each nation? The top four paper producers are also the four largest consumers of paper, in the exact sequence (see column "c"). The self-sufficiency rate (column "g") of three largest producers (China, United States, and Japan) ranged from 103% to 96%. It is striking that all top 15 consumer nations are also among the top 20 producing nations. Simply put, even in the globalized economy, paper is largely produced where it is consumed, though the extensive mutual trade among nations makes the actual situation more complex owing to specialization into diverse grades.

Table 11.1 Production, Consumption and Trade of Paper, Pulp, and Wasted Paper (World's Top 20 Paper Producing Nations in 2013)

Ranking of Paper Production	Country	Paper and Paper Board							Export and Import				
		Production		Consumption									
		a Production (million tons)	b World Share (%)	c Consumption (million tons)	d World Ranking	e World Share (%)	f Per capita Consumption kg/year	g Self-Sufficiency Ratio (%)	h Export Amount (million ton)	i Export Value (billion USD)	j Import Amount (million ton)	k Net Export (million ton)	l Net Export/ Production Ratio (%)
1	China	104.7	26.0	101.4	1	25.1	75	103	6.2	6.6	2.8	3.3	3.2
2	US	73.7	18.3	71.8	2	17.8	226	103	11.9	10.1	9.9	1.9	2.6
3	Japan	26.2	6.5	27.3	3	6.8	214	96	1.1	1.6	2.2	-1.1	-4.1
4	Germany	22.4	5.6	19.5	4	4.8	240	115	13.2	13.3	10.3	2.9	12.8
5	S. Korea	11.8	2.9	9.6	9	2.4	195	124	3.3	2.4	1.0	2.3	19.1
6	Canada	11.1	2.8	5.9	15	1.4	169	190	8.3	6.5	3.1	5.3	47.4
7	Sweden	10.8	2.7	1.8	n.a.	0.4	197	599	9.7	9.6	0.7	9.0	83.3
8	India	10.6	2.6	12.4	5	3.1	10	86	0.4	0.3	2.2	-1.8	-16.6
9	Finland	10.6	2.6	1.1	n.a.	0.3	212	946	9.9	9.1	0.5	9.5	89.3
10	Indonesia	10.6	2.6	7.2	12	1.8	29	147	4.0	3.4	0.6	3.4	32.1
11	Brazil	10.4	2.6	10.2	6	2.5	52	103	1.4	1.7	1.2	0.3	2.5
12	Italy	8.6	2.1	9.7	8	2.4	157	89	3.8	3.6	4.8	-1.0	-11.9
13	France	8.0	2.0	8.9	10	2.2	141	90	4.3	4.5	5.2	-0.9	-11.2
14	Russia	7.7	1.9	6.8	13	1.7	48	113	2.5	1.7	1.6	0.9	11.7
15	Spain	6.2	1.5	5.9	14	1.5	127	105	3.2	2.7	3.0	0.3	4.4
16	Mexico	4.8	1.2	7.5	11	1.9	66	64	0.3	0.3	3.0	-2.7	-55.6
17	Austria	4.8	1.2	2.1	n.a.	0.5	258	228	4.3	3.4	1.5	2.7	56.3
18	Thailand	4.6	1.1	4.7	18	1.2	68	97	0.9	0.7	1.1	-0.2	-3.5
19	UK	4.6	1.1	9.8	7	2.4	154	47	1.2	1.6	6.3	-5.1	-112.1
20	Poland	4.0	1.0	5.0	17	1.2	129	82	2.6	2.1	3.5	-0.9	-22.2
Total: 20 nations		356.4	88.5	328.5		81.4			92.4	86.0	64.4	–	
World		402.6	100	403.6		100	56.5		110.9	102.2			

(Continued)

Table 11.1 (Continued)

	Pulp					Waste Paper			
	Production			Export		Recycling and Trade			
	m	n	o	p	q	r	s	t	u
	Production (million ton)	Ranking of pulp production	World Share of Pulp Production (%)	Export Amount (million ton)*	Pulp Production/Paper and Paper Board production Ratio (%)	Collected Waste Paper (million ton)	Consumption of Waste Paper (million ton)	Waste Paper Net Export (million ton, r-s)	Waste Paper Consumption/Paper and Paper Board Production Ratio (%)
China	17.5	2	9.6	0.0	17	45.43	74.48	-29.04	71
United States	48.2	1	26.5	7.9	65	45.79	26.60	10.86	36
Japan	8.8	7	4.8	0.5	33	21.79	16.93	4.86	65
Germany	2.6	12	1.4	1.3	12	15.36	16.48	-1.13	74
South Korea	0.6	28	0.3	0.0	5	9.16	10.32	-1.16	87
Canada	17.3	3	9.5	9.8	155	4.17	2.68	1.4	24
Sweden	12.0	5	6.6	3.7	111	1.22	1.38	-0.15	13
India	4.0	11	2.2	0.0	38	3.43	5.96	1.02	56
Finland	11.1	6	6.1	3.1	105	0.69	0.61	0.08	6
Indonesia	6.8	9	3.7	3.8	64	4.06	6.25	-2.19	59
Brazil	15.1	4	8.3	9.8	145	4.55	4.53	0.3	43
Italy	0.6	27	0.3	0.0	7	6.06	4.71	1.35	55
France	2.6	15	1.4	0.5	33	7.24	5.15	-1.13	64
Russia	7.6	8	4.2	1.9	98	2.99	2.65	0.3	34
Spain	2.9	14	1.6	1.2	46	4.26	5.14	-0.89	83
Mexico	0.2	38	0.1	0.0	3	4.17	4.88	-0.72	101
Austria	1.6	16	0.9	0.4	32	1.45	2.33	-0.87	48

Thailand	1.1	0.6	22	0.0	2.89	3.71	−0.81	81
United Kingdom	0.2	0.1	36	0.0	7.88	3.80	4.08	83
Poland	1.2	0.6	21	0.1	2.19	2.05	0.14	50
Total:20 nations	161.8	89.1		29	194.78	200.6		
World	181.6	100.0	45	57.6	232.86	233.1		57.8

Source: The numbers of production, consumption, and trade of paper and paper board; those of the collection, consumption, and trade of waste paper are based on the data by *RISI Annual Review 2014* and *Paper Promotion Recycling Center* (Tokyo). (www.prpc.or.jp/menu05/linkfile/sekainotoukei.pdf). The export value of paper and paper board, and the production and export numbers of pulp are aggregated by authors using FAOSTAT (http://faostat3.fao.org/download/F/FT/E). The other data are aggregated by authors using the same sources. Per capita consumption of some nations is calculated by the national consumption amount obtained from the RISI statistics mentioned above and demographic statistics by WHO.

Notes

1) 'Pulp production' of South Korea, Italy, Mexico, Thailand, UK, and Poland does not show the production amount, but the production capacity in 2013 (dissolve pulp is excluded). The global production capacity is the sum of the data obtained from FAO statistics and production numbers in China. For FAO statistics, see FAO (ed.), Pulp and Paper Capacities, 2015 (www.fao.org/docrep/014/i2285t/i2285t00.pdf).

2) From 17.47 million tons of pulp production in China, 8.28 million ton is non-wood pulp.

The strong presence of thinly populated forest-rich nations in the northern hemisphere as regards both high self-sufficiency rates (column "g") and export/production ratios (column "l") is noteworthy. Finland (946%) and Sweden (599%) have exceptionally high export/production ratios, followed by Austria (228%) and Canada (190%). They hold even stronger positions in pulp production and export.

However, it is interesting that some nations enjoy a strong position on the paper markets despite their limited pulp production capacity. Germany (ranked first in the export of paper with 115% self-sufficiency rate), and South Korea (11th, 124%) are good examples.

Next, a closer look at the production and consumption of paper in each continent reveals high levels of self-sufficiency. In 2013, fairly balanced supply and demand were observed in East Asia (China, Japan, South Korea, and Taiwan) with 36.5% share in the world paper production and 102.5% of the self-sufficiency ratio, Europe (25.0% and 109.8% respectively) and North America (21.1% and 109.2% respectively). The total of these three regions accounts for 83% of the production and 78.6% of the consumption globally. In the rest of the world, other Asian regions (8.3% share in the world paper production and 74.6% of the self-sufficiency ratio) and Latin America (5.2% and 74.1% respectively) are relatively large.

A geographical shift in the global market over time is evident. A half-century ago, in 1965, the global production share of paper and paper board were 47.9% for North America (40% in the United States; 7.9% in Canada), 37.5% for Europe (7.3% in the three Nordic nations; 4.8% in the United Kingdom), 7.9% for Japan, and 14.6% for the rest of the world. East Asia expanded dramatically, and North America and Europe saw their shares reduced.

1.2 Enterprises

How will this picture change when we focus not on nations but on enterprises? Table 11.2 shows the world's top 20 pulp and paper-related firms (by revenue) in 2013. The composition of the listed firms reflects not only the presence of firms from North America, Europe, and East Asia but also the emergence of new players from the southern hemisphere. The top company in the United States is International Paper. International Paper and Oji Paper, the largest Japanese paper company, have kept their top positions in the world and in Japan, respectively, for longer than a century. Except for Procter & Gamble (ranked second), Kimberly-Clark, and Marubeni (a Japanese general trading company), most companies on the list have a clear focus on the pulp and paper industry.

Table 11.2 Global Top 20 Firms in the Paper and Pulp Industry (2013)

Ranking			Revenue in paper and pulp (million USD) (a)	Total Revenue (million USD) (b)	Ratio of paper and pulp (%) (a/b)	Total Assets (million USD)	Production (thousand tons)		Employees
Region	World						Pulp for market sales	Paper and Paper board	
North America									
1	1	International Paper (US)	29,080	29,080	100	31,528	1,700	19,600	65,000
2	2	Procter & Gamble (US)	16,790	84,167	20	139,263	n.a.	n.a.	121,000
3	7	Kimberly-Clark (US)	9,960	21,152	47	18,919	n.a.	n.a.	57,000
4	10	Rock Tenn (US)	9,077	9,545	95	10,733	392	8,116	25,800
5	15	Domtar (Canada)	5,391	5,391	100	6,278	1,445	2,957	9,400
6	16	MWV (US)	5,287	5,287	100	10,285	0	2,719	16,000
Europe									
1	3	UPM (Finland)	13,100	13,346	98	19,379	1,900	10,288	20,900
2	4	Stora Enso (Finland)	12,768	13,966	91	16,930	1,086	9,911	27,900
3	5	Smurfit Kappa (Ireland)	10,562	10,562	100	10,927	0	5,090	41,000
4	9	Svenska Cellulosa (Sweden)	9,596	13,656	70	21,825	318	5,090	34,000
5	14	Metsä Group (Finland)	8,596	6,546	87	6,855	1,409	2,576	12,200
6	17	DS Smith (UK)	5,925	6,307	83	5,525	0	2,719	21,400
Japan									
1	6	Oji Holdings (Japan)	10,190	13,651	74	19,625	581	8,733	31,000
2	8	Marubeni (Japan)	9,826	139,670	7	74,328	485	582	42,000
3	11	Nippon Paper (Japan)	8,688	11,077	78	15,171	539	6,882	13,000
4	19	Rengo (Japan)	4,767	5,359	89	6,444	0	2,478	13,000

(Continued)

Table 11.2 (Continued)

Ranking			Revenue in paper and pulp (million USD) (a)	Total Revenue (million USD) (b)	Ratio of paper and pulp (%) (a/b)	Total Assets (million USD)	Production (thousand tons)		Employees
Region	World						Pulp for market sales	Paper and Paper board	
Other Regions									
1	12	Mondi (South Africa)	8,596	8,596	100	8,283	535	5,283	24,400
2	13	Sappi (South Africa)	5,925	5,925	100	5,727	945	6,672	13,600
3	18	Empresas CMPC (Chile)	4,779	4,974	96	14,188	2,596	1,259	16,700
4	20	Nine Dragons Paper (China)	4,636	4,636	100	10,395	85	11,090	17,800

Sources: *Japan Paper Association* (www.jpa.gr.jp/states/global-view/index.html#topic05).

International Paper's production volume comes close to the entire production amount in Germany, the world's fourth largest paper producing country. About half of the listed firms from developed countries are born from mega-mergers. However, the market structure is still far from a global oligopoly. International Paper's market share in the world is merely 4.9%, less than a half of the global top firm from the automobile industry (Toyota, 11.5%), and it is even smaller than that of the top firm in the steel industry (Arcelor-Mittal, 5.9%), which is known for a low degree of concentration. Although Germany is the world's fourth paper producing nation, it has only three companies in the world's top 100 paper producing firms, and none in the top 50. In other words, the size of the companies can explain the competitiveness of nations and regions only partially.

2 'Industry Specific Time and Space' of Pulp and Paper

In the introduction of the book, the author argued that each industry has its own time and space. Then, what kind of 'time and space' do the pulp and paper industry have and how did it shape the above described global landscape of the industry?

First, the industry is marked by a long time horizon. Paper is an extremely mature and stable product/commodity (Kurlansky 2016). While epoch-making innovative products create new markets every now and then, paper has always been paper. The basic principle of its manufacturing process remained unchanged over centuries: both its demand and consumption patterns have been stable, and the time-horizon of the investment is long. Drastic changes in the competitive landscape triggered by transformation of products, materials, and processes have rarely occurred (Lamberg and Ojala 2006; Kurosawa and Hashino 2016).

However, as witnessed there was a geographical shift in the global market, though it took place rather late in comparison with some other industries, and it reflected the second feature of this industry: paper is a typical product for developed economies. The demand for newsprint and printing paper postulates a literate population, and it is significantly correlated with the level of income. The market of paperboard also grew together with the emergence of the modern distribution system and marketing, and mass consumption of packaged products. Furthermore, the third market, namely the wide range of household papers for hygiene purposes presupposes the existence of consumption habits of disposable goods. For example, the peaking-out of per capita consumption of paper occurred only lately: with 264 kg/year in 2004 in the United States and 245 kg/year in 2006 in Japan (Kurosawa and Hashino 2012). As the demand expands even after the country becomes a middle income economy, it takes longer for latecomers to catch up with the size of the demand in developed countries than in other industries with different patterns; thus limiting the effects of the 'advantage of backwardness.'

The technological feature of the industry also defines the temporal characteristics of the industry, by making it a typical 'installation industry,' where decisions on investment play a vital role. The economy of scale is significant both in pulp and paper industries, and a continuous production process has its advantages. The installation of a large-scale production facility is decisive: initial investment is gigantic, and the ratio of fixed capital is very high. Although the actual operation of the plant requires special know-how, the technologies are basically embedded in the plant design, and the plant and facility are usually long-lasting. In combination with the maturity of products, both the elements of labor and product development play only limited roles. Accordingly, the focal point of the competition is investment: when and where companies build their plants, for what type of product and raw materials, and by what kind of processes.

Furthermore, material procurements of this industry also require a very long time horizon and it has to be coordinated with the investments to the facilities and plants. The payout period of investment for forestry resource is extremely long, though the recent innovations in the bio-botanical technology have dramatically shortened the cycle. The decades-long time horizon of the industry is derived not only from stability of products, technology, and consumption but also from the long lead-time of the forestry resource cultivation.

What kind of spatial feature does the industry have? First, paper is generally a low-priced product on amount of its weight and volume, meaning it can bear only a little transportation cost. This is one of the main reasons for the afore-mentioned geographical structure of the industry. Each continental region, which has sub-regions with favorable conditions for either supply or for demand, tends to have its own self-sufficient market area.

The second spatial element characteristic for this industry is the geographical distribution of the raw material, and availability of other factors/conditions, such as clean water and low cost energy. The raw material is a significant determinant for the competition, because both processes and products are largely constrained by it. The pulp and paper industry is based on the processing of biological resources, including forestry resources, agricultural residue, and waste paper. All of them are unevenly distributed geographically, suggesting that economic actors (or networks of them) that enjoys advantageous access to raw materials and/or actors equipped with high capability to control multi-step material flow can become competitive.

Unlike mineral resource industries, not only the extraction (logging) but also plantation is possible, and recycling of materials has a technological limit, making constant input of virgin material indispensable. Especially after late 20th century, the plantation capability became crucial for competition.

3 The Three Major Regions: Historical Features

3.1 Europe: Intra-Regional Division of Labor

The modern paper industry was born in Europe. A literate population, publishing culture, and printing industry were decisive for the rise of the paper industry. The supply of rags was crucial. Europe pioneered in the invention and application of paper machine and the introduction of the wood pulp in the 19th Century. Some paper, printing, and publishing clusters with long traditions have survived until today. In addition, most globally competitive equipment and engineering firms for the paper industry are European (e.g., Metso in Finland and Voith in Germany). Though European nations share a common history in this industry, there are major differences among various European countries.

The United Kingdom

The United Kingdom had been the largest paper producer in Europe until the 1960s. The rise and decline of the British paper industry was greatly affected by the tariff policy and the pattern of international division of labor (Owen 1999). With the exception of newsprint, it enjoyed the protective tariff of 1932. Three decades later, the industry suffered from the 'EFTA shock' in 1959–1960, due to the foundation of European Free Trade Association. The EFTA abolished tariffs on imports from Nordic countries, triggering massive imports. Because the United Kingdom had shifted its source of raw material to the imported market pulp from Nordic countries and Canada long before that, the industry had no cost advantage against vertically integrated factories in Nordic countries. Although some firms saw opportunities in recycled paper and packaging materials, the industry witnessed a sharp decline. The production picked up since the mid-1980s facilitated by inward foreign direct investment (FDI). However, the recovery was very limited in comparison with the once strong position in Europe (Särkkä 2012).

Germany

The history of paper industry in Germany is marked by a series of external shocks, discontinuities, and vibrant expansion after World War II (Turunen 2012). Although Germany was ranked high in paper production until World War I, it suffered damages caused by defeats in the two wars, loss of territory, and division of the land. More than half of the pre-World War II production capacity was located in East Germany. In order to offset this loss, post-war Germany pursued a steady expansion of investments. However, unlike Japan, post-war German paper industry had only a little wood pulp production. Instead, it utilized imported market pulp and recycled pulp and fully exploited the advantage of European integration.

Nordic Countries

The rise of the Nordic pulp industry started in the second half of the 19th century with the commercialization of wood pulp technology (Järvinen et al. 2012). As early as World War I, Sweden became the world's largest pulp exporter. The paper production also expanded in the first half of the 20th century, and newsprint and craft paper were exported. After World War II, the integrated production of pulp and paper grew further. During 1970s—1980s, Nordic enterprises intensified their FDI to address the European integration and the appreciation of currency. Since the 1990s, when market saturation and the decline of performance became evident, a wave of cross-border mega-mergers and consolidation took place.

3.2 North America: Resources, Investments, and Innovations

In the mid-1960s the world production of paper was approx. 100 million ton/year, about one-fourth of today's output. One half of it was produced in North America, and the United States solely had a 40% share of the world production. The preponderance after the late 19th century was brought about by multiple factors. On the supply side, the following elements were important: 1) unmatched natural resources, 2) investment in the infrastructure and dynamic expansion and shifts in paper producing regions, 3) R&D of technology for raw material use and the extensive use of economies of scale in facilities, and 4) product innovation. On the demand side, 5) income and population growth and 6) emergence of new markets through a series of product innovation were decisive. As strategic decisions to connect the supply and demand, 7) horizontal and vertical integration among firms and the formation of modern business organizations were important.

Although the modern paper industry has its origin in Europe, radical product innovations to diversify the use of paper were achieved in the United States during the first half of the 20th century (Toivanen 2012). Kimberly-Clark in Wisconsin invented cellucotton—a cotton-like absorbent material—in 1915 and created a new market of hygienic papers—a segment of consumer nondurables. In 1919, feminine hygiene products and cleansing tissue were also commercialized. In the segment of packaging, Hinde and Dauch and other companies in the Midwest took an initiative in corrugated paper for packaging use. Due to these innovations and with the modernization of the distribution system and revolutionary change in packaging and shipment, the size of this segment surpassed that of newsprint.

The formation of modern corporate organizations was observed early in the United States. The merger of 18 pulp and paper mills in the northeastern states established International Paper. During the boom years after World War II, major producers diversified their businesses into almost all segments and pursued vertical integration. The geographical expansion of leading firms integrated the national market. Consequently, a limited number of large firms with s similar business domain, behavior, and organizational structure dominated the market.

3.3 Japan: Tradition, Technology Transfer, and Self-Contained Development

The history of modern paper industry in Japan is marked by rapid and steady expansion. The first machine-made paper was produced in 1874. Subsequent expansion continued for one and a quarter century until 2001. This growth was largely self-contained. The import dependency was low from the beginning (approx. 30% in the 19th century) and dropped further (approx. 10% since the 1910s and less than 5% in the second half of the 20th century). Inward FDI was virtually absent (Suzuki 1967). The geographical and cultural distance from major paper producing countries entailed this development.

Both technology from abroad and adaptation of the Japanese production system contributed to the competitiveness of Japanese firms in the local market. Because these firms purchased the main equipment from Western engineering firms or locally produced them through licensing, there is no special technological advantage in the core technology. However, Japanese firms have been accumulating special knowledge in a variety of ways: sourcing and mixture of raw materials, customized installation of equipment, and incremental improvements in daily operations and products. These functioned as important elements for competitiveness against imports, especially because the capability of flexible manufacturing high-quality products has been very important in the Japanese market (Kurosawa and Hashino 2012).

4 Variation of Integration and Location

4.1 Consumption-pull, Resource-push, and Integrated Types

In terms of both material flow and value chain, the pulp and paper industry can be understood as a flow from biological resource (e.g., forest resource) into pulp, into paper, into a paper product, and then to the end-user. The flow from waste paper to recycled paper also derives from the abovementioned main flow. From the viewpoints of specific countries or regions, there are questions about what part of this flow is located in its territory and who controls it.

Studies on other process industries with similar conditions can provide useful insights on this issue. Akira Tanaka's analysis on the iron and steel industry and his analytical concept of the 'resource procurement system' are good examples of such works (Tanaka 2008). He categorized a widely acknowledged feature of Japanese steel makers as a 'Japanese model,' classifying it to three levels, namely *production system, corporate system,* and *competitive behavior* (Tanaka 2012). Although the similarity between paper and steel industry in Japan is conspicuous at all of these three levels, the *production system* provides special insights for the analysis of paper industry. Tanaka characterized production system of Japanese iron and steel industry as follows: the investment strategy to seek state-of-the-art plants with a rational layout at a coastal location for the integrated production of iron- and steel; integrated quality control for flexible and efficient multi-product/ multi-specification production; the long-term-contract based raw material procurement system); This characterization of the steel industry can be applied to the pulp and paper industry in Japan with a little modification.

Furthermore, Tanaka's resource procurement system concept is highly useful to understand the abovementioned material flow in the pulp and paper industry. By using this concept, the following section tries to clarify the inner structure of the regional markets (Europe, North America, and Japan). For this purpose, the authors categorize a variety of integration and location patterns and the base of competitiveness into three types. Both North America and Europe have two types within their regional market: 1) The *consumption-pull* type, in which countries, regions, and firms have strength in the downstream of the entire value chain and 2) the *resource- push* type, in which countries, regions, and firms have strength in the upper part of the entire value chain. The post-war Japan can be classified as the third category, namely 3) the *hybrid-integration* type, in which the capabil- ity to combine advantages of the abovementioned two types contributed to its competitiveness. In this third category, the resource procurement system is similar to the one for the abovementioned 'Japanese model' in the iron and steel industry.

How can we distinguish these three types? An effective litmus test for the classification of these types is the ratio between the pulp and paper pro- duction. Table 11.3 shows ten largest paper—and paperboard—producing countries and the size of their pulp production, which is shown by index number in relation to paper production. In 1975, the index numbers in West Germany (29%), the United Kingdom (10%), and Italy (31%) were small, suggesting that these countries with relatively small pulp production that specialized in paper production belonged to the consumption-pull type. In contrast, in Canada (145%), Sweden (181%), and Finland (125%), pulp production exceeded paper production, and so these countries can be classi- fied into the resource-push type. Brazil (145%) is also included in this type based on the data from 2013, as shown in Table 11.1. Finally, the United States (80%), China (78%), and Japan (61%) are regarded either as a mix- ture of these two types or the hybrid-integration type.

4.2 Consumption Pull: Diverse Outcomes

In the consumption-pull type, the downstream part of the value chain drives the expansion of the industry. Most countries in this category do not have a large pulp industry and have a trade deficit in paper products (Tables 11.1 and 11.3). On the other hand, this type has a favorable procurement condi- tion of waste paper, being the location for the final consumption of paper (Table 11.3 shows the recycled paper ratio in 2005 [marked by "*"]).

Table 11.3 Pulp and Paper Production Ratio: Index of Pulp Production of Ten of the World's Largest Paper Producers, When Paper and Paperboard Production Is Taken to Be 100

	1956		1975		1995		2005		
1	US	70	US	80	US	70	US	65	*54
2	Canada	124	Japan	61	Japan	37	China	28	*36
3	UK	n.a.	Canada	145	China	86	Japan	35	*72
4	W. Germany	50	USSR	95	Canada	136	Germany	13	*66
5	USSR	101	W. Germany	29	W. Germany	13	Canada	130	*14
6	Japan	86	Sweden	181	Finland	92	Finland	90	*5
7	France	41	China	78	Sweden	111	Sweden	102	*13
8	Sweden	260	Finland	125	France	33	S. Korea	5	*67
9	China	35	UK	10	S. Korea	8	France	24	*58
10	Finland	186	Italy	31	Italy	9	Italy	7	*55

Source: The number for 1975–2005 is calculated by authors using data from the Food and Agriculture Organization of the United Nations Statistics Division (http://faostat3.fao.org/download/F/FO/E). Data for 1956 are based on Toyo Keizai Shinpo 1966, 'Kami-parupu no jissai chishiki' [Handbook of paper and pulp industry], Tokyo. The index of the United Kingdom in 1958 was four, and there is good reason to guess that it was less than six in 1956.

Note: The numbers with '*' in 2005 show the ratio of recycled paper production against paper and paperboard production.

Accordingly, many of these countries increased the ratio of recycled paper, especially after the 1970s, and some even became net-exporters of paper and/or waste paper.

In the formation process of vertical integration, the pattern 'from downstream to upstream' dominates the consumption-pull type. Two groups of firms, namely those that belong to the user industry of paper—such as newspaper companies and consumer goods producers—and paper companies that became the main players in paper production enter the market not through pulp production but with papermaking. Then, they integrate the upstream process into their business to ensure stable procurement of intermediate goods and raw materials. The vertical integration takes place in multiple forms and scopes: 1) integration of paper production by paper users, 2) integration of pulp production by paper makers, 3) integration of forestry by players based in the downstream, and 4) integration spanning more than two sections of the value chain (e.g., paper use to pulp production). As for location, the main actors of this type usually originate from densely populated, high-income regions. Proximity to the users and logistics centers are often crucial.

Which countries belong to the consumption-pull type? Except for Nordic countries, most European countries belong to this type, as indicated by the import dependency ratio (import/consumption) of paper. The numbers in 1964, 1975, and 1984 were, respectively, as follows: the United Kingdom, 48%, 44%, and 60%; (West) Germany, 30%, 35%, and 41%; France, 15%, 24%, and 37%; and Italy, 14%, 10%, and 30%. The figures stayed generally high and increased gradually.

The consequences of the 'consumption-pull' development are diverse. The United Kingdom is a conspicuous case, in which the consumption-pull type of industrial structure worked as a negative condition for competitiveness. In this country, considerable numbers of paper mills were founded and owned by paper users, such as newspaper publishers and producers of consumer goods (cigarettes, foods, toiletry, etc.). In the 1960s, when Nordic countries and Canada emerged as competitive paper exporters, these companies—for which paper-production is not the core-business—switched from in-house production in the United Kingdom to procurement from abroad, either by shifting the production to their overseas factories or by sourcing from other companies. The export of the end products of these user industries stagnated, due partially to declining competitiveness of the whole manufacturing sector and the delay in the United Kingdom's entry into the European Communities/European Union. In short, the United Kingdom lost its competitiveness in two ways: it suffered not only from unfavorable conditions in the upstream (supply side) but also dysfunction of their linkage with the related industries in the downstream, which could have been an advantage of the consumption-pull type.

On the other hand, the case of Germany shows that the consumption-pull type can improve its competitiveness significantly and even achieve 'export-pull' growth. The domestic procurement of pulp, the integrated production of pulp and paper, and the full-lineup strategy were not the priority of German paper producers. Instead, they pursued the utilization of imported market pulp and recycled paper and adopted a specialization strategy on the premise of international division of labor. The existence of user industries with a strong export activity worked positively. The German paper industry comprised of small and medium-sized enterprises (SMEs), and these firms supplied their customized products to wide-ranging SMEs (including highly localized newspaper, printing, and packaging firms) in each local market. In sum, the German paper industry kept its strong competitiveness not through vertical integration or economies of scale but through optimization of their scope to utilize their ties with specialized customers.

North America as a whole is featured as 'resource-push' type. Canada has a huge export of pulp and newsprint. The United States is the world's largest producer of pulp (Table 11.1) and fulfills approx.70–80% of the domestic consumption. However, it is also possible to find elements of consumption-pull in the United States, with the exception of its southern states. The utilization of wood pulp was pursued to address the expansion of newsprint demand and chronic scarcity of raw material, and thus it could be considered consumption-driven development. The leading actors of this process were newspaper publishers that established integrated mills, tracing the value chain from downstream to the upstream. After the import tariff repeal in 1913 on newsprint, American newspaper publishers procured their newsprint from factories in Canada, which were owned mostly by American paper companies or American newspapers. Another feature of the consumption-pull is the aforementioned product innovation. While the expansion of the market was first brought by innovative actions on the supply side, the subsequent expansion of demand necessitated the enlargement of the supply base.

In East Asia, South Korea can be classified into this type. Korean paper producers mainly use imported pulp and export proportionally large amounts of paper products. Similar to Germany, South Korea transformed itself from a consumption-pull type into an export-pull type by capitalizing on the international division of labor.

4.3 Location-based Resource Push: Advantages and Limits

Paper producing nations of the 'resource-push' type emerged with the commercialization of wood pulp. Nordic countries, Canada, and more recently major pulp producers in the southern hemisphere typify it (Ojala et al. 2006). Southern states of the United States have similar features to some extent. It also exports diverse forestry products (timber, lumber, wood chips, and wood boards).

In these resource-push type of countries, the establishment of a pulp industry often preceded that of the paper industry, and the forestry industry had started even earlier. The majority of paper factories are integrated pulp and paper factories and often connected with sawmills (forestry cluster). Firms on the upstream took the initiative for integration, though many cases of inward FDI (from the United States to Canada, FDI to South America) can be seen as important exceptions.

Canada is a good example of the competitive advantage of the resource-push type and its limits. The development of the Canadian paper industry was historically based on the following elements: 1) availability of low-cost and high-quality raw material (softwood) and proximity to the large market (the United States); 2) access to the world market, including the Commonwealth; 3) inward FDI; and 4) support by the government (e.g., favorable forest and water use concessions). After World War II, while pulp export expanded, the attempted diversification of paper production from newsprint to other products largely failed (Kuhlberg 2012).

Since the 1970s, the Canadian pulp and paper industry witnessed growing difficulties. Industrial decline of nearby Midwest of the United States dampened the demand. The inflation and rising labor costs discounted the cost advantage, and the environmental movements and cessation of government support worsened it. Since the 1990s, the newsprint market shrank dramatically after the information technology revolution. Finally, in the 21st century, competition with the newly emerged pulp producing nations intensified. A series of large-scale M&As did not improve its performance. A few firms such as Cascades and Domter survived by shifting their core businesses from traditional segments to new ones, including hygienic paper in the European market and recycled-paper products.

The high-quality and low-cost forestry resources are accessible also to outsiders through inward FDI. Which means, the competitive advantage of the raw material is 'transferrable.' However, the advantage of the resource itself is inseparable from the location, because the forest is irremovable. As rare as it may be, if the raw material of such a region loses its competitiveness, the advantage of that location will be lost. Such a once-in-a-century kind of upheaval has been occurring since the late 20th century with the rise of the southern hemisphere based on short-growth-cycle species, silvicultural innovation, and high yield plantation.

5 Japan as the Hybrid-Integration Type

5.1 Hybrid Integration as the Third Type

It might be possible to position post-war Japan as a mixture of the above-mentioned consumption-pull and resource-push types. However, it is more appropriate to classify it as the third category ('hybrid-integration' type)[2] for the following reasons. Despite its constraints in forest resources, Japanese firms pursued integration in production by expanding pulp production capacity and adopting the coastal location strategy. This pattern is different from both coastal locations for product exports, which can be observed in some forest-rich (resource-push type) countries and user proximity in consumption-pull type countries. In the hybrid-integration type, wood chip and not market pulp is procured globally with the uniquely developed infrastructure (e.g., the specially designed gigantic wood-chip carriers and port facilities). This is a conspicuous feature of the Japanese pulp and paper industry even today. Although the pulp and paper production using imported raw material can also be observed elsewhere, the scale of investment and consistency of strategy in Japan are outstanding.

This 'hybrid-integration type' is inherently universal and not necessarily bound to a specific country. However, there are two reasons to associate this type with the aforementioned Japanese model in the iron and steel industry defined by Tanaka. First, it exemplifies a new pattern of world trade in the post-World War II era: new regions for raw material supply (e.g., Latin America) and new paper-making/consuming population-rich countries (Japan) emerged hand-in-hand, becoming a prototype for today's global shift of industries to East Asia and its industrial hinterland. Furthermore, once we focus on other process industries in post-war Japan, this imported material based integrated production on the coast is a familiar setup. For example, in both Japanese steel and petrochemical industries, not the intermediate goods (pig iron or oil products) but primary raw material and energy (iron, coal, and crude oil) are imported from abroad through long-distance shipping. The characteristics of the Japanese paper industry—global resource procurement, coastal location, production across multiple processes, systematic and coherent investment strategy, and utilization of know-how of the so-called Japanese production system—are widely shared features for most process industries in post-war Japan.

5.2 Why and How Did the Hybrid-Integration Type Emerge?

Why and how did this unique type emerge and become the standard in Japan? Before World War II, Japan had both consumption-pull type and resource push type in its territories. Similar to Europe and North America, the commercialization of wood pulp transformed the softwood-rich northern land into the production base of pulp and paper. Since the 1910s, a dozen integrated pulp and paper factories with state-of-the-art equipment were built in Hokkaido and Southern Sakhalin, which supplied newsprint and other mass-market-oriented products to densely populated Honshu. Three major players—merged into Oji Paper in 1933—invested massively into these northern islands, enjoying the favorable concessions of forest and water. As a result, the self-sufficiency ratio of pulp in Japan jumped from 62% (1913) to 87% (1921) (Kurosawa and Hashino 2012).

On the other hand, the rest of Japans pulp and paper industry had consumption-pull type features. There were two types of suppliers: 1) small and medium-sized producers of machine-made *Washi* (Japanese paper) that used indigenous and local raw materials and 2) medium-sized makers of Western paper and paperboard that used mainly rice straw pulp and imported pulp. While these 'non-Oji' firms were excluded from access to the forestry resource in the northern islands, they could utilize their proximity to the users.

At the end of World War II, Japan lost Southern Sakhalin, where 44% of pulp capacity of Japan was located. The monopolistic Oji Paper was divided under the occupation and its monopoly came to an end. Accordingly, the dualism of the two models weakened significantly. Under the scarcity of foreign currency through the 1950s, import of pulp was impossible. Together with pine and a variety of hardwood in the main islands, indigenous non-wood fibers and recycled materials became important for pulp production.

The combination of pulp production and paper-making was realized from 1945 to the 1950s through intensive mutual entries—by both pulp producers and paper producers—into the upstream and downstream. As early as the 1950s, both groups became almost identical in their business portfolios and strategies.

The procurement of raw material for pulp from abroad shifted to a high gear in the 1960s, when the domestic supply was no longer sufficient. The use of wood chips—an eminent indication of the hybrid-integration type—launched in early-1960 and virtually replaced the use of timber in the 1970s. Toyo Pulp was the world's first mover to deploy a specially designed wood-chip carrier, and its Japanese rivals soon followed suit. In 1973, Japan had 51 carriers owned by 16 firms to import wood chips from 10 countries. Wood chips was the second largest imported item by volume in Japan after crude oil (Daishowa-Seishi 1991). Even in 2015, approx. 75% of wood-chip carriers in the world were under control of Japanese paper producers (World Resources International LLC 2015). Other features, such as long-term procurement contracts with overseas suppliers (usually local forestry firms), plantation at home and abroad, and optimal global procurement became indispensable aspects of this raw material procurement system. In this model, unlike the resource-push one, paper producers can reshuffle their sources to profit from the emergence of new forestry countries, as long as they have the capability to reorganize the network.

6 Global Structural Change in the 21st Century

In the 21st century, the global paper industry entered a new phase. First, on the demand side, emerging economies with a large population increased their presence. In particular, the expansion of the Chinese market was dramatic. Due to the demand at home, China became the world's second largest paper producer in 2000, and the largest in 2007, surpassing the United States. Today, it produces more than a fourth of the total paper output in the world (Table 11.1).

The features of Chinese paper industry present both similarities and contrasts with Japanese ones. The similarities are obvious: the growth was achieved by rapid expansion of demand, under significant constraints in domestic raw material supply (i.e., the consumption-pull element). Despite this drawback, the dependency on imported wood pulp was very low in China until 2009, and it is relatively limited even today. However, there are noticeable differences. In the case of China, not wood chip but waste paper—another internationally tradable good—is imported massively and used for pulp production. This became possible only after the establishment of paper recycling infrastructures abroad. Rich countries with high per capita paper consumption (especially the United States and Western-Europe) became its major suppliers. The variety of raw material is extremely wide in China, and the use of indigenous low quality material (e.g. agricultural residue such as bagasse) continues even in the 21st century. The basic elements of the competitiveness of the hybrid-integration type, namely integrated production of pulp and paper, coastal location, and extensive exploitation of economies of scale, are still limited in China. Above all, organizational capability for the optimized global sourcing of high-quality virgin material—another hallmark of hybrid integration—is largely missing.

Second, the structural upheaval on the supply side also changed the competitive landscape of the global paper industry. In addition to the worldwide expansion of paper recycling, the following changes brought about fundamental impacts: the emergence of new forestry countries in the southern hemisphere and tropics; increasing importance of planted forests and use of fast-growing, high yield species; and impact of bio-technological and silvicultural innovations. These three elements are mutually related, and they are affecting the over-a-century-long advantage of the northern forest-rich countries (Lima-Toivanen 2012).

Third, new dynamics can also be observed on the level of firms. While existing paper producers intensified their multinational characteristics, new players from the emerging markets expanded their presence (Kurosawa and Hashino 2016).

In Europe, Nordic companies like UPM (Finland) and Stora Enso (Finland/Sweden) consolidated themselves and improved their positions through successive acquisitions in Central and Eastern Europe. Although both these companies are active in FDI toward China and South America, sales in Europe still account for 70–90% of their global sales. In this respect, they are still European firms, rather than global ones.

Likewise, North America is trending toward consolidation to cope with the dramatic contraction of paper consumption after the digital revolution. In 2015, Rock Tenn and MWV were merged into West Rock. Similar to Europe, a truly global firm has not appeared yet. For International Paper, the largest paper producer in the world, the sales share of North America is still dominant at 72% (Europe and Russia, 13%; Asia, 7.2%; and Latin America, 5.9%) in 2015.

Japan also witnessed a series of M&As at the turn of the century to address similar difficulties. Since then, two top makers (Oji Paper and Nippon Paper, each with approx. 25% share), together with the second group comprising four companies (each with approx. 10%), account for approx. 90% of the domestic market.

In the high-income economies, the structural change in the last three decades is well exemplified by the growth of firms that specialized in recycling, recycled paper, and packaging materials. DS Smith (ranked sixth in Europe) is a good example. Since the 1990s, the company expanded its European business through a series of M&As in the continent and greenfield investments in Southern Europe. Smurfit Kappa (ranked third in Europe) has its roots in the Irish box maker, Jefferson Smurfit. The company made FDIs in the United States in 1964 and merged with Kappa, a Dutch packaging material maker with pan-European business, in 2005. Both examples reflect not only industrial integration in Europe but also the success of the strategy to exploit consumption-pull type market conditions (i.e., [neutralization of] the disadvantage in wood-pulp sourcing and advantage in recycled paper).

The most impressive change is the rise of firms with backgrounds in emerging economies. In particular, South Africa has two globalized firms that grew through M&As in the northern hemisphere. One is Mondi (ranked 12th in the world) that expanded its business through a series of M&As in Eastern Europe since the 1990s. Its regional composition of sales is now 60% in Europe, 30% in North America, and 10% in South Africa. Another example is Sappi (ranked 13th in the world), founded in 1936 in South Africa. After the 1990s, it expanded in Europe and North America via a series of M&As. Nowadays, its proportion of sales in Europe, North America, and South Africa are 2:1:1. Both South African multinationals combined the advantage of their home country in the south (forestry and pulp) and focused on products to maximize the condition of their targeted market in the north (recycled paper and packaging material as well as coated paper).

The advantage of the newly emerging supply-push growth in the southern hemisphere, as well as the continent-wide integration, are exhibited by the rise of Empresas CMPC (ranked 18th in the world), which was founded in Chile in 1920. This company pioneered in the plantation of radiate pine and eucalyptus and became the first pulp exporter from Chile. Since 1991, it has acquired many firms in Latin America and became a major player in forestation, lumbering, and pulp and paper production.

In Asia, Asian Pulp & Paper (APP) is a representative of the newly emerging MNEs, with its home in Indonesia and FDI in China. The firm has its origin in a pulp and paper plant in Java, a joint venture between a local Chinese-Indonesian entrepreneur and a company from Taiwan. In 1992, the firm became the first foreign paper producer in mainland China and is now listed on the Singapore Stock Exchange. Reflecting respective raw material supply conditions, it uses wood pulp in Indonesia and recycled paper pulp in China.

Conclusion

In the paper industry, not only the geographical distribution of production and consumption but also the competitive landscape directly reflects the product features of paper and the characteristics of the industry. On the demand side, countries with large consumption (mostly rich nations) also have dominant positions in production when the global structure is observed with a bird's eye view. In comparison with other products with smaller transportation costs, the geographical concentration of paper production to a specific nation is limited. In that sense, global competition is less intensive in this industry.

Despite the considerable inter-continental trade, Europe, North America, Japan, and China can be largely regarded as self-sufficient regional markets for paper, possessing their own suppliers and consumers. Each region has built up organizational capabilities to fulfill its demand for paper. In contrast, in the trade of raw materials (wood chips and waste paper) and semi-finished products (pulp), these markets are more integrated globally due to strong material flow from forest-rich regions (especially the Americas) to regions with large populations and high purchasing power (China and Japan).

The competitive landscape and sources of competitiveness in this industry have been stable due to the stability of the product and longer time horizon of the industry. The material flow and value chain that run from forestry resources to paper consumption are the key to understanding the competitiveness. Access to raw material and the consumption market, as well as the capability to connect these two, have been crucial for the competitiveness. This chapter demonstrated how three analytical concepts, namely resource push, consumption-pull, and hybrid integration can explain the historical dynamics of the industry.

However, this analysis does not suggest any determinism. There have been many nuances in the story and enough room for innovative actions. Both the emergence of hybrid integration and the different trajectories of Germany and the United Kingdom exhibit not only the significant role of historical contingency but also the importance of organizational capability to overcome the initial condition. In addition, the new reality in the 21st century suggests that the century-long framework of competition is changing in both raw material supply and consumption.

The industry-level analysis of this chapter can be easily connected to firm-level analysis. Historically, enterprises based in Europe, North America, and Japan have been the major players, and newcomers from the emerging markets are joining up. The top companies in the industry engage in world-wide activities, and transnational, pan-continental companies have emerged, especially in Europe. However, most of these firms are still regional (European or North American) or national (Japanese) rather than truly global, except for their material procurement networks.

Finally, the methodological implication of this chapter should be mentioned. The chapter tried to clarify the industry-specific features in order to determine the crucial determinants for competitiveness. The abovementioned three categories ('types') are the most important outcome of these steps of analysis. In addition, inter-industrial comparisons were made by applying an analytical concept developed by studies on other industries with similar characteristics. We argue that conscious application of inter-industry comparison will enrich studies on individual industries.

Notes

1 Each county has its own way of categorizing pulp and paper industries. Those with strong pulp industry tend to use the term "pulp and paper industry" and analyze them together. In Japan, the sequence of words is reverse ("paper and pulp industry"). In countries where pulp industry is weak, these two industries tend to be analyzed separately.
2 The authors once categorized this type as a 'Japanese model' (Kurosawa and Hashino 2012). This chapter avoids the use of this term, considering the universal nature of this model to other places. "Hybrid" implies not only the combination of "consumption-pull" elements and "resource-push" ones, but also this has its original advantages (e.g. exchangeability of raw material sourcing areas). Integration means that the vertical integration of multiple processes (pulp and paper making) is the essential feature of this model.

References

Daishowa-Seishi 1991, *Daishowa seishi goju-nen Shi* [50 Years History of Daishowa Paper Ltd.], Daishowa Seishi, Fuji.
Järvinen, J., Ojala, J., Melander, A. and Lamberg, J.A. 2012, 'The evolution of pulp and paper industries in Finland, Sweden and Norway, 1800–2005', in J.-A. Lamberg, J. Ojala, M. Peltoniemi and T. Särkkä (eds.), *The Evolution of Global Paper Industry 1800–2050: A Comparative Analysis*, Springer, Dordrecht, Heidelberg, New York and London, pp. 19–48.
Kuhlberg, M. 2012, 'An accomplished history, an uncertain future: Canada's pulp and paper industry since the early 1800s', in J.-A. Lamberg, J. Ojala, M. Peltoniemi and T. Särkkä (eds.), *The Evolution of Global Paper Industry 1800–2050: A Comparative Analysis*, Springer, Dordrecht, Heidelberg, New York and London, pp. 101–134.
Kurlansky, M. 2016, *Paper: Paging Through History*, W.W. Norton, New York.
Kurosawa, T. and Hashino, T. 2012, 'From the non-European tradition to a variation on the Japanese competitiveness model: The modern Japanese paper industry since the 1870s', in J.-A. Lamberg, J. Ojala, M. Peltoniemi and T. Särkkä (eds.), *The Evolution of Global Paper Industry 1800–2050: A Comparative Analysis*, Springer, Dordrecht, Heidelberg, New York and London, pp. 135–166.
Kurosawa, T. and Hashino, T. 2016, 'Bei-Ou-Ajia Sandai Shijo-to Kyousoryoku-no Mittsu-no Kata' [Three regional markets in America, Europe, and Asia and three

types of competitive advantages], in T. Kikkawa, T. Kurosawa and S. Nishimura (eds.), *Gurobaru keieishi: kokkyo wo koeru sangyo dainamizumu* [Global Business History: Industrial Dynamics Beyond Borders], Nagoya University Press, Nagoya, pp. 32–63.

Lamberg, J.A. and Ojala, J. 2006, 'Evolution of competitive strategies in global forestry industries: Introduction', in J.-A. Lamberg, J. Näsi, J. Ojala and P. Sajasalo (eds.), *The Evolution of Competitive Strategies in Global Forestry Industries: Comparative Perspective*, Springer, Dordrecht.

Lima-Toivanen, M.B. 2012, 'The South American pulp and paper industry: The cases Brazil, Chile, and Uruguay', in J.-A. Lamberg, J. Ojala, M. Peltoniemi and T. Särkkä (eds.), *The Evolution of Global Paper Industry 1800–2050: A Comparative Analysis*, Springer, Dordrecht, Heidelberg, New York and London. pp. 243–285.

Ojala, J., Lamberg, J.-A., Ahola, A. and Melander, A. 2006, 'The ephemera of success: Strategy, structure and performance in the forestry industries', in J.-A. Lamberg, J. Näsi, J. Ojala J. and P. Sajasalo (eds.), *The Evolution of Competitive Strategies in Global Forestry Industries: Comparative Perspective*, Springer, Dordrecht.

Owen, J. 1999, *From Empire to Europe: The Decline and Revival of British Industry Since the Second World War*, HarperCollins, London.

Särkkä, T. 2012, 'British paper industry, 1800–2000', in J.-A. Lamberg, J. Ojala, M. Peltoniemi and T. Särkkä (eds.), *The Evolution of Global Paper Industry 1800–2050: A Comparative Analysis*, Springer, Dordrecht, Heidelberg, New York and London. pp. 167–190.

Suzuki, H. 1967, *Kami parupu sangyo: gendai sangyo hattatsu shi* [Paper and Pulp Industry: History of Modern Japanese Industries], Kojyun Sha, Tokyo.

Tanaka, A. 2008, 'Tekko. Nihon moderu-no hakyu to kakusan' [Iron and steel: transfer and modification of Japan model], in H. Shioji (eds.), *Higashi ajia yui sangyo-no kyousou-ryoku: sono youinto kyoso, bungyo* [The Competitiveness of East Asian Dominant Industries: Its Bases and Structure], Minerva Shobo, Kyoto. pp. 15–49.

Tanaka, A. 2012, *Sengo Nihon no shigen bijinesu* [Postwar Japan's Mineral Industry: A Comparative History of Its Procurement System and Sogo Shosha], The University of Nagoya Press, Nagoya.

Toivanen, H. 2012, 'Waves of technological innovation: The evolution of the US pulp and paper industry, 1860–2000', in J.-A. Lamberg, J. Ojala, M. Peltoniemi and T. Särkkä (eds.), *The Evolution of Global Paper Industry 1800–2050: A Comparative Analysis*, Springer, Dordrecht, Heidelberg, New York and London. pp. 49–80.

Turunen, O. 2012, 'The paper industry in Germany, 1800–2000', in J.-A. Lamberg, J. Ojala, M. Peltoniemi and T. Särkkä (eds.), *The Evolution of Global Paper Industry 1800–2050: A Comparative Analysis*, Springer, Dordrecht, Heidelberg, New York and London. pp. 81–100.

World Resource International LLC 2015, 'The family of global wood chip carriers is becoming smaller and younger', *Business Wire (Berkshire Hathaway Company)*, 7 February. Available from: <www.businesswire.com/news/home/20150207005016/en/Wood-Resources-International-LLC-Family-Global-Wood> [13 September 2015].

Conclusion

Bram Bouwens and Pierre-Yves Donzé

The globalization process, since the last decades of the 20th century, is one of the most striking phenomena in recent economic history. The widening, deepening, and speeding up of global interconnectedness, measured in terms of, say, FDI or numbers and size of multinationals were more widespread and intensive after 1980 as compared to the earlier decades of the 20th century. The global diffusion and acceleration of international business competition were accompanied by major shifts in economic activities and markets around the globe. It led to changes in the composition of industries and the division of labor and production across different regions of the world.

The impact of globalization on the development of international business has received much attention, especially from the point of view of MNEs. This volume has another starting-point, which indicates that the specificities of an industry are decisive with respect to both the location and the competitiveness of companies in this industry in a certain time period. The reciprocity of these characteristics at an industrial and entrepreneurial level is demonstrated in many cases. New organizational structures, ranging from global production networks to the incorporation of competencies to broaden the scope of operations enabled some regions and firms to safeguard or strengthen their competitiveness. The industry, which was defined as an arena for competition and cooperation, and characterized by its products, common technology, economic function and/or market, was in many cases not a static feature, but a flexible concept. The industry can be redefined to enable the development of new capabilities to ensure the competitiveness of various firms and regions.

The process of transition in most industries was not simply a matter of decline or catching up, of winners and losers. In some industries, firms remained competitive even without relocating their operations overseas. Further, the transformation process was not initiated solely by MNEs. Small- and medium-sized enterprises (SMEs) played a role in the internationalization of business and the transition of the industrial landscape. This volume explores the main drivers of transition and transformation. Why did some industries and their firms move to other parts of the world, while others did not? Relocation was not the sole determinant of success or failure of firms and regions. The transformation of some industries made it possible for some companies and regions to build new competitive advantages. The three patterns of the evolution of firms in particular industries—move, not-move, and transform—were studied in eleven chapters.

The first part of this volume contained four cases of industries that relocated their activities or reorganized their business in new locations to meet the international competitive challenge. The firms in these industries (tobacco multinational enterprises, Canadian automobile makers, Japanese electrical equipment companies, and French vaccine producers) invested in business beyond national borders to follow their customers, enter new unexplored markets, or maintain and safeguard their position in the domestic market.

Part I shows that the globalization process forced these industries to rethink the location of their activities. Internationally, each of these industries was rather homogeneous, but with the speeding up of regionalization and globalization and the development of emerging economies, the market that defined the boundary of the industry was stretched. Thus, the global nature of these industries created strong competitive demands that could not be ignored. The cases clarify that the dynamics and direction of this development of interconnectedness and shifting competitive advantages were not a linear evolution of regional and global integration, but a process of continuities and discontinuities influenced by path dependent trajectories. The industries reacted in different ways to the competitive challenges they faced.

The specificities of the industries turned out to be decisive in the strategic choices made by the firms. Nevertheless, regional differences could occur within an industry. In contrast to their American competitors, who relied on exports, the Japanese manufacturers of electrical equipment followed the traditional path of an MNE and built production facilities in emerging markets to secure their sales. Foreign direct investments, joint ventures, and strategic alliances were used to simultaneously exploit competitive advantages and reduce costs. The chapter on tobacco indicates a similar trend. This industry was dominated by three large global companies (Philip Morris, British American Tobacco, and Japan Tobacco) that produced and sold similar goods. Their internal organization, as well as home-based advantages, had a major impact on the way they implemented their expansion in the global market.

However, the influence of national governments on global firms can have different effects on their competitiveness. In some cases, like Japan Tobacco, we observed a high productivity due to effective manufacturing capabilities, but low profit margins as a consequence of marketing strategy (discount brands in overseas markets). However, in the global vaccine industry, characterized by the absence of large companies and the dominance of non-competitive laboratories, the French company Mérieux (Sanofi Pasteur since 2004) benefitted from the protection of the state to grow in the domestic market through technological innovation and takeovers, before expanding overseas through mergers and acquisitions. Moreover, in Canada, the automobile sector, with its long history of inward FDI and fragmented domestic network of suppliers, became an important part of the continental car industry. It was able to strengthen its position in the international market for automobiles through active governmental support for widening the geographical scope of their agreements, particularly with the US. Hence, Canada was able to attract Japanese car makers, who were aiming to enter the North American market. Therefore, the specificities of these industries, along with the location factor and the necessity to accomplish a new competitive edge, determined the responsiveness of companies to global challenges.

Part II addressed the case of industries in which firms retained their competitiveness over time (Dutch water management, European publishing, and Japanese functional chemicals). Despite the globalization of markets, the rise of competitors in other nations and regions as well as technological and marketing innovations, some companies were able to maintain their dominant position since the end of World War II.

The three examples analyzed in this part clearly highlight the role of localized knowledge as a lasting competitive advantage. The localization of such knowledge results from various factors. It can be geographic conditions, like in the case of the Dutch water management industry. The necessity to carry out large-scale engineering works since the 19th century, for the protection of the Netherlands from the sea, led some companies to accumulate knowledge related to the construction of canals, harbors, and other maritime constructions. Culture is another factor, as indicated by the example of the European publishing industry. Language areas offered an opportunity for publishers, especially from France, Germany, and Spain, to expand beyond their national borders, and thus, strengthen their competitive advantage before moving to global markets. In other cases, such as the Japanese functional chemical industry, localized knowledge did not result from specificities related to the nature of a territory, but to specific circumstances, which gave some companies the occasion to build and strengthen their competitive advantages at a given moment. For the Japanese functional chemical companies, this was the cooperation and the co-development of material with the Japanese electronics multinational enterprises during the 1980s and the 1990s. This closeness made it possible for them to establish oligopolies in niche markets and maintain their competitiveness when the electronics industry moved from Japan to other countries of East Asia after 2000.

However, localized knowledge is not enough to establish and retain competitive advantage in global markets. All the examples analyzed in this part highlight the importance of institutional support from large MNEs and/or the state. First, the key role of MNEs is clear in the cases of the Dutch water management companies and the Japanese functional chemical companies, despite this relationship manifesting with very different features. In the case of the former, the closeness of Royal Dutch Shell gave firms that dredged, drained, and reclaimed land the opportunity to expand internationally, especially in Asia. These MNEs needed the expertise of firms like Boskalis around the world. The functional chemical companies in Japan indicate the opposite form of evolution. This industry did not go directly into the global markets through the development of materials for the Japanese electronics companies. Until the 1990s, companies like Sony and Panasonic had access to the global markets, while the functional chemical companies did not. However, despite the global leadership shifting from Japanese to Korean and Taiwanese firms, the accumulated knowledge and the oligopolies founded by chemical firms helped them retain their competitive advantage.

Second, the role of the state explains the development of firms in industries like European publishing. Protectionist policies, such as fixed prices for books, led to an organized competition between domestic firms and it nurtured national champions. These policies had a positive effect in the cases observed in this book; however, they failed in many industries, like electronics, where national companies had no specific localized advantage. In this sense, organized competition and protectionism contributed to the development of strong companies in the national market, which were then competitive enough to enter foreign markets through mergers and acquisitions.

Finally, part III focused on industries in which the competitiveness of firms changed along with the building of global value chains. The companies that were able to adjust to changes in industrial organization established themselves as the dominant players in their respective sectors. Hence, this transformation gave the newcomers an opportunity to emerge, while the first movers faced the challenges in which some survived, while others declined.

All the four industries mentioned in this part have a global perspective (watch industry, department stores and apparel industry, shipping industry, and paper industry) that underlines the major impact of changes in the value chains on their industrial organization. Two main causes of this transformation are highlighted in different chapters in part III. First, one must stress the importance of institutional change. The building of global value chains did not exclusively result from the global dominance of free market forces. The impact of privatization by national authorities on the processes of globalization cannot be ignored. For example, the withdrawal of the State was a major event in the watch industry. The decline of custom protectionism in the US and Japan, together with the end of state-controlled cartels in Switzerland during the 1960s, opened borders for companies with enough resources to invest overseas and delocalize production in South-East Asia. In the apparel industry, the opening of China for inward FDI was a major institutional change that gave way to the relocation of apparel production to this country. Japanese department stores lost their traditional suppliers, with whom they used to co-develop fashion for the domestic market, and as a result, their competitiveness. The case of the shipping industry indicated another feature, an institutional innovation (the system of "flags of convenience" or "open register") adopted by different European countries enabled their companies to retain their competitive advantage, while the core of this industry was moving to East Asia.

Second, technology played a major role in the transformation of these industries, but rather than product innovation, it seems that process innovation had the widest impact. Apart from the watch industry, the cases addressed here did not present any major product innovation during the last decades. Apparel, shipping, and paper are mature goods and services. However, the institutional changes mentioned above made it possible to mass produce standardized goods for global markets. Attaining economies of scale was an important objective of these industrial reorganizations. Producers of watches and apparel build new factories in China, while European shipping companies re-positioned themselves as active firms throughout the world, connecting not only Europe with other regions, but also non-European nations between them.

The watch industry is the only case in which product innovation played a major role in terms of the emergence of global value chains. The advent of quartz watches, during the 1970s, strengthened the relocation of watch parts manufacturers to Asia and lowered the entry barriers in this industry, as electronics modules were far cheaper and easier to acquire than mechanical movements. Consequently, newcomers emerged, particularly in Hong Kong, and established a competitive advantage on the management of value chains. However, despite high costs, the Swiss watch companies were able to retain their competitiveness, thanks to an institutional innovation (Swiss Made law in 1971) that forced them to produce half of their parts in Switzerland, and allowed the simultaneous procurement of the other half from foreign countries, thus making a fervent use of global value chains.

Moreover, one must stress the originality of the chapter on the paper and pulp industry, which is characterized by the coexistence of various models. Here, industrial organization did not change much over time, but rather across space. The existence of a large market or/and of natural resources (mostly wood) gave birth to different kinds of competitive companies, such as firms focusing on the manufacture of downstream products to respond to a large domestic demand (e.g., in Europe except Nordic countries, or in South Korea), firms from countries that have large resources (e.g., Nordic countries, or Canada), and Japanese firms, which combine advantages of the two aforementioned types.

The objective of this book was to discuss how the specificities of a given industry and the location of particular resources were related, and how this relationship evolved over time. Based on a broad variety of case studies, this volume has demonstrated that there is no definite answer to these questions. Unlike scholarly works in management and economics, which offer general theories to explain the competitiveness of firms and regions, we argue that each industry has its own dynamics and that a proper understanding of its global evolution requires paying attention to its specificities. Industry history is a powerful approach to analyze global competition and we hope this book will invite more researchers to follow it.

Index